Naples

In recent years Naples has been the subject of a sort of hyper-narration, particularly when it comes to film and literature, which has added to the existing imagery of the city in the collective consciousness. The pendulum here has always swung wildly, and it is difficult to work out any kind of average, any idea of what a Neapolitan normality, if such a thing exists, might be. Naples has become the most filmed city in Italy. What lessons can be learned and what conclusions drawn from this? Where to look for this much-sought-after normality? Perhaps we need to 'climb up' to Vomero, a neighbourhood regarded as almost separate from the city, precisely because it is assumed to be 'normal', home to a calm, homogeneous middle class, in stark contrast to the excesses of life in the historic centre, with its countless layers of stratification – architectural, historical and social. And yet there is another interpretation there, too, that the centre, with its subterranean city and artworks embellishing its metro stations, is a model for the cohabitation of past and present rather than yet another variation on Naples' own narrative of exotic exceptionalism. Take the regeneration of old industrial areas. Which is the norm and which the exception in the cases of Bagnoli – which, after thirty years, is still waiting for one of the countless proposed projects to come to fruition – and San Giovanni a Teduccio, where a former tomato-canning plant is now home to a university innovation hub that has had a positive impact on its neighbourhood? This is the same kind of difference that the film industry has made, with many productions being filmed in the city's most troubled districts. One major success story is *Fanpage*, the website that has established a reputation as a highly innovative news outlet, emblematic of a city that is at long last attracting talent rather than scaring it away, that experiments with new ways of doing things and colonises instead of being colonised. On the level of governance, too, the 'city state' and its powerful mayors constitute a political laboratory that often prefigures future trends at a national level. Whether positive or negative, Naples is always full of surprises, even when trying its hardest to be 'normal'.

UÀ NÈ MÀ

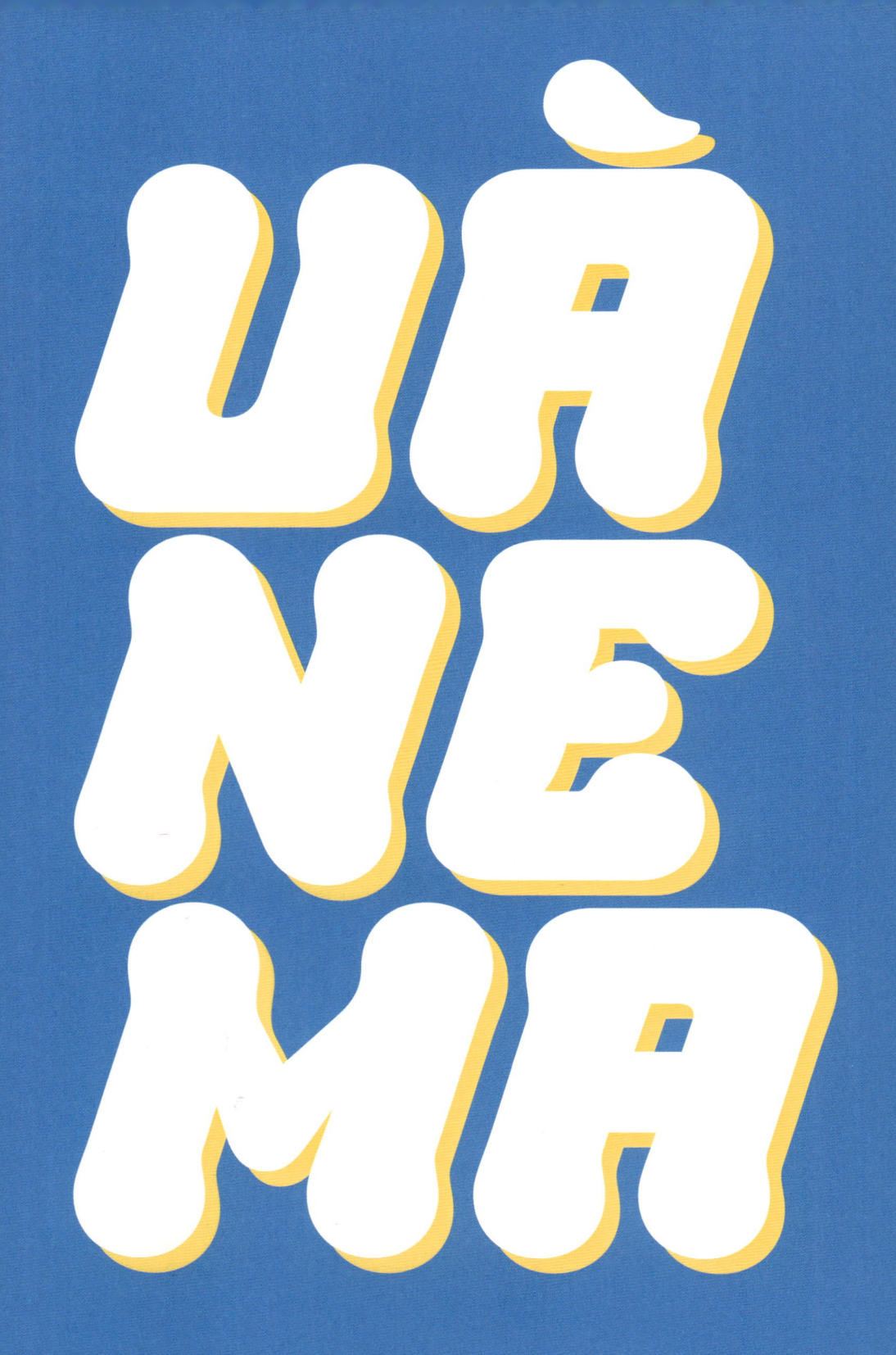

Contents

Some Numbers — 6

Republican Kings — Paolo Macry — 9
Historian Paolo Macry chronicles the careers of Achille Lauro, Antonio Bassolino and Luigi de Magistris, charismatic mayors often hailed as the 'new sovereigns' of Naples.

Minor Saints — Alessandra Coppola — 33
From the walls lining the streets and alleys of Naples, images of murdered teenagers watch over the city's residents like guardian angels. They are all considered victims – of the Camorra, the police or fate. Some of them, however, were criminals, and the authorities want their portraits erased.

The Neapolitan Janus — Lorenzo Colantoni — 47
Naples, one of the cultural capitals of the Roman Empire, has one of the most complex histories of any city in Europe. Here ancient artefacts are not locked away in museums but are indissolubly linked to the present.

Going to Naples — Cristiano de Majo — 67
Is Vomero part of Naples, and are the Vomeresi Neapolitans? That depends on your perspective.

Nero a metà — Francesco Abazia — 83
The presence of US armed forces in the city since the Second World War has had a profound effect on the culture of Naples, from jazz to the African American influences on the Neapolitan Power movement and up to today's rap and trap.

Napuletana — Cristina Portolano — 97
What does it mean to be Neapolitan but to leave? And what is it like to return to the place you call home and yet feel like an outsider? A colourful and personal journey along the streets of a city, stuck somewhere between past and present.

Naples, the Sacred Ground — Carmen Barbieri — 105
The cult of the dead is central to Neapolitan society. Carmen Barbieri guides us through the necropolis of Poggioreale, a city of the dead comprising ten cemeteries and many centuries of history.

Cages of Metal and Cages of Paper — Piero Sorrentino 121
Between crumbling structures and mountains of red tape, the writer Piero Sorrentino guides us through the two greatest economic and ecological rifts in Naples, in San Giovanni a Teduccio and Bagnoli. Between them they exemplify the importance – and the difficulties – of redeveloping the old industrial areas of the city.

Napolisphere — Peppe Fiore 137
Since the success of *Gomorrah*, the television and film industries in Italy are increasingly choosing the regional capital of Campania for their stories and their locations.

A View of the City Through Its Newspapers — Raffaella R. Ferré 153
In the past fifteen years Naples has witnessed the birth of *Fanpage* and *NapoliMonitor*, two often diverging entities that nevertheless share the desire for journalistic experiment and the ambition to achieve national relevance. It is all in the rich tradition of Neapolitan publishing, which comprises both long-running newspapers of its own and the local desks of national newspapers.

Blue Voices — Gianni Montieri 167
SSC Napoli brings Neapolitans together but also drives them apart in an era when being a football fan is increasingly an individual act lived in front of a television screen rather than collectively at a stadium. Between nostalgia and madness, however, the passion for Napoli remains special.

The Centro Direzionale — Ester Viola 182
The Dark Side of Neapolitan Cuisine — Cristiano de Majo 184
The Playlist — Francesco Abazia 188
Digging Deeper 190

The photographs in this issue were taken by **Mario Spada**, a Neapolitan photographer who graduated in 1998 from Milan's Riccardo Bauer Institute, the same year he began his ongoing project on low-level criminality in Naples. In 2001 he won the Canon Young Photographers Best Portfolio award for a feature on the Mastiffs, a group of Napoli ultras, a project that was selected for the Perpignan Festival of Photojournalism. In 2006 he published *Made in Italy* (Trolley), alongside fellow photographers Emiliano Mancuso, Massimo Berruti, Riccardo Scibetta and Giancarlo Ceraudo. The book also became an exhibition held in Naples, Rome and Livorno. He has worked as a stills photographer on films including *Leopardi* and *Gomorrah*, and in 2009 he published the book *Gomorra on Set* (Postcart). He is the founder of the Centro di Fotografia Indipendente, an association that promotes photography in Naples, and has worked with *D - la Repubblica*, *Libération*, *L'Espresso*, *Vanity Fair* and *Der Spiegel* among numerous other publications.

NAPULE È MILLE CULURE/ NAPULE È MILLE PAURE/ NAPULE È A VOCE DE' CRIATURE/ ☞ CHE SAGLIE CHIANU CHIANU/ ☞ E TU SAI CA' NUN SI SULO/

'Napule è' by Pino Daniele (1977)

Some Numbers

I NEED SOME SPACE!

The 10 most densely populated municipalities in Italy, 2022

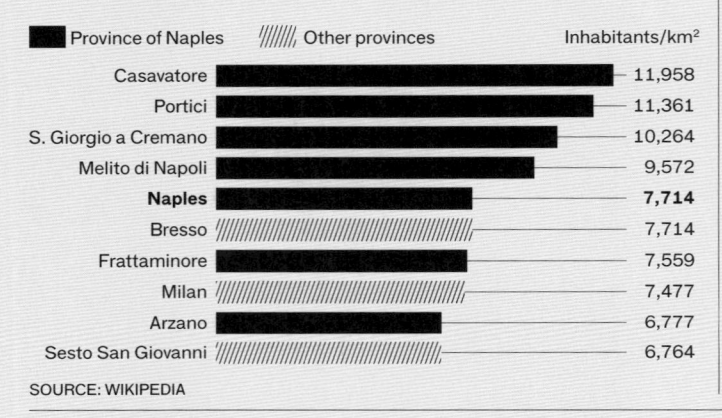

■ Province of Naples ▨ Other provinces   Inhabitants/km²

Municipality	Inhabitants/km²
Casavatore	11,958
Portici	11,361
S. Giorgio a Cremano	10,264
Melito di Napoli	9,572
Naples	**7,714**
Bresso	7,714
Frattaminore	7,559
Milan	7,477
Arzano	6,777
Sesto San Giovanni	6,764

SOURCE: WIKIPEDIA

NO COUNTRY FOR AN ONLY CHILD

Average number of household members, 2011 (latest data)

#	City	Members
1	Naples	2.73
2	Palermo	2.65
3	Catania	2.57
4	Bari	2.53
5	Rome	2.19
6	Turin	2.06
7	Florence	2.06
8	Genoa	2.03

SOURCE: WIKIPEDIA

UNSORTED

Upward trend of separated waste collection %

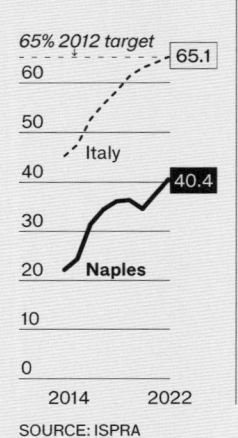

65% 2012 target — Italy 65.1; Naples 40.4 (2014–2022)

SOURCE: ISPRA

Cities with the highest waste-disposal tax, 2023 (€)

1	Catania	594 ↑
2	Genoa	492 ↑
3	**Naples**	**491 ↑**
4	Pisa	481 ↑
5	Brindisi	464 =
6	Latina	460 ↑
7	Messina	453 ↓
8	Salerno	451 ↓
9	R. Calabria	443 =
10	Benevento	442 ↓

POOP!

European cities that manage dog excrement best

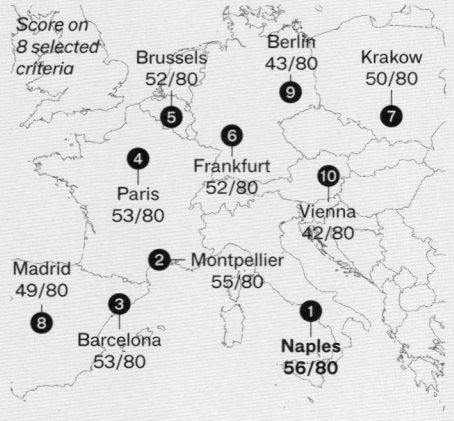

Score on 8 selected criteria:

- Brussels 52/80
- Berlin 43/80
- Krakow 50/80
- Paris 53/80
- Frankfurt 52/80
- Vienna 42/80
- Madrid 49/80
- Montpellier 55/80
- Barcelona 53/80
- Naples 56/80

SOURCE: TAILS.COM

STUDENTS

Number of students registered in the 2019–20 academic year

- Milan Polytechnic: 47,453
- University of Milan: 62,853
- University of Padua: 61,957
- University of Turin: 76,865
- University of Bologna: 82,167
- University of Pisa: 45,684
- University of Florence: 52,753
- Sapienza University of Rome: 104,700
- University of Naples Federico II: 75,542
- University of Bari Aldo Moro: 42,687

SOURCE: WIKIPEDIA

THE SWEETEST TOOTH

Number of confectionary manufacturers, 2019

1. **Naples** — 2,447
2. Rome — 1,875
3. Milan — 1,844
4. Turin — 1,540
5. Palermo — 1,416

SOURCE: CHAMBER OF COMMERCE OF MILAN, MONZA, BRIANZA, LODI

'O NAPULITANO

5.7 million people speak Neapolitan

SOURCE: ETHNOLOGUE

COST OF DRIVING

€758

Average premium for motorcycle and scooter insurance in the province of Naples, April 2024. The Italian average is €346. The price difference is down to the number of accidents and the level of fraud.

SOURCE: OSSERVATORIO ASSICURAZIONI AUTO E MOTO FACILE.IT

CRIME INDEX

The *Il Sole 24 Ore* crime index classifies Italian provinces based on the number of complaints/100K inhabitants for various types of crime, 2023

Final ranking: 1. MI = Milan   3. RO = Rome   6. TU = Turin   **10. NA = Naples**   24. PA = Palermo

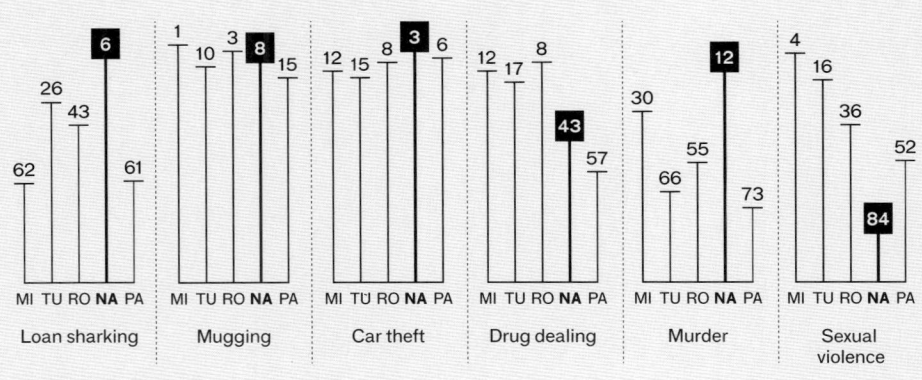

Loan sharking — MI 62, TU 26, RO 43, **NA 6**, PA 61

Mugging — MI 1, TU 10, RO 3, **NA 8**, PA 15

Car theft — MI 12, TU 15, RO 8, **NA 3**, PA 6

Drug dealing — MI 12, TU 17, RO 8, **NA 43**, PA 57

Murder — MI 30, TU 66, RO 55, **NA 12**, PA 73

Sexual violence — MI 4, TU 16, RO 36, **NA 84**, PA 52

SOURCE: IL SOLE 24 ORE

Some Numbers

REPUBLICAN KINGS

PAOLO MACRY
Translated by Ned Darlington

A view of Vesuvius from the Salita Moiariello
with the Centro Direzionale and Miracoli
neighbourhoods in the foreground.

For centuries Naples was the capital of a kingdom, and even after Italian Unification it never forgot its monarchical past. Historian Paolo Macry chronicles the careers of Achille Lauro, Antonio Bassolino and Luigi de Magistris, charismatic mayors often hailed as the 'new sovereigns' of Naples, who left deep impressions on the city and turned it into a political laboratory.

Naples has never had great municipal power nor a strong civic attitude, not least because these were historically overshadowed by the far more relevant political, administrative and judicial powers that it held as the capital city of the Kingdoms of Naples and the Two Sicilies. And when it lost this role in 1861 and could no longer enjoy its historic influence over the Mezzogiorno, it seemed to turn inwards on itself. It did not become the centre of a regional *territorium* as did Milan or Turin. Almost as if it did not want to face facts, it bemoaned its lost noble status. And somehow, whether deep down or superficially, it embraced its monarchical past and at times even promoted its own monarchic ambitions.

Naples was Bourbonic in that dynasty's heyday but also during its decline. And the city became nostalgic for the Bourbons once the kingdom collapsed, with a sentiment bubbling under – genuine at times, ironic at others – that is still apparent today in certain segments of public opinion and which has motivated a singular strand of ideological activism (see 'Skewed Nostalgia' on page 16). Later Naples welcomed Victor Emmanuel II with the generous response of the 1860 plebiscite and fêted him when he visited the city with Garibaldi by his side, although the new king did little to earn the city's goodwill. Thanks to the presence of the dukes of Aosta, who resided in Capodimonte, Naples was able to maintain the illusion of still having its own court, where 'there was dancing, receptions, garden parties in the woods, horse races and fox hunts', as the daily newspaper *Roma* once wrote. Right up to her death in 1951 the Duchess of Aosta, Elena d'Orléans, was a well-known figure in the city, admired and respected from the working-class neighbourhoods to the salons of Chiaia. Even during the fascist *Ventennio* (the twenty-year period when Mussolini was in power), Naples seemed more monarchist than fascist, so, naturally, in the 1946 referendum on whether to retain the monarchy or become a republic it fervently affirmed

---

PAOLO MACRY is a historian, political commentator and professor of contemporary history at the University of Naples Federico II. He is on the editorial board of the *Journal of Modern Italian Studies* and writes for the *Corriere del Mezzogiorno* and *Il riformista* as well as for a number of magazines. Notable publications include *Ottocento. Famiglia, élites e patrimoni a Napoli* (2002, '19th Century: Family, Elites and Heritage in Naples'), *Gli ultimi giorni. Stati che crollano nell'Europa del Novecento* (2009, 'The Last Days: States Collapsing in 20th-Century Europe'), *Unità a Mezzogiorno* (2012, 'Unity in the Mezzogiorno') and *Napoli. Nostalgia di domani* (2018, 'Naples: Nostalgia for Tomorrow') from which this article is adapted. He co-edited with Pasquale Villani the volume on Campania in the Einaudi series on the history of Italy.

THE 'VICEROYS' OF NAPLES

In the 1980s, aided by the huge flows of public development funds for the Mezzogiorno (southern Italy) and the Irpinia earthquake emergency, Naples became one of the centres of power of the First Republic. And the men who ran the show became known as the 'viceroys': two Christian Democrats (Antonio Gava and Paolo Cirino Pomicino), a liberal (Francesco De Lorenzo) and a socialist (Giulio Di Donato). Some also include Giuseppe Galasso and Vincenzo Scotti in their number. Gava was so powerful that he really did deserve the viceroy moniker: he grew up in opposition to Achille Lauro, becoming president of the province, then senator and holding seven ministerial roles, even though his Christian Democrat rival Pomicino was the one nicknamed *'o ministro*, 'the minister'. Legend has it that when the viceroys returned from the corridors of power in Rome, they met their 'court', composed of fixers and Campanian entrepreneurs, to hand out contracts, plot political schemes and do deals. Gava is said to have received guests at his home in the exclusive Posillipo neighbourhood dressed in a long red-silk dressing gown, smoking a cigar. When the *carabinieri* came to arrest him, he was asked the routine question, 'Are you Antonio Gava?' 'I was,' he replied. The system collapsed with the Tangentopoli bribery scandal, even though Gava had been accused of collusion with the Camorra as early as the 1980s. Pomicino went through forty-two trials and was found guilty twice. One historian described him as 'secretary of the cross-party public expenditure party', and, in fact, the viceroys, the city's 'republican sovereigns', did build a network of local power independent of national parties, which would prove useful following their legal issues as a means of continuing their political careers, no longer on the front line but with their positions secured.

its monarchist stance, giving the House of Savoy 80 per cent of its vote.

But Naples has had sovereigns of its own – albeit unique – kind in the republican era, too. Thus did Naples experience them and thus were they labelled. In current lore, Achille Lauro became 'the last of the Bourbons'; Antonio Gava, whose ring his devout followers were said to kiss, was 'the viceroy'; and in the late 20th century three influential personalities – Paolo Cirino Pomicino, Giulio Di Donato and Francesco De Lorenzo – were 'viceroys', too, not just big shots, not simply political leaders, but 'viceroys'. As for Antonio Bassolino, he became likened to a Renaissance prince. And Luigi de Magistris was likened to Luigi Masaniello, the famous Neapolitan peasant revolutionary. They were all rulers because of their strong personalities, their charisma, their aptitude for paternalistic leadership, their intense connection with the people and because they were inclined to present themselves as standard bearers for the community.

Yet, like a chameleon changing its colours, the city that seemed continually to promote the nostalgic myth of the monarchy was simultaneously open to experimentation. In fact, Naples quite frequently became a kind of laboratory for political experiment. It has always reacted to the changing times, even anticipated them, has nimbly switched allegiances and has been strikingly volatile in elections, and its experiments sometimes anticipated political models and languages that would manifest only later across the rest of Italy.

THE COMMANDER

It was surrounded by the ruins of the war that Il Comandante, 'the Commander', was crowned. When he became mayor in 1952 Achille Lauro had a respectable business career behind him. The son of a small-scale shipowner from Sorrento, he had managed during the *Ventennio* to put together a sizable shipping business thanks to his mastery of the market and his entrepreneurial shrewdness. When peace returned, despite having lost almost his entire fleet during the hostilities, he did not stay idle, nor was he deterred by the political turnaround that took place. Accusing him of illegally profiting under fascism, the Allies seized his villas in Naples and Sorrento and arrested him, and Lauro spent a couple of years between prison and internment camps. But then, in quick succession, he was acquitted by an appeals court in 1945, succeeded in obtaining substantial public reparations for war damages, reconnected with British finance, returned to buying ships and recovered his trade routes. By 1950 he was already master of a merchant fleet of more than 600,000 tonnes, the largest in Europe.

An inexorable rise. It was an opportune time to be in politics, and Naples was ready to crown its king. The political and cultural climate of a city still licking its wounds from the war appeared to be a tricky mix of foot-dragging and anticipation. Lack of involvement in the Resistance combined with the old anti-northern stance turned into hostility towards the 'wind of the north', towards the parties of the anti-fascist Comitato di Liberazione Nazionale (National Liberation Committee), towards the republic and thus towards parliamentarianism and politics in general. Serious trouble had erupted in the aftermath of the 1946 constitutional referendum, when the headquarters of the Partito Comunista Italiano (PCI, Italian Communist Party) were stormed by monarchists, which resulted in seven killed and sixty wounded. The dispute with the 'northern' parties was being stirred up in sometimes crude tones by the local press, fuelling the myths and passions of traditional Neapolitan claims. Furthermore, the city was still raw from the agonising months of the Allied occupation, and yet it managed to remain in some ways a free zone, intolerant of rules and capable of providing its own unwritten laws and practising often illegal forms of self-organisation. The social and cultural fabric was frail, but the government and the Democrazia Cristiana party (DC, Christian Democracy) nevertheless seemed to underestimate it, and the left never effectively managed to dismantle it. Neapolitans, rightly or wrongly, felt alienated by the national political stage – or, worse, felt abandoned.

Lauro latched on to those sentiments. After surfing the wave of the Fronte dell'Uomo Qualunque (the Common Man's Front) movement he became president of the Partito Monarchico Nazionale (Monarchist National Party) and was able to involve the neofascists of the Movimento Sociale Italiano (MSI, Italian Social Movement), putting together an unlikely cartel of those nostalgic for the monarchy and heirs to the Nazi puppet state of the Republic of Salò. In this way he was able to win the 1952 local elections by a landslide, capturing over 40 per cent of the vote and being elected mayor on the strength of his more than 100,000 preferential votes. His coronation by the people was not in question, and the DC took this into account, deciding to take a soft line in opposition. Then, in 1953 Lauro was also successful in the general elections, and the following year he founded his own

A BRIEF HISTORY OF CONTEMPORARY NAPLES

☞ **FOR THE PREQUEL SEE PAGES 56-7**

1943 During a four-day uprising (the Four Days of Naples), the Neapolitans drive the Germans out of the city and allow the Allies in.

1944 The last eruption of Vesuvius to date.

1946 In the referendum held on 2 June, an overwhelming majority in Naples vote for the return of the monarchy. A few days after the republican victory, a popular protest in Via Medina leads to a violent clash, leaving nine people dead.

1952 The shipowner Achille Lauro becomes mayor, signalling the start of the period of large-scale property speculation denounced by the filmmaker Francesco Rosi in his thriller *Hands Over the City*, released in 1963. The city expands in all directions.

1973 A serious cholera epidemic breaks out followed by a mass vaccination campaign. During this period the Nuova Camorra Organizzata (NCO, New Organised Camorra) is founded by Raffaele Cutolo, who attempts to take control of all illicit activities in the region. In response, other criminal organisations band together under the name of the Nuova Famiglia (New Family). The violent war between these two criminal groups ends in the early 1980s with the defeat of the NCO.

1980 A powerful earthquake, with its epicentre in Irpinia, damages buildings and the city's artistic heritage, and major construction projects planned to support the city's development are redesigned to meet new anti-seismic standards. These include the Centro Direzionale (the business district completed in 1995) and the first line of the city's metro. In 1983 a second bradyseismic uplift (a rapid rise in ground level caused by the movement of magma or geothermal activity), following the event in 1970, occurs in the Phlegraean Fields, a volcanic area to the west of Naples, leading to evacuations and an exodus of inhabitants, particularly in Pozzuoli.

1987 Diego Armando Maradona leads Napoli to the first Serie A title win in the club's history.

1993 After a long period under external administration, the city elects Antonio Bassolino in its first direct mayoral election, signalling the beginning of the 'new Neapolitan renaissance'. The first section of the new metro serving several of the city's hilly districts is inaugurated (later renamed Line 1). The historic centre is added to UNESCO's World Heritage list.

2001 The metro's first 'art stations' are inaugurated: Quattro Giornate, Salvator Rosa and Museo.

2004 The first so-called Scampia feud breaks out between rival Camorra clans, the subject of Roberto Saviano's TV series *Gomorrah*. Naples is rocked by a second feud in 2012.

2007 The waste emergency comes to a head in the metropolitan area of Naples, and images of the city buried under tonnes of uncollected rubbish are beamed around the world.

2011 Luigi de Magistris is elected mayor. A new tourism boom begins.

2023 Napoli wins its third Serie A title, while mayor Gaetano Manfredi, elected in 2021, supported by a similar centre-left coalition as his predecessor, struggles with the municipality's disastrous public finances. A small earthquake in 2024 spreads anxiety and fear in and around Pozzuoli.

Republican Kings

party, the Partito Monarchico Popolare (PMP, People's Monarchist Party), supporting Prime Minister Mario Scelba's centrist government and obtaining financial resources for Naples in return. When he finally stood again in 1956 in the municipal elections, it was a triumph. The PMP garnered almost 300,000 votes. Naples had become a 'Laurin' city.

The material roots of consensus. Il Comandante had been able to build robust networks of support around himself through policies that responded to the interests of large swathes of the citizenry: he improved the dilapidated public transport system; he promoted a vast urban-planning project, creating new working-class districts and new elite residential areas; he made extensive use of the opportunities for high-density construction provided by the 1939 General Regulatory Plan, which aimed to redevelop the city's urban landscape, quickly had the new neighbourhoods equipped with roads and sewer systems and became a symbol of unscrupulous use of the land. But the massive supply of housing was in response to a much-felt need in a city that had been badly damaged during the war. Lauro set up a kind of pact between developers and

Naples, 1958: Achille Lauro addresses his supporters. Credit: Jack Garofalo/Getty Images

city planning that incorporated building planners, landowners, money attracted by the real-estate prospects and then numerous bourgeois white-collar workers with the opportunity for new – potentially high rise – apartments and, finally, the mass of workers who saw in construction the only growing sector, that is, the only remedy for the tough postwar industrial crisis.

Simultaneously, Lauro increased the ranks of municipal employees with an employment policy that was also highly appreciated by the citizens. In return for guaranteeing the survival of the DC-led national governments with the votes of his own elected members in parliament, he had been given substantial funding for Naples from the government in Rome. His support network was growing by the day. Administrators, professionals, technicians and workers were always local people: *giving Naples back to the Neapolitans.*

Il Comandante's huge popularity and his political entrenchment stemmed no less from his methods of governance. The administration appeared efficient in its own way: first, because it enforced bureaucratic procedures and legal constraints to the hilt – what mattered was getting things done – and, second, because it relied on personal ties, first-hand introductions and absolute discretion. Public construction and maintenance contracts were handed out in private negotiations. Additional favours, such as permission to increase the height of buildings, were granted on a case-by-case basis. The beneficiaries, in turn, made voluntary contributions to a fund for welfare activities that was managed directly by the mayor without going through the city council. Alternatively, they would be used to finance the famous Piedigrotta Festival.

The Laurin period was later put to shame in Francesco Rosi's 1963 film *Hands Over the City*, which depicts the urban growth of those years as a morass of corruption, speculation and illegal entanglements between private and public interests. The film received fervent praise from the left – and didn't displease the DC and the government either. The parties were only too happy for the opportunity to shatter the Comandante's image, notwithstanding their political agreements, complacency and under-the-table handouts which had left no one unsullied. The film was – as it is to this day – the definitive condemnation of Lauro's legacy in the eyes of posterity, but at the cost of serious omissions. Indeed, while new construction projects had been launched for a couple of million cubic metres in the 1950s, it was in the following decade, when the municipal government was now controlled by the DC, that building permits reached unprecedented levels: almost eleven million cubic metres. The 'goldmine' had therefore not closed

'Lauro's support network was growing by the day. Administrators, professionals, technicians and workers were always local people: *giving Naples back to the Neapolitans.*'

down with the shipowner-mayor's departure – even though it was during his time that such property speculation began – and it would continue.

The idol. In addition to responding to widespread material interests, Lauro built his reign on an effective identity-based strategy. The people of Naples, the writer Anna Maria Ortese stated, are 'either hungry for bread or for idols', and Lauro gave them an idol. He became the noisy champion of the accusations which, since 1860, the former capital had traditionally hurled against the wealthier northern regions and against a government accused of working for the north at the expense of the south. But, in Lauro's parlance, these were not recriminations, they were simply Naples' rights, and, in defending those rights, the mayor pulled together the entire population, regardless of political affiliation. His vindicatory rhetoric worked like a charm. The city obtained its special law, and Lauro was given free command of public resources. Naples seemed able to hold its own against Rome, which served to burnish Naples' self-image.

The mayor promised the splendours of a tourist city, saying he would make Naples 'Europe's garden'. He organised and revived large street festivals. He funded popular music. He made himself a film producer. He staked his hopes on the huge public following of the game of football, becoming president of the city's football club, promising 'a great team for a great Naples'. He became a regular presence on the sidelines during his team's games. He built the great Stadio San Paolo for them.

It felt like a leap into the past, and a poster put up by the DC controversially suggested as much, depicting the mayor

SKEWED NOSTALGIA

Not everyone knows that in 1860, when Garibaldi entered Naples in triumph, annexing the city to the new Kingdom of Italy, the Kingdom of the Two Sicilies was the world's third-largest power, a nation at the forefront of technology in Europe, and that the 'northerners' immediately set about destroying its economy and exterminating a million southerners under the false premise of repressing brigandage – actually a spontaneous popular liberation movement – by establishing concentration camps. These, at least, are the beliefs of the neo-Bourbons, a 'cultural movement' that became more prominent in the 1990s at the same time as the regionalist Lega Lombarda emerged in the north but without the Lega's political and electoral apparatus. It claims to stand 'on the difficult side of the vanquished rather than the very convenient side of the victors'. The alleged 'firsts' achieved by the southern kingdom are listed on a page of the movement's website and constitute a sort of Bourbon mythology, seasoned with a dash of conspiracy theory, which is promoted in numerous revisionist pseudo-historical books. Genuine historians have repeatedly disproved or contextualised the data and debunked some of the neo-Bourbon theories, such as the supposed massacre of Fenestrelle, the Savoyard military prison in which tens of thousands of former Bourbon soldiers were allegedly held in conditions worthy of a Nazi death camp. The historian Alessandro Barbero, the author of a book on what he terms a 'historical invention', even agreed to a bizarre debate (available on YouTube) with Gennaro De Crescenzo, president of the neo-Bourbon movement, who had called for a boycott of the book.

under the age-old adage: *feste, farina e forca*, give the people merry-making, flour and the gallows. But all this was perhaps an illusion. Laurism was yet another reflection in the taunting game of mirrors that Naples often plays. His era was pilloried on all political fronts, by the liberal intelligentsia of the magazine *Nord e Sud*, by the great northern newspapers such as *Corriere della Sera* and *La Stampa*, by historians. It was the expression of a plebeian, archaic, reactionary city, nostalgic for the monarchy and for fascism. The kingdom of lawlessness. And Lauro was the last of the Bourbons.

Political innovation. The Laurin period, on closer inspection, constituted a remarkable political experiment. The shipowner-mayor had created a groundbreaking model of political participation based on direct contact with voters and the ability to fully tune in to the common man's culture, of being ostentatiously anti-elitist and averse to the language of professional politics. Il Comandante launched tirades against corrupt parties, dithering parliamentarianism and useless intermediate bodies, contrasting all this with an ethics of common sense, the coarse irreverence of getting things done and making a mockery of procedures – and, what is more, a paternalistic authoritarianism. Today we would call it a populist approach and charismatic leadership. Lauro built a party fully dependent on its leader. He was adept at using his ownership of the local press and football team. His messages were simplistic, and he often used crude rhetoric to denigrate communism, the anti-fascist hegemony, the rapacious north and the centralist state, while he systematically appealed to the vindictive sentiments of the erstwhile capital city. He would promise them jobs, homes, incomes. His authoritarian, even ostentatious, public image seemed to suggest that he would make good on those promises. It guaranteed unquestioned and swift decisions – that is, efficiency. And, of course, his track record offered reassurance. Lauro presented himself as a successful entrepreneur, the leader of an industrial organisation that provided jobs for thousands of people, one who had contracts in oil company Eni, power provider Ansaldo as well as Fiat and was on good terms with international finance. His name stood for competence and managerialism. Someone who had been able to create such an economic empire would also achieve great results in the administration of public affairs – and his wealth shielded him from corruption. His populist model and his business model went hand in hand.

It was the first experiment in mass politics in Italy – a visionary leap forward in many ways. Image played a huge and early part in creating Il Comandante's charismatic profile and a role in constructing the demonic profile that his opponents attributed to him – reminiscent of the dynamics that surrounded Silvio Berlusconi in a more recent period of Italian history. Lauro foreshadowed many of the phenomena that would resurface forty years later: a populist demagogy steeped in anti-institutionalism, the myth of civil society and the party in thrall to one individual. His was the pioneering project of an Italian right-wing *rassemblement* through the legitimisation of the neo-fascist MSI, not dissimilar to the way Berlusconi would legitimise the right-wing politics of Gianfranco Fini, who served in a number of roles in Berlusconi administrations. Lauro sought to be a coalition-maker, and at first the strategy seemed successful. Those who later came to govern the city, such as Antonio Bassolino or Luigi de Magistris, would be indebted to his political model, but so would national leaders of diverse political persuasions, including Berlusconi, Romano Prodi, Umberto Bossi and Beppe Grillo.

Put side by side, the stories of Lauro and Berlusconi explain one another. In the working-class Naples of the 1950s Lauro represented an advanced, fierce, successful entrepreneurial attitude, while in the cosmopolitan Milan of the 1980s Berlusconi would represent the intersection of private capital and state protection. 'Making the comparison with Berlusconism,' wrote the historian Salvatore Lupo, 'shows that Laurism was not a mere by-product of backwardness' and, conversely, 'the comparison with Laurism shows that Berlusconi's modernness does not represent what was once called progress'. Indeed, things are never so simple. What is certain is that Naples produced a political experiment of unusual social and cultural flexibility. A city that was in several respects lagging behind the rest of the country but was open to every experiment of the boldest kind. Perhaps in no other city in post-war Italy could Il Comandante have built his own kingdom.

And then it ended in Rome. But the way it all came to an end is also significant, because it puts the myth back into perspective – or rather to the particular nature of that Neapolitan monarchy which often made proud claims of self-sufficiency while, in truth, remaining fatally subordinate to the Roman state and politics. As mayor, Lauro was initially faced with a difficult budgetary situation. But he was not deterred, and he asked for and eventually obtained special measures from the government, taking ample advantage of the political debt owed him by the DC and the government in Rome – and he was never known to be light handed in this regard. Yet, despite the favours from Rome, by 1956 the municipal deficit was around thirty billion lire (*c.* $540 million today), so high that the finance offices thought it best to alert the government authorities. Naples' public accounts were on the verge of collapse. The minister of the interior alerted the premier of the day, Antonio Segni. This was an embarrassment for the DC, as their governments continued to rely on support from Lauro's parliamentarians and those of the MSI. Finally, in 1957, after yet another round of censorship by the central bureaucracy to keep those irregular accounts under wraps, Rome took action.

And this didn't happen by accident. The political winds were changing, the DC was moving to the left, Il Comandante's votes were no longer of any use to it and his plan to create a great rightist monarchist social movement obviously did not please the Catholic party, so national events were immediately reflected in Naples. In December 1957 some monarchist city councillors switched support to the DC, putting Lauro in the minority and forcing his resignation. Then the prefect dissolved the administration and appointed a commissioner. The authorities feared that the fall of the ruler would cause street uprisings, but nothing happened. Once again, the city proved fickle – or it was simply being pragmatic.

Antonio Bassolino during the electoral campaign of 2021.

THE COMMUNIST OF THE SALONS

Naples proves as slippery as an eel if you try to lock it into any rigid scheme. It consistently produces myths but is just as capable of disowning them. Even Lauro was disowned in a flash. Having left behind the era of populism, the city entered fully into the national realm of DC politics, which in this case meant Silvio and Antonio Gava, and it remained there throughout the 1960s. Later it had a communist mayor, Maurizio Valenzi, and with the 1980s, in the political climate following the powerful 1980 earthquake, it experienced the period of the socialist-dominated 'Pentapartito', the five-party coalition government. In elections the city pandered to the government coalitions and was repaid by the parties' administrative offices: important ministers were Neapolitans.

But it was clear that the rituals of politics failed to excite public opinion. The city derived undoubted material benefits from them and yet it disliked them. Nor was it particularly excited, truth be told, when in 1993 the judicial storm of the Tangentopoli scandal saw many heads roll on corruption charges. There were no torchlight processions in front of the courthouse demanding that revenge be exacted by the new heroes of the prosecution as there had been in Milan, and yet the consequences of Tangentopoli were devastating for Naples as well.

Parties and the political class melted like snow in the sun. The time was ripe for the return of the monarchy. In 1993 Antonio Bassolino became mayor – the first to be directly elected. Bassolino had had a career as a communist leader in the central committee of the PCI from

Republican Kings

THE 'OBLIGATORY MUSEUM'

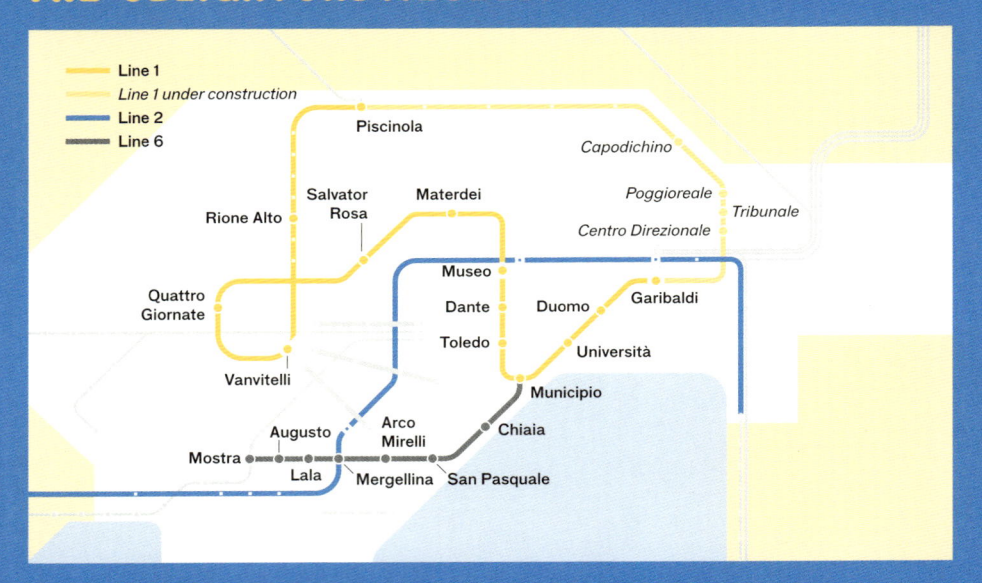

LINE 1

Garibaldi — 2013
ARCHITECT
Giorgio Gradogna
ARTIST
Michelangelo Pistoletto

Duomo — 2021
ARCHITECT
Massimiliano and Doriana Fuksas
ARCHAEOLOGY
Ancient gymnasium and temple of the Isolympic Games (1st century CE)

Università — 2011
ARCHITECT
Karim Rashid
ARTIST
Karim Rashid

Municipio — 2015
ARCHITECTS
Álvaro Siza and Eduardo Souto de Moura
ARTIST
Michal Rovner
ARCHAEOLOGY
Outer defensive constructions of the Maschio Angioino (Torrione dell'Incoronata). The finds from excavations of the ancient port of Neapolis are on display at Museo station; however, remains of the Roman ships unearthed here will be restored and exhibited at Municipio.

Toledo — 2012
ARCHITECT
Oscar Tusquets Blanca
ARTISTS
Achille Cevoli, Francesco Clemente, Ilya and Emilia Kabakov, William Kentridge, Shirin Neshat, Oliviero Toscani, Lawrence Weiner, Robert Wilson
ARCHAEOLOGY
Remnants of the Aragonese city walls. Neolithic finds are on display at Museo station.

Dante — 2002
ARCHITECT
Gae Aulenti
ARTISTS
Carlo Alfano, Nicola De Maria, Jannis Kounellis, Joseph Kosuth, Michelangelo Pistoletto

Museo — 2001
ARCHITECT
Gae Aulenti
ARTISTS
Antonio Biasiucci, Luciano D'Alessandro, Fabio Donato, Mimmo Jodice, Raffaela Mariniello

THE PASSENGER — Paolo Macry

ARCHAEOLOGY
Reproductions and casts of Graeco-Roman statues. 'Neapolis station', a free museum space within the station, displays finds from the excavations for Line 1, particularly around Via Toledo, Piazza Bovio, Piazza Nicola Amore and Piazza Municipio.

Materdei   2003

ARCHITECT
Alessandro Mendini (Atelier Mendini)

ARTISTS
Mathelda Balatresi, Domenico Bianchi, Sandro Chia, Lucio Del Pezzo, Anna Gili, Stefano Giovannoni, Robert Gligorov, Sol LeWitt, Luigi Ontani, Denis Santachiara, Innocente Maria Scardoni, Luigi Serafini, George Sowden, Ettore Spalletti

Salvator Rosa   2001

ARCHITECT
Alessandro Mendini (Atelier Mendini)

ARTISTS
Inside: Enzo Cucchi, Santolo De Luca, LuCa, Fulvia Mendini, Raffaella Nappo, Perino & Vele, Anna Sargenti, Quintino Scolavino, Natalino Zullo; outside and in the surrounding garden: Renato Barisani, Riccardo Dalisi, Lucio Del Pezzo, Nino Longobardi, Lello Esposito, Ugo Marano, Alex

Mocika, Mimmo Paladino, Salvatore Paladino, Gloria Pastore, Augusto Perez, Gianni Pisani, Mimmo Rotella, Ernesto Tatafiore

ARCHAEOLOGY
Roman bridge

Quattro Giornate   2001

ARCHITECT
Domenico Orlacchio

ARTISTS
Marisa Albanese, Renato Barisani, Betty Bee, Maurizio Cannavacciuolo, Baldo Diodato, Sergio Fermariello, Nino Longobardi, Umberto Manzo, Anna Sargenti

Vanvitelli   1993 [2005]

ARCHITECTS
Michele and Lorenzo Capobianco

ARTISTS
Olivo Barbieri, Gabriele Basilico, Gregorio Botta, Isabella Ducrot, Mario Merz, Giulio Paolini, Vettor Pisani, Gilberto Zorio

Rione Alto   1993 [2004]

ARCHITECT
Renato Miano

ARTISTS
Marco Anelli, Bianco-Valente, Achille Cevoli, Donatella Di Cicco, Danilo Donzelli, Pina Gigi, Ivan Malerba, Pennacchio Argentato, Katharina Sieverding, David Tremlett, Marco Zezza, Giuseppe Zevola

Piscinola   1995

ARTISTS
Since 2013, following a citizens' petition, it has displayed works by artist Felice Pignataro

NEW STATIONS

Centro Direzionale   2024

ARCHITECT
Benedetta Miralles Tagliabue

Tribunale   2024

ARCHITECT
Mario Botta

Poggioreale   2024

ARCHITECT
Mario Botta

Capodichino   2026

ARCHITECT
Richard Rogers

LINE 6

Mergellina   2007

ARCHITECT
Vittorio Magnago Lampugnani

ARTISTS
Alan Fletcher, Gerhard Merz

Lala   2007

ARCHITECT
Studio Protec

ARTISTS
Nanni Balestrini, Monica Biancardi, Luca Campigotto, Salvino Campos, Vincenzo Castella, Ousmane Ndiaye Dago

Republican Kings

> 'The man who had previously been described as a grey communist official now flaunted completely unexpected political and cultural attributes.'

1972 and then in parliament from 1987. His face was well known by the left, less so by the public. Bassolino's charisma was evident immediately. He was surrounded by the political desert created by the court investigations, and he shrewdly kept his distance from the parties, especially his own, building a strong, direct and personal rapport with the people, something Naples has always appreciated.

Reformative tensions. Discontinuity was the watchword: starting afresh from ground zero. The past was described as Absolute Evil, with its rampant corruption, clientelistic public spending, the ravenous appetites of the parties and the arrogance of the business lobbies. It was said that Naples had lived in the shadow of a vile liaison between the Camorra and politics and that the resurrection of politics would also require the defeat of the Camorra. 'Naples was a dark city,' Bassolino would write years later, recalling his impression of it upon arriving at the mayoral residence of Palazzo San Giacomo. 'With dim lights not only in the most working-class neighbourhoods furthest from the centre but also in the more bourgeois quarters. Dark outside and dark inside.' The previous council had just declared City Hall bankrupt. 'Can't doism' was spreading, said the mayor, quoting the writer Antonio Genovesi, but now was the time to start over. In contrast to the demonising portrayal of the past, the journalist Marco Demarco wrote that Bassolino's city was depicted as a kind of paradise on earth. Public discourse took on millenarian tones, and the myth of a Renaissance was born. Naples went over the top, as it sometimes does. The work of a public administrator was likened to nothing less than the glories of the 15th century.

Bassolino's charisma was coming into its own. The man who had previously been described as a grey communist official now flaunted completely unexpected political and cultural attributes in a skilful sleight of hand that, piece by piece, helped build his monumental image. He was the man of rules, and he distanced himself from a sociological approach to law-breaking, combating absenteeism among the municipal workforce, declaring himself ready to crush even small-scale abuses, cracking down on cigarette smugglers who asked for exemption and condemning riotous marches by the unemployed. He was in favour of the army's support in upholding law and order. He routinely discredited the political culture of the left, declared himself for the market economy and praised meritocracy. Empty slogans? Not from the mouth of a communist of yore. He privatised the airport, selling it to the British Airports Authority. He placed municipal treasury bonds on Wall Street and used the proceeds to fund public transport.

The image he built for himself was in some ways astonishing. Seemingly transformed by his new role, he became anti-statist, tougher on welfare, liberal, legalist, security minded – and equally astonishing was his rapport with the city, as if the city really identified with its mayor's unequivocal message of modernisation. It is unlikely that it voted for him for these reasons, but – whether it was his stepping in at the right time, the zeitgeist of the moment or the city once again changing its colours – Naples took him very seriously.

Symbolic policies. Bassolino showed that he had the attributes of a monarch and was a skilled communicator. He staked everything at first on symbolic policies, his first moves aimed at plucking the sensitive chords of public opinion. He immediately wanted to confront one of the cultural scourges of Naples, an original character that had perhaps first moulded the city aeons ago: the *crowded space*. In a densely populated city, he wanted to create more room. He turned emptiness into a resource.

When he took office, open and clear public squares were pretty hard to find. They were covered with illegally parked cars and frozen queues of traffic. He liberated them from vehicles and turned them into pedestrianised zones. He became the sorcerer who conjured up a new Piazza San Domenico Maggiore, a new Piazza Dante and so on. Above all, he invented a new Piazza del Plebiscito, transforming it from an immense car park into a wide-open empty space with no private cars, no public transport, no permanent activity, no cafés, no restaurants, no shops. Emptiness. It was an effective idea. In Naples the void suggested freedom, freedom from age-old urban bottlenecks, and it conjured up images of the leisurely stroll of the elderly and of children playing. An entire population went to visit that void as if it were a museum. Piazza del Plebiscito, with its new lava-stone paving and the restoration of the Royal Palace and the church of San Francesco di Paola, became the symbolic centre of the city for Neapolitans and visitors alike, something it had never been. A textbook case of the invention of tradition. But the pedestrianisation of Via Toledo was also a success and was rewarded with the fervent support of the crowd. Other restorations were made to the Umberto I Gallery, the Municipal Villa and fourteen monumental fountains in the historic centre, which were put back into operation.

Bassolino was shaping both the city's and his own charismatic image at the same time. He was changing the collective perception of the environment. Pedestrian areas, historic squares closed to traffic, blooming public flowerbeds, fountains with actual water, restored parks, road surfaces without potholes, functioning traffic lights, legitimate car parking, new public transport, more police, clean streets: it was much more than a well-intentioned effort to spruce up the surroundings, and it affected a significant proportion of the populace. It confirmed the broken-windows theory: just as decay attracts more decay, an improved environment encourages ordinary people to enter a virtuous cycle of self-discipline. Now it seemed that Neapolitans stopped at red lights, observed traffic lanes and dropped fewer cigarette butts on the ground. 'Bassolino had an edge, he was a leader,' wrote the essayist Giorgio Bocca.

But the renaissance went further still. It was cultural. Bassolino intended to build and promote Naples as a city of great cultural relevance and reputation. Culture was offered to the whole city, publicised, popularised and then, thanks to the immortal charm of the Bay of Naples and an excellent press office, it was picked up by national and international news. Clearly, the path was carefully designed. It had a symbolic quality that was fascinating to commentators and social scientists as well as to ordinary folk.

The culture project. Unlike the political landscape Bassolino first came into, the cultural environment was anything but barren. In the 1970s and 1980s, after the post-war chaos, the city had become a powerful point of reference, a place where cultural institutions and private initiatives multiplied. Bassolino could therefore rely on a rich cultural bedrock, and he made shrewd use of it during his terms as mayor, from 1993 to 2000, and later as president of the region of Campania between 2000 and 2010. He made the *Monumenti porte aperte* initiative (designed to open up cultural and historical sites to the public through special events) his own by turning it into an annual event with a strong tourist appeal, the *Maggio dei monumenti* (Monument May). For the Christmas season he filled the empty space of Piazza del Plebiscito with exciting installations by Mimmo Paladino, Anish Kapoor, Jannis Kounellis, Sol LeWitt, Rebecca Horn, Richard Serra and many others. Steel spirals, famous quotes in neon lighting, huge red sails, gleaming white mountains of salt studded with brown horses: installations that brought contemporary art out of the museums and into the public squares, from the intellectuals to the people. In 2005 a charming little museum of contemporary art, the Madre Museum, was opened in the middle of the historic centre, where visitors could admire a collection of paintings, sculptures, videos, drawings and performances by many 20th-century masters.

More than anything, however, the mayor wanted to see his name associated with the creation of a unique 'art metro', Line 1, with stations where the engineering structures merged with the architecture, sculptures, paintings and the large quantity of archaeological finds that were unearthed during the excavation of the metro's tunnels. It's not just an underground line; rather, the idea is to have an actual contemporary-art museum that filled up with crowds of commuters and which at the same time became the reason for their visit – 'an obligatory museum', as Achille Bonito Oliva, the project's coordinator, said.

The open-air structures of the stations erupted across the cityscape with bold, sometimes invasive signs: Gae Aulenti's glass structures, the colourful spires of Atelier Mendini, Dominique Perrault's huge steel canopies, Anish Kapoor's big red crevice, frescos on adjoining buildings, high-tech crossings and squares. And then, down the escalators and into the galleries, awaited Joseph Kosuth's neon installations, Jannis Kounellis's metal panels, Mimmo Jodice and Oliviero Toscani's photography, Michelangelo Pistoletto's canvases, Nino Longobardi's bas-reliefs, Sergio Fermariello's wiry warriors, Mario Merz's prehistoric creatures, and then more mosaics, silkscreen prints, ceramics, mirrors, polychrome totems, giant flowers, fibreglass automobiles, reproductions of classical sculptures, light boxes, meteorites. Art noisily overpowered, almost crushed, the architecture. It became part of the everyday, a subliminal landscape. To those who observed Naples from the outside, Bassolino's metro-museum offered a rich vision of the city's *genius loci*: sunshine and gloom, clarity and darkness, the high and the low, the ancient Graeco-

JUSTICE SERVED?

After Silvio Berlusconi, Antonio Bassolino has been perhaps the most prosecuted politician of the Second Republic: nineteen trials, 140 hearings, 150,000 pages of investigative text, years of shuttling between different courts. Unlike Berlusconi, however, his criminal record remained remarkably spotless: nineteen acquittals out of nineteen! And another difference also stands out: more than once he decided against an acquittal on the basis of the statute of limitations, agreeing to a longer timescale in order to obtain a full exoneration on the merits of the case. All this without playing the victim or levelling accusations at the judiciary, even though his experience raises questions about the slow pace of justice and about the impartiality of some prosecutors. The cases related mainly to his role as extraordinary commissioner during the waste emergency between 2000 and 2004 (when he was also president of Campania). As well as interrupting his political career, the actions also undermined his relationship with the Democratic Party, which was somewhat timid in its demonstrations of support for him. In fact, at the height of the legal storm, during a rally in Naples held by party leader Walter Veltroni around the 2008 general election, Bassolino was even asked not to make an appearance on the stage. In 2016, after the first major acquittals, he decided to stand again for mayor, against the will of his party, losing the primaries by a small margin. He filed an appeal when two videos were published by *Fanpage* showing electoral fraud and the trading of votes in favour of his rival. The following year he left the party he had helped to found, and in 2021 he stood again in the municipal elections, this time as an independent, but only managed third place.

Roman stones of underground archaeological parks and the kitsch plastics of contemporary artists.

It was also an operation of unprecedented gigantism. The first acts of the new municipal government had been minimalist – 'one step at a time', Bassolino kept repeating – but then they changed scale and ended up promoting a vision of the city that hid unlimited, almost shameless ambitions. Neapolitan exceptionalism once again. The Line 1 project sent a strong ideological message that was intended to seduce citizens by its spectacular nature, to remind them of a more noble identity, to bring the elite and the people closer together – and to celebrate *sovereignty* – as the first Bourbon had done with the Teatro di San Carlo. Perhaps an overstatement? What is certain is that the 'art metro' became the flagship of an entire era of politics, as the international press remarked in sometimes triumphal tones. And yet the fact remains that later bureaucracy and funding streams have continued to delay its construction. Thus, decades after the first stone was laid, it remains unfinished and fills the squares with its intrusive building works and has travel times completely at odds with any other metro system. This, however, is a recurring feature of the city: the gap between form and substance, between the passion for glory and the drudgery of everyday life.

Nonetheless, Line 1 offered an entire population high-end culture and sophisticated art and filled the city with abstruse experimental forms of expression. And, of course, the educated classes sided with the apparatchik-turned-Renaissance-prince, supported him, voted for him, at times worshipped him. The city's pride came flooding back. The mayor was its undisputed leader, a communist loved

A De Magistris rally in 2016 at the cloister of Santa Maria la Nova between the first round of voting and the run-off with Gianni Lettieri.

both by the people and in the salons. In post-Tangentopoli Italy, his adviser Mauro Calise ascribed the formation of a new political model to the radical restructuring of traditional parties, to leaders being elected by the people, to the direct relationship between the voters and the elected and to the role played by the media. Bassolino ended up as the national benchmark for the era of directly elected mayors, of a longed-for 'Republic of Cities', as he wrote in a 1996 pamphlet, in which he hoped that the profound political crisis of those years would be solved by the new leadership class that had emerged in the administrations of large cities. Bassolino's Naples was the prototype. It became the workshop of the so-called Second Republic.

Disappointment. It was the high point of that era, an international success that eclipsed all other events. Even as the process of deindustrialisation was at its height and the historic Bank of Naples was being absorbed by the northern Sanpaolo banking group, the city managed to present itself as a triumphant model of urban policies. The prince's PR strategy had been highly effective. The administrative limitations of the councils passed into the background, and efficiency gave way to a seemingly unlimited capacity for hegemony. A kind of conformism emerged that spread like wildfire among intellectuals and academics, artists and the local press, the clergy and the people, the left and the right. In 1997 Bassolino was again crowned mayor and ruler by more than 70 per cent of voters,

'Luigi de Magistris had very little in common with Bassolino – except, of course, the regal throne awaiting him at Palazzo San Giacomo.'

an extraordinary result that did credit to the leader's media strategy.

The following year, however, this relationship between the citizens and the administration broke down, although not because of a critical shift in public opinion. Bassolino was not blamed for the shortcomings of his administration but for betraying the responsibilities of his power. It happened in 1998, when the mayor fell for the temptation of leaving the confines of his own kingdom, accepting the post of labour minister in the new government of Massimo D'Alema, thus becoming the ruler who abandoned his people. Bassolino seemed to forget that from 1799 to 1860 Naples had a long history of fugitive sovereigns. His decision caused a kind of collective trauma, eliciting sentiments of disillusionment, accusations, controversy. As is often the case in Naples, the churning urban identity enfolded current political affairs.

In 2000 Bassolino decided to run in the regional elections, becoming the president of Campania, but he received almost 20 per cent fewer votes compared with the magical year of 1997. The king could be forgiven for anything – even a government that turned out to be underwhelming, even the very rocky start of the grand redevelopment projects in the eastern suburbs and of the abandoned Bagnoli steelworks – but not his desertion. The legitimacy of an absolute monarchy, as the old texts say, sometimes runs on something other than pure reason.

LOVE AND REVOLUTION

As if any confirmation were needed of the capacity of Naples to mutate, the long Bassolino experience was followed by a very different, in some ways antithetical, political model. Luigi de Magistris, who was elected mayor in 2011 and again in 2016, had very little in common with Bassolino – except, of course, the regal throne awaiting him at Palazzo San Giacomo.

The ex-prosecutor's good fortune. Coming from a family of magistrates, de Magistris decided to follow in his father's footsteps, and in 2003, as a young deputy prosecutor, he was attached to the offices of the Calabrian city of Catanzaro. There he attracted press attention for a number of inquiries he led into the connections between politics, business and Freemasonry involving government figures, party secretaries, senior officers of the Guardia di Finanza (the law-enforcement agency that deals with financial crime), magistrates as well as the then president of the European Commission Romano Prodi – and it did not go down well. He was reported, interrogated in parliament and investigated by ministers. Eventually, the Higher Council of the Judiciary stepped in, stripping him of his position as a prosecutor in 2008 and transferring him to Naples. 'I felt the world collapse around me,' de Magistris would later recall on social media. 'The bourgeois mafia had won, the state was stabbing us to death.' He resigned from the magistracy. His case went national, backed by the former public prosecutor Antonio Di Pietro, the comedian Beppe Grillo and the popular television host Michele Santoro. Thanks to Santoro's talk shows, the young de Magistris's face and personality became familiar to millions of Italians, and it was not surprising when in 2009 Di Pietro himself offered him a candidacy for the European Parliament. De Magistris collected something like 500,000 votes – the most after Silvio Berlusconi. It was even less of a surprise when two years later the former magistrate decided to run for mayor of his city.

Naples seemed to expect nothing less. Public opinion was ready for one of its sudden changes of heart. It had happened before. The city would grudgingly bear witness to the rituals of local politics without showing any signs of life – like a grumpy, listless, sleeping creature – suddenly awakening and ousting the old rulers and raising the new king high. It had happened with Lauro who, after a run of victories, had ended up with just 8 per cent of the vote, and with the powerful DC of the 1960s, wiped out by the communist victory of 1975, and with Bassolino, disowned after his flight to Rome. If Naples was ever, as they say, an immutable city, that is certainly not true politically.

By 2011, when de Magistris stood in the municipal elections, public opinion had shifted dramatically: the prestige of the left had sunk under the weight of the resounding waste crisis of 2007–8; political mistakes, administrative inefficiencies and local pockets of resistance had reduced Naples to an image of two-storey-high piles of rubbish bags. Nor was the centre right in any better shape: internally divided, its liberal components fragile by tradition, incapable of

De Magistris in a room at the Hotel Vesuvio, Naples, as votes are counted after the first round of the mayoral election.

choosing an adequate ruling class. De Magistris was lucky. The city's political picture was clear – something not dissimilar to what had happened with Bassolino in 1993. Just as Bassolino had arrived in the wake of the Tangentopoli crisis, de Magistris arrived in the wake of the waste crisis, and he – thanks to his age, background in the justice system and his political-outsider status – had a winning combination of being legalitarian, anti-party and open to younger people. He won unexpectedly, but his adversaries had been in a weakened position. He collected the votes of the leftist electorate and of the broader public that was willing to give the magistrate-mayor a try. And so came about the first experiment in leftist populism in Italy.

Mayor of the streets. De Magistris immediately tapped into an effective ideological language, picking up on the anti-political, anti-capitalist and anti-elitist tensions that spread across the West in the third millennium. He interpreted these tensions on the scale of the city and upon them built his image as a charismatic leader.

The mayor is the unsullied, fearless champion of his community, he declared with a studiedly naive rhetoric. 'Enough of the attacks on Naples and Neapolitans,' he tweeted. He blamed all the city's problems on the policies of the government in Rome, the European Union and international financial institutions as well as on corrupt white-collar circles and mafias. He called for a popular rebellion against what he called 'the unfair debt', that is, the struggling state of the municipality's accounts. 'Governments want to strangle us,' he insisted. The fault always lay with forces outside the city, appealing to the resentful temperament of public opinion, describing Naples as a beacon of civilisation besieged by a maelstrom of short-sighted or hidden agendas, a treasure trove of resources shackled by the chains of central power, life vs. death. 'Naples is as intense as the most wonderful love affair. Here you feel most deeply, here you find your humanity, here your heart beats, here you live,' he wrote.

He declared himself a defender of the people. He legitimised everything he thought contributed to the urban community: spontaneous gatherings, community centres, street processions. He defined public buildings occupied by dissidents as 'liberated spaces'. The people, he said, must 'not only be heard but also be granted power to make decisions'.

In 2014, having been convicted of abuse of office, he was suspended under the Severino Law for corruption prevention, but he had every confidence. 'I am the mayor of the streets,' he proclaimed on social media, turning his legal issues into a formidable exercise in popularity. 'I will not give up, I will not allow politicians and entrepreneurs to get their hands on the city,' he wrote. He constantly raised his game: 'Resist, resist, resist gangs, mafias, political castes, corrupt entrepreneurs and Freemasons.' Far away from his lofty headquarters he hit the city's neighbourhoods, met families in poor areas, visited hospitals and accompanied refuse collectors at night. It was a triumph. 'Thank you to the women and men who strengthen my will to resist,' he wrote at the time, 'thank you for your looks, touches, hugs, kisses, hands.' He quoted Che Guevara: 'If it is worth the

> 'The mayor with the bandana, the one who had wrapped his head in a flashy orange sash on victory day, built a populist model of very broad appeal.'

risk, I'll even bet the last fragment of my heart.' Finally he was reinstated. 'The people have won, Neapolitans have won. Naples, I love you. I will never stop being the mayor of our streets!'

Pop culture. Meanwhile problems began to emerge in local government. Public services entered a spiral of grave inefficiencies. Waste was exported at great expense rather than disposed of, and waste recycling increased only very modestly. The profitability of the municipality's real estate decreased noticeably, while public accounts were on the verge of bankruptcy and local taxes at the maximum allowed. All this, however, did not seem to dent the popularity of the leader who, for his part, played on the politics of image, but this time, in contrast to Bassolino's reign, a popular rather than cultured image. He closed large stretches of the waterfront to traffic, and these areas filled up with cafés and pizzerias and attracted large Saturday-night crowds, hawkers displaying their wares and large food trucks with gaudy neon signs. To those who reminded him that public transport was in poor shape, that parks were deteriorating and that public order and law violations had worsened, he responded with concerts for the youth, large food fairs on Via Caracciolo and festival apparatus built at the Diaz roundabout. The vitality of 'pop' Naples seemed to have won out over the cold accounting of the Ministry of Finance or the European Commission.

And the city seemed to join in with this latest statement of its identity. The same city that in the 1970s and 1980s had given birth to a widespread lively and experimental culture and then had eagerly adhered to the Bassolinian renaissance now seemed to embrace the turn suggested by de Magistris: a popular culture that appeared light years away from the days of film director Mario Martone, art dealer Lucio Amelio or sculptor Richard Serra and which made its own mark on the urban landscape and the anthropology of the community, presumably involving also the middle and educated classes themselves, however silent they remained. This, once again, was a sign of the city changing its spots with its usual combination of adaptation and realism.

The Orange Movement. But it should not be forgotten that de Magistris's narrative of identity held a firm grip on public opinion, expressing as it did the tensions and moods that were being felt simultaneously in many Western countries, and it is to his credit that he grasped them and applied them to his own context. Piece by piece the mayor with the bandana, the one who had wrapped a flashy orange sash (the colour of his political movement) around his head on victory day, built a populist model of very broad appeal. He brought together sections of a society and culture that were stratified, diverse, even contradictory, that were hardly definable by conventional right–left parameters and that were culturally and sociologically mixed. His approach was far-reaching.

De Magistris' 'people' were the youth, the fervent nonconformists and militants of community centres, the students, the young entrepreneurs of a micro-tertiary sector spilling out on to the busy night-time streets, the crowd, adeptly controlled through social media, the street theatre, the countless musical events, the joggers on the pedestrianised seafront, the cyclists on their newly built cycle paths. His voice was heard in the living rooms of the old anti-Berlusconi left and the pro-Bourbon intellectuals. Those he spoke to were the leftist movements of the 21st century, those nostalgic for Third Worldism, the pro-Castroists, the pro-Palestinians, the pro-Kurds, the supporters of Varoufakis, the anti-capitalists and those against neoliberalism, the Latouche-style degrowth supporters, the enemies of globalisation and of the IMF. They were the theorists of public property, of public services, of direct democracy, of people's assemblies. They were the defenders of personal rights, of gay unions, of euthanasia, of living wills. They were the autonomous trade unionists, the labour movement, the defenders of Article 18 against discriminatory layoffs and the seekers of justice, the activists of the no-mercy war on corruption, the lovers of the constitution, the anti-government, those against (former prime minister) Renzi: '*Derenzizzare Napoli*' (de-Renzify Naples) became one of the most popular slogans. But even descending from the realm of idealists to the more materially concerned, de Magistris spoke to the more than twenty thousand city-hall employees and their plethora of associations, along with the café, pizzeria, restaurant and B&B owners who took advantage of the kind of tacit laissez-faire that had settled in, and even the taxi drivers who could service those who waited endlessly for public transport or the illegal car parkers who took over streets and squares by force.

A seemingly incoherent, jumbled list of supporters, yet this was the real picture of politics in the era of post-politics and of popular opinion at a time when parties were disappearing. A paradigm that was anything but local and which at the same time showed an underlying reflection of Naples, of its soul, attitude and behaviour, the paradigm of a conscious lack of order. De Magistris triumphantly became the Masaniello – the 17th-century Neapolitan insurrectionist hero – of the third millennium because he made that lack of order his own, perfected it. Even in the blatant contradiction between his effective and charismatic leadership and the meagre results his administration achieved, the mayor seemed to represent Neapolitans, their low expectations regarding normality, their mistrust of development and their tendency to look outside for someone to blame for their local problems.

But we must not forget the relationship between Naples and the country. What would later be called populism blossomed early in the city. Naples foreshadowed phenomena that would later become prevalent across Italy, outlining their political and governmental evolution. Rather than being an exception, therefore, Naples once again served as a laboratory, paving the way for things to come. If today the populist model – in its various expressions – appears widespread in much of the European and Atlantic West, the case of the 'orange' mayor was one of its first and most potent examples. The perfect champion for a time when tweets matter more than policies.

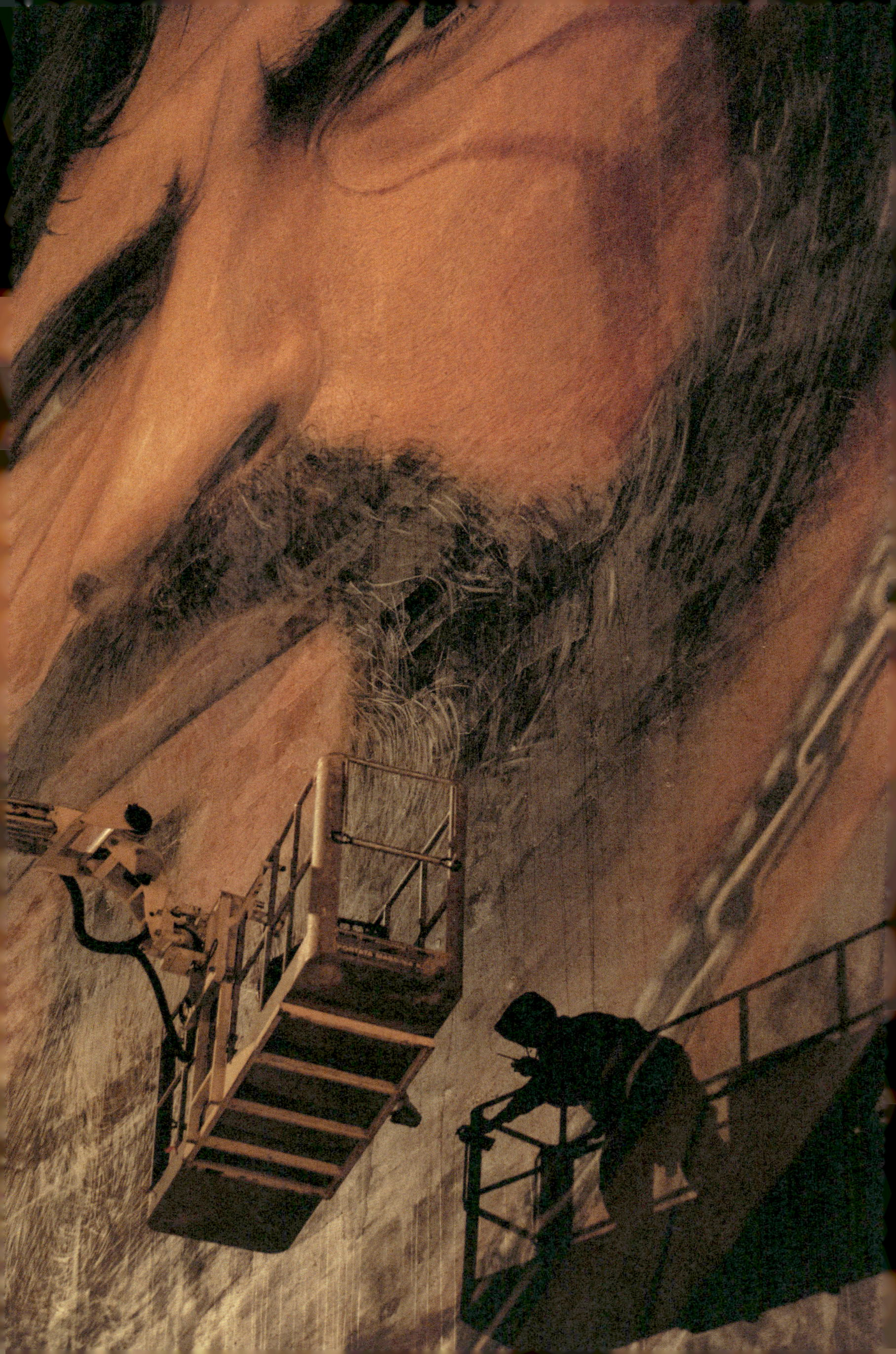

Minor Saints

From the walls lining the streets and alleys of Naples, images of murdered teenagers watch over the city's residents like guardian angels. They are all considered victims – of the Camorra, the police or fate. Some of them, however, were criminals, and the authorities want their portraits erased.

ALESSANDRA COPPOLA
Translated by Eleanor Chapman

The artist Jorit works on restoring the mural of Diego Maradona on the façade of a block of flats in San Giovanni a Teduccio, a social housing complex that became known as the Bronx.

In these narrow streets kids grow up fast and – sometimes – die young. Emanuele Sibillo, the serious, bearded leader of the Paranza dei Bambini – a Camorra gang made up of teenagers – reckoned with this when, barely of age, he tried to beat the bosses at their own game and conquer Forcella, a neighbourhood in the historic centre of Naples. Antonio Criscuolo remembers working with him as an educator with the Chance Project, a sort of street school for 'rehabilitating' students considered to be lost causes. 'They're just children,' he remarks. 'It's unbelievable that we're talking about giving them a second chance.' What happened to their first?

In middle school Emanuele was polite and calm, the natural leader of a group of friends who spent their afternoons hanging out on Via dei Tribunali, the main *decumanus* (or east–west street) of the ancient city. He was obsessed with respect, dignity and justice – or, at least, with the warped way such things are understood in these enclaves. At one point he wanted to be a journalist. There's an old video clip of him with thick hair, holding a microphone, question at the ready. Instead, after his chance at middle school, a conviction for possession of a firearm and a stint in a juvenile detention centre, it was a race to the end.

The infatuation with the crazy idea of taking the city centre from the powerful Mazzarella clan, the real bullets, the raids, the war with the Camorra. A teenage father, his girlfriend pregnant for the second time, the fantasy of easy money, many sleepless nights. Ultimately, an ambush, a wound to his back and the futile transfer to the Loreto Mare hospital. On 2 July 2015, not yet twenty years old, Emanuele bled to death.

Sanctified by his criminal ambitions, by his carefully curated hipster-jihadi style and ultimately by his untimely death, today, still, 'Sibillo rules' – at least according to the graffiti on the Vico Santi Filippo e Giacomo, where his remains were laid to rest in a small shrine to the Virgin Mary in an alcove near the entrance to the building where his family still lives. The white urn, the flowers, the candles, a bust with his black heavy-rimmed glasses on his forehead and his mohawk hair. Legend tells of throngs of worshippers but also of shopkeepers forced to pay *il pizzo* (protection money) and to bow before the shrine out of fear of reprisals. (News reports offer no corroboration of these accounts, which

---

ALESSANDRA COPPOLA has been a journalist for the Italian daily *Corriere della Sera* since 1999. She has mainly worked as a reporter and editor on the international desk, covering stories from Latin America to the Middle East, and for the *Metro* section, where her work focuses on migration. She is now in charge of the paper's podcast series, the most recent being 'Cinema Eros: La strage dimenticata' ('Cinema Eros: The Forgotten Massacre').

> 'There are no longer baby bosses but rather part-time drug mules, petty thieves learning on the job, aspiring gangsters caught up in the system of the Mazzarella clan, who calmly took back control during the pandemic.'

seem more like something out of a television series.) But then, in the spring of 2021 a police operation disrupted the half-hearted attempts to reorganise the family clan and dismantled the shrine to its boss.

When we return to take a photograph a few days after the raid, there are still the remains of broken photo frames, large vases of white and red roses and a Nursing Madonna in a marble frame that, according to the plaque, dates from 1884 and was restored – presumably in thanksgiving for grace received – by a Serafina Napolitano in 1956. A collage of photographs of the deceased, who are all fairly young, includes the singer-songwriter Pino Daniele. There is a note signed by Enzuccio 'o Lupen, 'your friend and brother'.

But there are no longer any images of Sibillo. Everything was confiscated, even the glasses. The urn holding his ashes was given to his mother, Anna, who now looks down, cursing, on to the interior courtyard from the communal balcony on the third floor. Barely forty years old, she hurries towards us, her long, sleek hair tied back in a ponytail, wearing a fleece dressing gown that seems almost like a uniform for the women in these narrow streets. Agitated, she tells us to leave and turns towards an older man whom she recognises, as if trying to calm herself down. 'Don Alfonso, give me a cigarette ...'

*

Investigators say there are no longer *paranze* – gangs of dangerously reckless boys with guns who want to do battle with the adults – like that of Emanuele Sibillo and his older brother Pasquale. The ages of those convicted, however, keep on falling, as if somehow related to the phenomenon of puberty starting earlier and earlier. Several years ago the police homicide unit created the 'baby gang' division. The officers working in this field speak of small gangs proclaiming themselves as 'the new Sibillos' or 'the new Giulianos' (a powerful Camorra clan from Forcella). Every now and again there will be a *stesa*, a burst of random shots fired from mopeds to assert dominance and stake out territory.

There are no longer baby bosses but rather part-time drug mules, petty thieves learning on the job, aspiring gangsters caught up in the system of the Mazzarella clan, who calmly took back control during the pandemic. They might grow up to be killers, but for now, more often than not, they are the victims.

Luigi Caiafa died during the night of 3–4 October 2020 – shot by a plainclothes motorcycle officer with the so-called *Falchi* (Hawks) special unit – as he was attempting a robbery on Via Duomo, wearing a full-face helmet and armed with a toy gun from which he had removed the red cap. He was seventeen years old. He had moved to Forcella with his family from Pallonetto. The story goes that his dad had problems with criminal gangs in the Santa Lucia

> 'Around the corner, a shop selling soap, buckets and Chinese hairclips displays a photograph of Luigi in the small shrine that the family manages, along with photos of their own lost ones and the godlike Maradona.'

district. Luigi seemed to fit in well with the local boys, given that his accomplice that night was Ciro, the son of Gennaro De Tommaso, known as Genny 'a Carogna (Genny the Swine), formerly leader of the Napoli ultras before being convicted for criminal association and drug trafficking.

Luigi's dramatic death shook his group of young accomplices, who decided to pay tribute by devoting a corner of Vico Sedil Capuano to his memory. They organised a collection and commissioned a mural depicting the boy bathed in celestial light – a modern-day version of the many religious shrines in alcoves on the sides of buildings and street corners across Naples. Photographer Mario Spada and I met the artist behind this mural as he was finishing a large painting of Diego Maradona in the Corallo neighbourhood, unusually in black and white at the request of the Fedayn, another ultras group, who had commissioned him and whose name stands out against the stadium depicted in the background of the mural. He didn't want his real name to be used – we will refer to him as LC – because his portrait of Caiafa had just been painted over with an abundant slathering of white limewash, something for which the *prefetto* (the main representative of national government in the city) and the chief prosecutor of the Court of Appeal had been calling, following a long and heated debate.

LC says he prefers to stay out of politics and doesn't want to take a position. It was the police raid that shocked him the most because, as he was working with his spray cans early that autumn morning, he got the impression there was a sort of tacit agreement with 'the cops'. He phones a friend of Luigi's to get him to talk to us, but he's at the paediatrician with his youngest son: another teenage father.

Meanwhile, Caiafa senior, who fought to stop the memorial mural of his son being painted over, was killed – old Pallonetto accounts being settled, those in control in Forcella confirm – and his mother hunkers down behind the iron door of her *basso*, a very small, windowless, street-level flat. Around the corner, a shop selling soap, buckets and Chinese hairclips displays a photograph of Luigi in the small shrine that the family manages – 'He was a friend of my nephew,' the shopkeeper explains – along with photos of their own lost ones and the godlike Maradona. Opposite, there is a cultural centre established by the father of Annalisa Durante, the fourteen-year-old girl who in 2004 was caught in the crossfire between two rival gangs and was killed by a bullet fired by Salvatore Giuliano. There is a memorial to her, too – although this one is untouchable – with a photograph, flowers and marble statuettes. Coming full circle, when Salvatore Giuliano got out of prison he came back to live here.

*

The altars scattered throughout the streets of Naples were installed during the Bourbon period. Rather than creating a street lighting system to reduce night-time crime, King Charles had many of these altars built, which the locals then lit up with oil lamps out of devotion.

Minor Saints

Above: A mural dedicated to Luigi Caiafa. Spotted by police in an unmarked car while mugging a couple, the boy was killed by one of the officers with a shot to the neck and one to the abdomen while he was trying to escape. The gun found in Caiafa's hands was a replica.
Below: Remembering Ugo Russo, who was killed during an attempted robbery. The intended victim was a plainclothes *carabiniere*, and he shot Ugo in the chest and the back of the neck. The officer is being investigated for voluntary manslaughter. Ugo was fifteen years old.

STREET SCHOOL

In Naples the school drop-out rate is higher than the Italian national average – 22 per cent as opposed to 14.5 per cent – but also higher than the average of 18.5 per cent in the surrounding Campania region. This phenomenon, which is linked to economic hardship, feeds the vicious circle of poverty. It is therefore no coincidence that there are numerous alternative educational projects in Naples, the best known of which is the charity Maestri di Strada (literally, Street Teachers), which started out in 1998 as the Chance Project. Operating primarily on the outskirts of the city, the charity – founded by Cesare Moreno, known as the 'teacher in sandals' – aims to help the most vulnerable young people, those with family issues who want to escape from a life of social exclusion. Working with the kids in the class, the volunteer educators and teachers aim to tackle marginalisation – an issue that became more acute during the pandemic with the closure of schools – as well as rethinking students' relationships to culture. In February 2021 Maestri di Strada presented the Patto educativo di comunità (Community Education Pact), signed by thirty associations based in eastern Naples, the municipal councillors with responsibility for schools and young people and local public-health institutions. The aim was to support community development and young people's personal development by means of study-support activities and workshops around subjects such as journalism and theatre. For those interested in digging deeper, two must-read Italian books are *Insegnare al principe di Danimarca* by Carla Melazzini (2011, 'Teaching the Prince of Denmark') and *Di mestiere faccio il maestro* by Marco Rossi-Doria (2009, 'I Am a Teacher by Profession').

Given this complicated proximity of victims and executioners, after the mural of Caiafa was painted over, national as well as regional authorities ordered the police to conduct a survey of 'unauthorised altars', those that depict criminals 'as heroes', in economically deprived parts of Naples. In the words of Luciana Lamorgese, the Italian minister of the interior at the time, 'It is our duty to respect the pain of all families, but when it comes to upholding the law, we cannot give an inch.'

In an interview with an *Il Mattino* journalist Gigi Di Fiore, the former *prefetto*, Mario Morcone, who later became regional police commissioner, explained how 'fairly often criminality works by trying to pass off its practices as religious … Prolonged tolerance has negative consequences.' In short, with some provisos – and with a certain coolness from the former mayor of Naples, Luigi de Magistris – an official 'zero-tolerance' campaign started to take shape, from the judiciary to the archbishopric, forcing even veteran anti-Camorra campaigners to take sides but also generating a protest movement and an open letter signed by Neapolitan intellectuals.

The open letter was prompted by a mural that stands out from the others, at least on an artistic level, and which was created after a similar incident prior to that of the young Caiafa. It is in a little square in an area of the city that climbs up towards the bends of Corso Vittorio Emanuele in part of the Quartieri Spagnoli that takes its name from the parish of Santa Maria Ognibene. In a low building two streets away, Ugo Russo, a handsome boy, as they are round here, was born, grew up, learned to ride a bike and played with his friends and three

STREET ART IN THE CITY CENTRE

MURALS AND OTHER PLACES MENTIONED IN THE ARTICLE

1 *Ugo Russo* by Leticia Mandragora
Piazza Parrocchiella Santa Maria Ognibene

2 *Annalisa Durante* Library and Children's Centre
Via Vicaria Vecchia

3 *San Gennaro as a Factory Worker* by Jorit
Piazzetta di Forcella

4 *Titta Cesarano* by Addi (the statue of her brother, Genny Cesarano, is also nearby)
Piazza Miracoli

5 *Ciro "o Spagnuolo' Esposito*
Supportico della Vita

6 *Emanuele Sibillo* (dismantled shrine)
Vico Santi Filippo e Giacomo

7 *Luigi Caiafa* (erased mural)
Vico Sedil Capuano

SELECTION OF MURALS NOT MENTIONED IN THE ARTICLE

8 *Fidel Castro* by Mono Gonzales and Tono Cruz
Via Mezzocannone (façade of the Mezzocannone squatted social centre)

9 *Angel* by Zilda
Vico San Giovanni in Porta

10 *Madonna with a Pistol* by Banksy
Piazza Gerolomini

11 *Pino Daniele* by Zemi
Largo Ecce Homo

12 *Mission Possible (San Gennaro and Caravaggio)* by Roxy in the Box
Piazza Cardinale Sisto Riario Sforza

13 *Anna Magnani and Maria Callas* by Roxy in the Box
Vico Mastellone

14 *Maradona* by Mario Filardi (restored by Salvatore Iodice in 2016)
Via Emanuele de Deo

15 *Eleonora de Fonseca Pimentel* by Leticia Mandragora
Via Sergente Maggiore

16 *Quore spinato* by cyop&kaf
Around 250 walls in the Quartieri Spagnoli

40   THE PASSENGER   Alessandra Coppola

brothers. He now looks down at passers-by with a concerned expression, shoulders bare and a rosary around his neck, painted against a blue background on a wall of the square.

He died on the night of 29 February–1 March 2020, still under sixteen. It was another attempted robbery, armed with a toy gun, his sidekick riding a moped. It was a Saturday night. They wanted to go dancing, but they had no money. They thought they could get some by following a man in his twenties wearing a Rolex to a car park in Santa Lucia, but he turned out to be an armed plainclothes policeman who pretended to take his watch off, grabbed his service weapon and shot Ugo in the chest and neck. He is on trial for voluntary manslaughter. Ahead of the trial, the neighbourhood – once again – organised a collection and commissioned a mural by the famous Italian-Spanish street artist Leticia Mandragora that calls explicitly for '*verità e giustizia*', truth and justice.

'If removing the mural would solve all the problems, I'd do it myself,' Ugo's father says. 'I know my son did bad, but he should have been punished, not killed.' He points at the wall. 'There's a local ordinance for revitalising public spaces – it used to be a dump here!'

The mural was painted over in March 2023 and replaced by two banners commemorating Ugo, despite the campaigning of writers such as Maurizio de Giovanni, Valeria Parrella and Maurizio Braucci (the screenwriter of, among other films, 2019's *Piranhas* – known as *La paranza dei bambini* in Italian – about children involved in Naples' crime underbelly and very much the story of Sibillo's gang) and the playwright Ascanio Celestini. The mural should have been preserved, they argued, not as a tribute to the young thief but as a piece of public art in a district often overlooked when it comes to improvements in the public realm.

Russo's mother, meanwhile, leads the way to a more secluded corner on the very street where Ugo grew up and now – according to the graffiti – 'lives on' in a little altar at street level. There are photos of him all dressed up lit by neon lights. 'He'd put on a bow tie for his friend's wedding. Wasn't he handsome? It was as if he was getting married himself! It was a neighbour of mine who gave me this photo, and now they all come here to pray to him. Ugo, you were good. Think of us ...'

*

This is what the famous Neapolitan anthropologist Marino Niola, after the noted historian Mircea Eliade, calls 'kratophany', referring specifically to the power wielded by those who suffer an early and violent death. 'These aren't just any old spirits,' he explains to me, 'but souls whose death imbues them with a particular power and who are therefore prayed to for grace and intercession.' Niola has studied this phenomenon and also witnessed it while wandering around the streets of Naples. 'One day, in the Pallonetto area, I noticed a woman in contemplation at a small shrine in an alcove in a wall,' he recounts. 'I went closer and noticed that she wasn't praying to the religious imagery but to a photograph placed lower down, at eye level, at the level of souls in Purgatory.'

In a liminal city such as Naples, on the threshold between this world and the next, this is an ancient and deep-seated ritual. It is entangled with the Camorra because of its everyday nature, but its history goes back much further, fuelled by centuries of disease and violence.

Those who died in tragic circumstances – from stabbings, boils or the gallows – inhabit this midway place.

'They are homeless spirits, lost souls, in need of veneration and care,' the anthropologist continues. 'They represent the archetypal *Ecce Homo*: vulnerable, suffering wretches exposed to injustice.' These *anime pezzentelle* [urchin souls] need prayers and veneration to be released from Purgatory, and yet, at the same time, especially if they died young and 'carry their lifeblood to the next world', they can accrue great power.

'This collective devotion elevates the marginalised – the last shall be first – and these dead souls go from bestowing graces to becoming guardian angels.' The faithful believe they are not entitled to any other form of protection, that no one else watches over them and that they can count only on their own 'minor saints'. 'There is nothing harder to eradicate than deeply embedded symbols,' Niola warns. 'These memorials, although they might be considered sacrilegious, are so deeply rooted that they're not going away.' Not with a lick of paint.

If today these shrines to lost young souls take the form of murals, it is because this older practice has merged with a new, widespread phenomenon that over the last few decades in Naples has developed in internationally significant ways.

*

Let's start in the east of the city, for example, in one of the rough, economically deprived, sprawling suburbs of high-rise tower blocks, vast walls and (almost) no windows: perfect. On the vast walls of the *phalanstère*-inspired tower block – known as the Bronx of San Giovanni a Teduccio – one of the most famous contemporary street artists, Jorit, with the assistance of Leticia Mandagora, painted a massive mural of Maradona, his cheeks painted with the artist's signature red 'human-tribe' markings. There are also the eyes of an autistic boy and, on the other side, two Che Guevaras. A man who lives in the tower blocks proudly remembers having contributed to renting the scaffolding that enabled the artist to do his work. A young man who gives his name as Ciro Esposito just as proudly recalls a group of Argentinian tourists coming to see the murals as well as some Paris Saint-Germain away fans.

Jorit has painted major and minor saints throughout the city – including a famous depiction of San Gennaro, the patron saint of Naples, as a factory worker, a Roma girl and the face of Davide Bifolco, a boy shot by a police officer when he didn't stop when ordered to – on a wall in the Traiano district. He started his career, however, as a graffiti artist in the outskirts to the north of the city – the reasons being more tower blocks, (generally) fewer patrols, greater dereliction and an abundance of walls on which to work undisturbed. A similar logic has influenced the development of urban art in suburbs the world over.

Our next stop, then, is Scampia – made famous as a film and television set, and before that, from the 1970s to the 1990s, as the site of one of the largest social housing estates established under Legge 167, a law passed in 1962 that provided a new planning tool for Italian municipalities to develop urban social housing. The notorious, rundown buildings of Le Vele – the Sails – along with mid-level cooperative housing make for a vast expanse of urban space to paint.

The pioneer of urban art in Scampia

'Street art is still fundamentally grassroots, emanating from the peripheries towards the centre for everyone's immediate enjoyment.'

was Felice Pignataro – the visionary co-founder of the cultural association GRIDAS (Gruppo di Risveglio dal Sonno, the Group for Waking Up), who from the 1980s used murals as an educational and expressive technique. 'Shouting your truth from the rooftops,' his wife Mirella put it during our walk around the area (Felice died in 2004). She also told me about the decision not to restore Felice's now fading murals. 'They're an effective way to communicate with someone in the moment.'

Street art, by its very nature, is ephemeral, but in the northern outskirts of Naples you can still see the traces of the influential Crew KTM – a new generation of artists (including, among others, the famous duo cyop&kaf) working in the 1990s, before this combination of symbols, sounds and attitudes became popular. In April 2021 one of the group's founders, Marcello Divano, known in the art world as Zemi, died at forty-five years of age. His partner-in-crime, Alberto 'Polo' Cretara, who now lives in New York, remembered him in *la Repubblica*: 'He was an accomplished artist. He was painting enormous murals before anyone else was drawing on buildings.' His friend, the Italian rapper Lucariello, stated: 'Thank you for having paved the way for the incredible story that is Neapolitan hip-hop. Sorrow and sadness in my heart. What a loss, Marce''.' Artists asked the council to name a space for teenagers to practise skateboarding and spray painting after Zemi.

Despite the exhibitions, galleries and praise from art critics such as Achille Bonito Oliva (who openly supports Jorit), street art is still fundamentally grassroots, emanating from the peripheries towards the centre for everyone's immediate enjoyment. Even the most famous street artists are still socially conscious, combining well-paid commissions with community fundraising. The quote on the mural of Pasolini in Piscinola, with Jorit's 'human tribe' streaks on his cheeks, reads: 'They'll teach you not to shine. But nonetheless, you shine.'

But because of the folk religiosity discussed above, everyone gets a halo, regardless of the divisions of earthly justice: the district of Rione Sanità dedicated a statue to the memory of the young Genny Cesarano, seventeen years old when he was hit by a stray bullet during a *stesa* in 2015. The Mexican street artist Addi painted a mural of his sister, Titta Cesarano, looking up at the sky. As Ivo Poggiani, president of the local administration commented, 'We should find comfort in beauty.' A few years later a portrait of Vincenzo Di Napoli appeared on a wall in the northern suburb of Miano. He is thought to have fired the fatal shot that night, and two months after Genny's death, concerned he might reveal the identities of the other members of the *paranza*, his boss had him killed.

*

Photographs, however, are better suited than murals to the narrow alcoves in the walls that house the shrines in the city centre. The portrait of Ciro ''o Spagnuolo' Esposito, on Vico Supportico della

Minor Saints

Vita, also in the Rione Sanità, has been retouched so that a golden light shines behind him. The iron railing around the shrine is rusty and the plastic flowers are dusty. His closest relatives died or ended up in jail after the boy was killed to get revenge on his father, 'Pierino', but there must be someone who still holds the keys and maintains the shrine to some extent. The shopkeeper in the traditional *acquafrescaio* stall on the main road tells us that the photograph was placed beneath an old altar dedicated to San Vincenzo "o Munacone' (St Vincent 'the Big Monk'), depicted wearing his fine clothes and donated by an unknown noblewoman. You can still admire it next to an image of the Madonna dell'Arco.

Some of the photographs in the shrines have been signed by famous Neapolitan photographers. A secluded display case on a corner of Vico Purgatorio Ad Arco houses the portrait of Antonio Capuano, lieutenant of Luigi 'Loigino' Giuliano, a former boss who made Camorra history. He sits for the photograph, stylish and smiling, his chin resting on his fist and his flashy watch on show. Photographer Mario Spada seems to recognise the stylistic composition of Gaetano Caso, who portrayed these families in the 1980s, or even that of Oreste Pipolo, one of the

A mural by the artist Jorit in the Traiano district dedicated to Davide Bifolco, killed by the *carabiniere* Giovanni Macchiarolo because he didn't stop at a checkpoint. The officer was sentenced to four years and four months for manslaughter. The bullet discharged accidentally when the officer fell during his pursuit of Davide.

44   THE PASSENGER   Alessandra Coppola

WATER SELLERS AND NUMBER MEN

The *acquafrescaio*, or *acquaiuolo* (water seller), is just one of the many ancient occupations that were a feature on the streets of Naples. Often taking to hawking their wares or skills as result of poverty – a circumstance in which inventiveness and originality can make the difference between putting food on the table and going hungry – the majority of these traders have now disappeared, although not all. The *acquafrescaio* – who could be an itinerant street trader or occupy fixed premises – sold lemonade and a variety of waters, such as *acqua addirosa* (flavoured water, sometimes mixed with wine) and *acqua appanata* (with toasted bread to be used for making meatballs and stuffing) but also rainwater (for laundry), seawater (for fishmongers) or river water. Another of these vanishing trades is the *numeraro*, literally 'number man', whose job it was to write the prices on signs for market stalls, shops, restaurants and pizzerias. There is still one person in Naples plying this trade, Pasquale De Stefano, a veteran craftsman whose workshop in Vico Finale has a hundred-year history behind it. With their swiftly executed but precisely drawn letters and a palette of vivid, sometimes fluorescent colours, his signs are instantly recognisable and a part of the city's iconographic legacy. After conducting photographic research and meeting the master signwriter on several occasions, the Neapolitan designers Alessandro Latela and Gianluca Ciancaglini created a font – which they christened, appropriately, Pasquale – based on the characteristic lines of the lettering produced by the last of the *numerari*. It is the same font we have used in this issue of *The Passenger* for the titles of sidebars like this one as well as the infographics.

most famous wedding photographers in the world. They are often extremely well-executed portraits.

Antonio's brother-in-law, Carmine, notices us at the shrine and politely approaches to give us some information. It is well known that Antonio fought for the Giuliano clan at the time the Naples clans formed an alliance against Raffaele Cutolo for the control of drug trafficking. The circumstances surrounding his death in 1991 are unclear but seem to have involved some punishable indiscretion to do with women. Next to his portrait there is a framed, more recent photograph of his widow, a good-looking blonde woman with her own criminal past who died from an illness. Next to the couple, there is photograph of their son, who died from an overdose in the mid-1990s.

Carmine has the keys to the anodised aluminium railings that protect the shrine. He points to the plaque detailing the year of its foundation, 1889, and the restoration commissioned by Antonio Capuano in 1982. He wistfully shares memories of a Camorra that didn't run rackets – that's his perspective – but distributed donations around the neighbourhood. He calls to an old woman lowering a basket from a first-floor balcony to give her account. 'Capuano? Ah, he was a good man, he always gave presents out at Christmas. He thought of everything, he did ...'

Carmine served time for the armed robbery of a bank. He studied while inside and is very articulate. He's still young, only in his fifties, but when we ask him about the *paranze*, the murals, the Sibillos, 'No, no, I don't understand them.' He closes the railings, smiles and bids us farewell. 'Pop in for a coffee next time you're here'. ◂

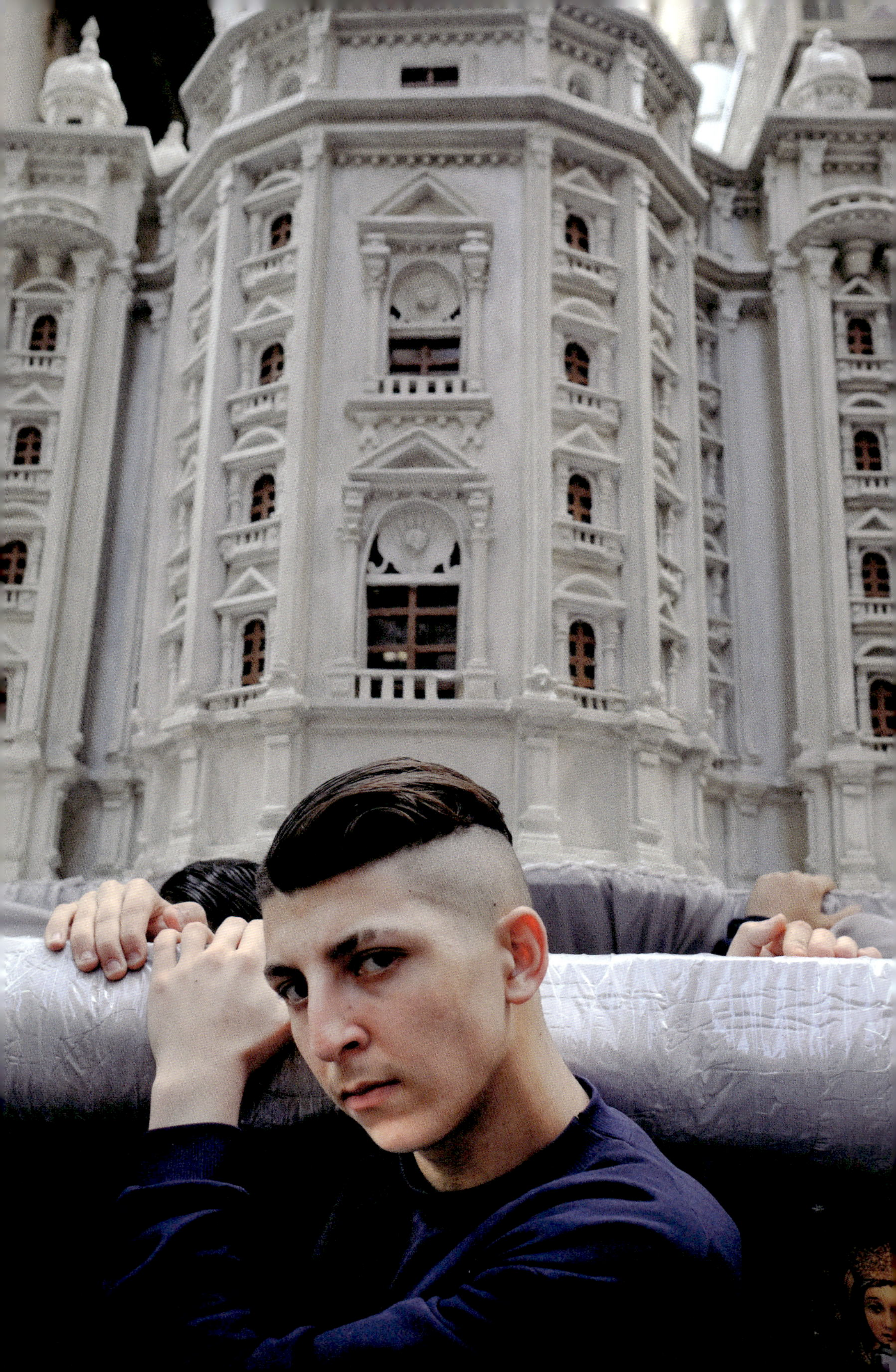

The Neapolitan Janus

Naples, one of the cultural capitals of the Roman Empire, has one of the most complex histories of any city in Europe, one where ancient artefacts are not locked away in museums but are indissolubly linked to the present, a unique and fragile coexistence that could serve as a model for the rest of Italy – and beyond.

LORENZO COLANTONI
Translated by Alan Thawley

Each district of the city has an association dedicated to the Black Madonna of Naples, and over the Easter period the streets are filled with processions honouring this protector of the poor. The events are real spectacles of music, dance and flag waving with participants carrying statues on their shoulders.

I am sitting in Bar Nilo in the centre of Naples, sipping an iced coffee and taking in the view of the little square and the ancient marble statue that presides over it. The figure is reminiscent of the famous personification of the Nile in the Vatican Museums but is not a large sculpture, and most tourists ignore it. Only the passing Neapolitans favour it with a slightly intimate, complicit gaze, because this is *'o cuorpo 'e Napule*, the body of Naples. It always has been and always will be the spirit of the city.

'It's the body of Naples because it's the centre of the city,' says Bruno Alcidi, who runs the bar. In spite of his passion for the past, he doesn't feel the need to go back over the statue's long history – it is a Roman monument dedicated to an Egyptian god that has undergone several alterations over the centuries – instead, he talks about it more as a timeless work that can no longer be attached to a specific period, because it has taken its rightful place in the life and fabric of the city. 'It's no coincidence that there's a little altar with one of Diego Maradona's hairs in it opposite the body of Naples,' says Ivan Varriale, the archaeologist having coffee with me, pointing out the brightly lit and heavily decorated glass case that is actually inside the bar. 'Both of them have become so much a part of the city's soul that they've escaped from their own temporal context, to the extent that they've both been made sacred by the Neapolitans, despite not being sacred objects.' And he starts to give me example after example of the way in which the city's present insinuates itself, gets stuck or blends into the city's myriad past incarnations: we discuss Roman theatres and gentrification, 16th-century cloisters and the Camorra and old, abandoned churches that have been catalysts for breathing new life into their neighbourhoods.

Ivan supplies me with further arguments to support an idea that I have had in my head for some time and have developed over long chats with him and his colleague, fellow archaeologist Daniele Petrella. All three of us are convinced that Neapolitans have a relationship with the past that, with some exceptions and nuances, is substantially one of continuity, almost harmony, in contrast to other cities in Italy and in other countries where the precious but oppressive legacy of the past creates scope for conflict. I am thinking in particular of my native

---

LORENZO COLANTONI is a journalist, researcher and filmmaker specialising in environmental and archaeological themes. He has worked with *National Geographic*, *Corriere della Sera*, *Internazionale* and the *Guardian*, among others, and is the author or co-author of eight books. His research has received two major Italian awards for journalism, the Tutino (2016) and Premiolino (2017). His latest publication is a book about the collapse of the Gulf Stream, *Lungo la corrente* (2024, 'Along the Current').

A reproduction of the Farnese Hercules at Museo metro station.

Rome, where the medieval past has been systematically erased and where even the omnipresent legacy of the Roman Empire struggles to integrate into the contemporary fabric of the city – from the finds discovered during excavations for the new metro lines (promptly buried again) to difficulties with opening spaces in private hands to the public. It is also a difference in attitude, because Neapolitans often engage with the past with a pride and naturalness that we Romans sometimes lack. And as victims of a stark dichotomy between the greatness of imperial Rome and our current circumstances, we also find it less easy to accept stratification, the blending of past and present, so we are also ignorant of everything that went between the two periods, perhaps with the exception of the Baroque era. Naples is different, thanks in part to the fact that the city's stratification is never linear: its Greek, Roman, Byzantine, Norman, Angevin, Aragonese and finally Bourbon eras are rarely superimposed but instead quite inextricably intermingled.

There are many places that encapsulate this unique perspective. They can be found in the centre, ancient Neapolis, where superimposition is continuous and inevitable, but they are everywhere, in the Quartieri Spagnoli, in the Rione Sanità, at the port or in the elegant Chiaia neighbourhood. For some time I have wanted to immerse myself in the city's profound but hidden soul, to take a journey into its present and its past. After finishing my coffee I decide that the time has come. And so I set off.

I start out from the notional central point of the city, the Largo Corpo di Napoli, with my first destination

The Neapolitan Janus

already in mind: Signora Anna's apartment and the great secret it conceals. My route takes me through the streets of the centre, which in themselves already tell us so much about the relationship between ancient and modern. 'The only real development plan in force in Naples is the one drawn up by the ancient Greeks,' says Ivan, joking, but only up to a point. He has tagged along, pleased to be able to visit a place that is currently difficult to access even for a noted archaeologist like him. Fundamentally, his assertion is true. The centre of Naples is famously arranged around three main streets known as the *decumani* (east–west roads), which, in spite of their Roman name, are actually the *plateiai* (main streets) of the ancient Greek city. The side streets, like the Via San Gregorio Armeno, famous for its traditional nativity cribs, are the *stenopoi*, the secondary streets, which still run at right angles to the *decumani* as laid out by Greek settlers in the late 6th century BCE. I make my way along them, trying to assimilate the awareness that is clear in the minds of many Neapolitans: the form of these streets has not changed since the days of Magna Graecia, and, with every step, I am following in the footsteps of the city's ancient inhabitants on their way from the *agora* to the *acropolis*. I know that there are various practical reasons behind this fact – first and foremost, the underground cavities frequently found in the subsoil (or created by quarrying for volcanic tuff), meaning that it has always been easier to build directly on top of pre-existing buildings rather than undertake the tricky task of constructing new foundations. But I also know that over the centuries this environmental constraint has insinuated itself into the Neapolitan mentality, creating the strange coexistence between past and present that now typifies the city. I am filled with Sartre's feeling of disorientation, *dépaysement* – which was the title of a novella he wrote about Naples and Capri – as I observe the countless pharmacies with timid curiosity. In so many of them, behind the modern medicine labels and the contemporary façades, you can still see the old briarwood shelves, half-hidden.

In fact, I had already felt this sense of disorientation, of being in limbo between past and present, the evening before in my apartment on a side street intersecting with Spaccanapoli (one of the *decumani*), with its modern Ikea furniture standing on a floor of antique maiolica tiles. On the narrow terrace where I had to stand because the thickness of the old walls blocked any kind of phone signal indoors, I watched a woman in the little alley tending to the 19th-century shrine, which has been transformed into a kind of garden. All of the city's shrines in private hands are tended in this way, whether they are modern or very old, such as the one containing an 18th-century *Ecce Homo* that is stuck under the awful Kimbo building in the Ponticelli neighbourhood. The Neapolitans look after these shrines and decorate them regardless of how old they are. The past is a constant part of their lives that cannot be separated from the present.

This superimposition is clearly visible from the terrace of Signora Anna's apartment, our destination, which we have finally reached. From the top of her block you can see the cathedral and countless other buildings that I try without success to get Ivan to date for me. 'For some it's impossible to say,' he replies. 'Here you can see one from the Bourbon era built on to elements from the 16th century. Over there a 1960s wall and a terrace built a few years ago. You don't know where one begins and the other ends.' The most surprising part, however, is not what we can see up high, in front of us, but what lies below: this block of flats contains the only visible section of the ancient Roman theatre of Neapolis. Built in the first century BCE, it was one of the emperors' favourite places – perhaps Nero even performed there. It is perfectly embedded in the building, with the marble terraces of the *cavea* – which some say could seat up to six thousand people – ending only where the building's wall begins. The structure of the building itself is tortuous and apparently disjointed precisely because it follows the ancient pillars of the theatre on which it rests. The view is unique and currently a rare privilege because the theatre has not reopened to the public since the beginning of the pandemic, and only the intervention of my friend Antonella Furno, an archaeologist who worked in the area, gave me access to the flat shared by Signora Anna and her son Luigi. This unique situation is a source of pride but also a natural part of their lives. While I go into raptures over the view, they notice the socks that have fallen from the laundry hanging directly over the terraces and which they will get their neighbour on the ground floor to pick up for them. Luigi also talks to me about the performances of classical drama that were staged right there in the theatre and how his mother would interact quite casually with the actors. 'In the end, before going on stage, some of them would be congratulating her on her pasta sauce,' he told me with a smile.

The centre of Naples gives the impression that it is still inhabited in the same natural way, its narrow streets the backdrop for the sort of everyday life that has now vanished from Rome or Florence, where the historic centres are increasingly sterile and focused exclusively on tourism. Here, however, tourism has yet to make its presence fully felt. So the *bassi* – the characteristic cramped apartments opening directly onto the streets on the ground floors of 17th-century buildings – still reveal untidy kitchens, the ever-growing numbers of restaurants still alternate with fishmongers and greengrocers, the souvenir shops with old bars and ironmongers. 'But, above all, it's the intellectuals who assert this connection with the past,' Ivan points out as we leave the theatre, suggesting we make a little stop to prove his point. We head towards the nearby Basilica di Pietrasanta, which in theory remains closed to the public but which Ivan can access in his capacity as scientific director. An impressive sight greets you inside. The church has the highest dome in Naples but is completely empty because of the work being carried out, including to the 18th-century hand-painted maiolica tiles on the floor. 'We're adding a protective layer so that people can walk on it freely,' explains Martina D'Aniello, one of the restorers from Artes, the all-female firm in charge of the works. A necessary measure, because even though the basilica is no longer used for religious purposes (despite not having been deconsecrated) it does play host to numerous exhibitions and events run by the association Polo Pietrasanta – an improvement on its treatment in previous decades when it was used as a storehouse and even for illicit motorbike races.

But this continuity of use is not what Ivan wants to tell me about, nor even the extraordinary superimposition that is also revealed by this building – Hellenistic houses, Roman townhouses, an early Christian church and the current 17th-century basilica all stand on the same site. He shows me a map in the old crypt, where, in association with the National Archaeological Museum, they are installing a permanent exhibition of the city's past. It shows the genuine instances of current Christian churches being superimposed on Roman places of worship as well as the – probably false – examples posited by many Neapolitan intellectuals. 'The churches were given legitimacy by the continuity of their sacred status, from paganism to Christianisation,' Ivan tells me, 'because scholars had to justify the present on the basis of antiquity. It happened in the 9th century, and it still happens in the same way to this day.' He goes on to mention the countless times he has found himself trying to unpick presumed connections between historical places and current buildings and their uses in discussions with intellectuals and journalists. 'I had an argument with one journalist who maintained that the Temple of Apollo was underneath the courtyard of Palazzo Carafa, whereas what you

A night-time stroll on the pier at Castel dell'Ovo.

THE SUBTERRANEAN CITY

can see is simply the foundations of the building. The allure of continuity with the past still lives on, because it is normal for Neapolitans. And it's quite difficult to make them believe otherwise,' he says, as I notice a long flight of stairs that takes you down underneath the vast pillar that holds up the basilica's dome. This is a passage that leads to the tuff quarries that provided the materials for the building but also gives access to a long section of the famous subterranean city, the ancient belly of Naples. I ask him to show me around the area that is still closed, and we set out for an hour's exploration that feels like it lasts a lifetime. Here you enter an alien world that seems to have nothing in common with the throngs of people in the *decumani* a few dozen metres above our heads. We walk through kilometres of tunnels lit only by the light of our torches, through gigantic 17th-century cisterns and Greek wells that descend from 18th-century *palazzi*. Here and there you can still see signs of the most recent use of this underground world, the ghostly remains of the bathrooms and even entire little apartments that many people built when these tunnels were used to shelter from bombing raids – after Milan, Naples was the worst-hit city in Italy during the Second World War, leaving wounds that have still not yet entirely healed. This was one of the rare instances of a rupture between past and present in Naples, because the tunnels filled up with the rubble from

Tuff is a type of rock composed of the compressed and compacted ash from volcanic eruptions, which develops different colours depending on where it was deposited. Neapolitan yellow tuff is the product of volcanic activity on the Phlegraean Fields, and it is made up of ash that became sediment in the sea and later re-emerged between 35,000 and 10,500 years ago and is found all across the Campanian Plain. As a result, veins of this light, strong, easy-to-work rock run underneath Naples. Since the time of the first Greek settlement it has been used to build the city on the surface, while, in a mirror image, its subterranean alter ego has been dug out underground, making way for sewers, cisterns, catacombs and tombs. As the centuries have passed, the buildings of the modern city have been constructed on top of earlier structures – including Roman aqueducts and theatres. Since the 1960s and 1970s it has been possible to visit the remains of these older constructions, after the association Napoli Sotterranea opened up an exploratory topographical route. One of the initial aims was also to evaluate the city's safety, given that it is in part built over empty space. The association now boasts a 'geothermic' pizzeria on the site of an old Roman bakery, an art gallery and an underground kitchen garden – an experiment in the cultivation of different plant species far from the pollution on the surface, but also far from daylight. Its popularity with tourists led to other similar projects, such as the reopening of the Catacombs of San Gennaro beneath the Rione Sanità by a neighbourhood cooperative that employs more than thirty young people from the local area and welcomes over 130,000 visitors a year.

the bombing and were gradually abandoned. The reclamation began twenty or so years ago but almost exclusively for the purposes of tourism. I have the feeling that one element of the city's life was lost for good.

This partial disconnection from its underground past has made the work of many archaeologists specialising in subterranean Naples particularly complicated, as I discover when I leave Ivan in the basilica and head away from the centre of ancient Neapolis in the direction of the Rione Sanità district. Waiting for me there are an engineer, Mario Cristiano, a speleologist, Mauro Palumbo, and the president of the association Celanapoli, Carlo Leggieri. I expected to meet them in a modern office, but instead I find them, somewhat incongruously, poring over a 19th-century tome in a former cobbler's shop, full of dusty old furniture and piles of maps. This is the operational base for their research into the ancient Greek necropolis, which stood right under our feet and which is the focus of the association's activities. In fact, it extends all around us. So far they have identified around ten funerary monuments, but there could be at least a hundred or so. Difficult to say, because they are wedged in between cellars, buildings, streets and cisterns, forgotten or perhaps absorbed by centuries of superimposition.

After a tour of the courtyards, distracted by the aroma of food emanating from the kitchens, Carlo opens a big metal gate and leads me underground, where an even more striking sight awaits. I find myself in front of a tuff-stone portal adorned with the figures of a married couple, as well defined as if they had been carved half a century ago but cut off halfway by the arch of the 17th-century *palazzo* that stands on top of the tomb so that you can barely make out the *dexiosis*, the gesture of greeting captured by the sculptor 2,500 years ago. Around them are piles of debris that the three men have painstakingly cleared away over time: you can still see an old chamber pot, a toy brought over by Americans after the war, scraps left by the cobbler upstairs over many decades of trading. Stratification within stratification. The other funerary monuments are even more hidden. You access them through the anonymous courtyard of a house – which dates from the 17th century but, from the way it fits into its surroundings, could have been built in the 1960s – through a hole made in the floor that reveals the old staircase that the owner had blocked up. To the right is the former studio of a tattoo artist, who was working there before Celanapoli rented the space to excavate the cellar, while to the left the shop's bathroom is still there. 'This is a section of the Augustan aqueduct,' says Carlo, pointing to the corner with tiles, WC and basin, which I had half thought about using, but looking again I can see Roman *opus reticulatum* stonework where the plaster is missing. A really amazing thing is to be found down two flights of stairs, however, where you enter another three tombs that still contain their sarcophagi and wall paintings, in some cases perfectly preserved. Were it not for Carlo's authoritative confirmation that they date back to antiquity, I might have imagined they had been painted by the lady slowly simmering her *ragù* above our heads. 'The sarcophagi here have been opened and looted, but in the tomb where we were earlier they might still be intact. We'll have to excavate. And we still don't know what the others could contain.'

An artists' dinner in Michele Iodice's laboratory-cum-studio.

Finding them will not be a simple task, though, because on top of the speleological, engineering and archaeological dimension, Carlo insists that his work is, more than anything, an 'anthropological' project. 'You have to build a rapport with the people who live in these buildings so that you can continue the investigations in what in the end are their homes,' Carlo says. 'If I hadn't talked to them, hadn't stopped for a coffee to say hello and give them a chance to get to know me, I wouldn't have been able to discover any of this. Sometimes it took a week, other times you don't get there even after twenty years. Near here there's one guy I'll convince sooner or later. I didn't manage it with the father, but if not him then I might have success with his kids.' For Carlo the only way to convince the locals to open their doors to him is to invoke this same sense of the continuity between present and past and the pride associated with it.

In its continual intersection with the present, the city's past inevitably also crosses paths with the live issues affecting the city, including criminality and the regeneration of its disadvantaged areas. This is also a matter I want to address, so I have arranged another meeting close by. I say goodbye to Carlo and his colleagues and make my way to the nearby Nuovo Teatro Sanità, where the theatre's director, Mario Gelardi, and Matteo Borriello, an art historian who often works around here, are waiting for me. The reason for our visit is the building: the theatre occupies an 18th-century church, which, once again, has not been deconsecrated. The young team who run the space have, however, been granted use of it by the parish. While Mario proudly shows me the

The Neapolitan Janus 55

A Brief History of Naples from Antiquity to the Second World War

☞ Graeco-Roman Period

9th–8th century BCE Greek settlers found their first settlement on the small island of Megaride (where the Castel dell'Ovo, the city's oldest castle, now stands). With assistance from the inhabitants of Cumae, they go on to establish Parthenope on the Pizzofalcone promontory.

6th century BCE The Cumaeans are also responsible for establishing the 'new city' of Neapolis, in the area corresponding to the current historic centre. It becomes one of the most important cities of Magna Graecia, the Greek settlements in Italy.

326 BCE The Romans conquer the city, although it retains its Greek character and institutions.

79 CE An eruption of Vesuvius destroys Pompeii, Herculaneum and Stabiae.

476 The Castrum Lucullianum (Castel dell'Ovo) was used to imprison the last Western Roman Emperor, Romulus Augustulus.

☞ Byzantine Period

536 General Belisarius conquers Naples (entering the city via the aqueduct), and the city remains under Byzantine rule over the following decades, although gaining evermore independence until it becomes an autonomous duchy (some say in 661 under Basil of Naples, others in 763 under Stephen II).

☞ Normans and Swabians

1139 The Neapolitans hand the city over to the Norman King Roger II of Sicily. His son William I has the Castel Capuano built in 1165.

1194 The city comes under the control of the Swabians. In 1224 Frederick II founds the first state university.

☞ The Angevin and Aragonese Periods

1266 Charles I enters the city: the House of Anjou comes to power and the capital of the Kingdom of Sicily moves from Palermo to Naples. In 1279 the construction of the Castel Nuovo (also known as the Maschio Angioino) begins.

1302 De facto birth of the Kingdom of Naples as a separate entity from Sicily.

In 1309 Robert of Anjou is proclaimed king. During the Angevin period the capital of the new kingdom is enhanced and expanded; many monumental churches are built, as well as a fourth castle (Castel Sant'Elmo) and a new port. Giotto, Boccaccio and Petrarch visit Naples.

1442 After Joanna II of Anjou-Durazzo dies without an heir, Alfonso of Aragon conquers the city. The Aragonese court under Alfonso and his son Ferdinand I (aka Don Ferrante) is among the most refined and influential of Renaissance Europe.

☞ Viceroyalty

1503 After repeated wars between the French and Spanish for control of southern Italy, troops loyal to King Ferdinand II of Aragon, led by Gonzalo de Córdoba, enter Naples, signalling the start of a long period of Spanish viceroyalty, during which the city is once again expanded.

1600 The construction of the Royal Palace begins. In 1606 Caravaggio arrives in the city and goes on to influence a generation of local artists. With around 220,000 people, Naples is Europe's third-largest city after Istanbul and Paris. It remains in the top five until the 19th century, despite an outbreak of the plague in 1656 that kills between a third and a half of the population.

1631 An eruption of Vesuvius threatens Naples. The Neapolitans express their gratitude to their patron saint for having saved the city by erecting the Obelisk of San Gennaro in Piazza Riario Sforza.

1647 The population of the city, led by the fishmonger Masaniello to the cry of 'Long live the king of Spain, death to misrule', rises up against the tax burden imposed by the viceroy's government. Masaniello lasts ten days before being killed, and the revolt is bloodily suppressed the following year.

☞ THE BOURBONS

1734 After a brief period under Austrian control, Naples regains its independence thanks to Charles of Bourbon, who begins an ambitious urban development programme both inside and outside the walls, with the construction of the Teatro di San Carlo, the palaces of Portici and Capodimonte (as well as the palace of Caserta) and the royal almshouse, the Real Albergo dei Poveri. Naples becomes one of the capitals of the European Enlightenment. In 1738 the excavations of Herculaneum begin, followed by those at Pompeii.

1759 Charles leaves Naples to claim the Spanish throne in Madrid; his son Ferdinand becomes king of Naples.

1799 A group of patriots and intellectuals proclaims the Parthenopean Republic, based on the French model, but within six months Ferdinand of Bourbon returns to the throne and the revolution ends, once again, in a bloodbath.

1806 The French conquer Naples, and Napoleon grants the kingdom to his brother Joseph Bonaparte. He is succeeded by Joachim Murat, who promotes administrative reforms and public works.

1815 Murat is executed by firing squad. Ferdinand retakes the throne of what is now known as the Kingdom of the Two Sicilies.

1839 Italy's first railway opens, running from Naples to Portici.

1848 Revolutionary uprisings lead to a parliament and a new constitution, but the following year the parliament is dissolved. In 1859 Francis II, the last king of the Two Sicilies, ascends the throne.

☞ THE KINGDOM OF ITALY

1860 Garibaldi enters the city, and the kingdom is annexed to Piedmont following a referendum. Florence is chosen over Naples as the capital of Italy, and twenty years of economic crisis begin.

1884 A terrible cholera epidemic in the city is followed by the urban renewal project known as the Risanamento to make the city a healthier place in which to live. Entire working-class neighbourhoods are swept away and the Corso Umberto and the Galleria Umberto I are created. In 1889 the city's first funicular railway begins operations (the Vesuvius funicular dates back to 1880), linking Vomero to the centre.

1918 Although far from the front, Naples is bombed by a German airship. Rather than hitting strategic targets (the Ilva steelworks in Bagnoli or the port structures, for example) the bombs fall on the city centre.

1934 The project to redevelop the Rione Carità is approved, giving rise to an entire neighbourhood of fascist construction, including the post office and other public buildings. During the fascist era Naples loses its position as Italy's most populous municipality, first to Milan and then to Rome. In 1940 the Mostra d'Oltremare exhibition complex opens in Fuorigrotta.

CONTINUED ON ☞ PAGE 13

(significant) work carried out to convert the church, I take in the production desk where the old organ would have been, the service corridors located in the matroneum and contemporary artworks everywhere in dialogue with the church's interiors. This is not just a theatre but one of the centres driving the regeneration of a tough neighbourhood, as the Rione Sanità was for many years and in parts still remains. Mario is a theatre director who has spent many years fighting against the Camorra, and he sees the Nuovo Teatro Sanità as the best way to keep young people off the streets and to give them an alternative to slipping into criminality. This is an idea that was initially met with a certain hostility; in the theatre's first year those who did not want the project to go ahead inflicted serious damage on the building. It was only Mario's determination – plus that of the young people and the support of their parents – that made it possible to continue, culminating in the successes of recent years. 'It is also the neighbourhood's social network that makes all this possible, and it could also perhaps give rise to a different form of tourism,' adds Mario, who sees the Rione Sanità as the epicentre of a sort of tourism 2.0, a suitable model for Naples but also for other places. Compared with the attitude of 'tourism at all costs' espoused by the former mayor Luigi de Magistris, the pair see the regeneration of the district as an opportunity to promote a slower, more thoughtful approach than that of the mass tourism that has robbed so many other cities of their souls. 'Only people who have already had contact with Naples come here,' says Matteo, who believes the starting point for tourism in the Sanità must be through promoting visits 'on a human scale'. 'The key to success will be in the coordination resulting from the autonomous approach that is intrinsic to this neighbourhood and our natural relationship to the past,' adds Mario, who contrasts such 'respectful' visits to the Sanità to the tourist explosion that has hit the historic centre, which, while still very much a place where people live, has nevertheless changed in recent years, and not for the better, according to some, with the original inhabitants increasingly pushed out of its *palazzi*, in part because of the growing number of short-term tourist lets.

This subject is close to my heart. As a Roman, I have seen Trastevere slowly disappear beneath the shock wave of

THE MIRACLE WITHIN A MIRACLE

Miracles abound in the story of San Gennaro, who was persecuted for his Christianity and martyred in 305 CE. There are stories of how he managed to escape his fate on previous occasions: in one instance he calmed the wild beasts who were about to devour him; in another he escaped unscathed from a burning furnace. Neapolitans – who honoured him with the Chapel of the Treasure in the early 17th century following an epidemic – remember him above all for the miracles he performed posthumously. For instance, in 1631, more than a thousand years after his death, a procession of his relics is said to have saved the city from destruction following an eruption of Vesuvius. And then, of course, every year there is the liquefaction of his blood. The chapel that contains the vials, relics and the treasure – miracle within a miracle – has been run since the early 17th century by a lay organisation, the Deputation of San Gennaro, rather than the Church itself. This scandalous independence from the Church authorities is jealously defended by the venerable institution, which consists of twelve members, two for each of the six *sedili*, the institutions that governed the city when it was established – five for the nobility, one for the people. After five centuries of resistance, in 2016 the privilege was due to be removed by a reform promoted by the then interior minister, Angelino Alfano, who wanted to alter the dynamic within the Deputation by introducing four members nominated by the city's cardinal. But the cardinal himself opposed this break with tradition. Cue a U-turn and apologies. But the Deputation could now do with one final miracle: for the municipality of Naples to pay its overdue contributions. The city, which has been taken to court over the matter, has failed to pay its annual fees of €89,000 for a number of years.

tourists, mostly Americans, while a similar fate has befallen many parts of Florence and the whole of Venice – two cities where I have spent a lot of time in recent years. So I decide to leave Matteo, Mario and the Sanità and dig deeper into the subject, but with a complete change of scene. I make my way to Chiaia, a neighbourhood that seems to belong not just to a different city but almost to a different planet. This is the place for the elegant calm of Gucci and Marinella boutiques, selfies with the latest Tramontana bag or a Louis Vuitton billiard table priced at €70,000. Chiaia is home to the Libreria Grimaldi, a bookshop that, like the Nuovo Teatro Sanità, also occupies a church that has not been deconsecrated.

Opened a few years ago, the shop contains books old and new as well as historic prints piled up in what were the different parts of the church – on the altar, in the pulpit, even in the matroneum – in a sort of elegant *horror vacui* perfectly in tune with the church's Baroque style. 'Over the past five years, 80 per cent of the bookshops in Naples have closed. The reason is the demand for premises to open up clothes shops and restaurants aimed at tourists. If this space wasn't granted to me by the church authorities perhaps I wouldn't have survived either,' Mario Grimaldi tells me. The owner of the bookshop and eponymous publishing house is sitting behind his desk, which is wedged in beside the altar. He lays the blame at the door of 'chaotic tourism', which is also exacerbated by the Camorra's involvement in the hospitality industry. By flooding the system with large amounts of money to be laundered, it further inflates prices, driving the emptying-out of the city. And, ultimately, this also breaks the relationship that exists between Neapolitans and the past by taking them away from the places they have lived for generations, destroying the thread that is simultaneously formed from continuity in the use of these places, pride in their own past and family tradition.

I discover these three interlinked factors in one of the last appointments I have organised, at La Pignasecca market. Yet another change of scene takes me to one of the oldest markets in the city, one which maintains a direct link with its 16th-century origins. Apart from the odd stall full of phone chargers and sunglasses and the endless stream of scooters, little seems to have changed over the centuries. My companion is Bianca Verde, a tough trade unionist and a well-known face in the market, who introduces me to a few of the historic Pignasecca families. It doesn't take long for them to confirm the existence of this interconnection between families, past and present. 'If you're born in the market, it's difficult to leave,' Francesco Varriale tells me. At thirty-three, he represents the fifth generation of greengrocers at Funcillo; the shop took its name from his grandfather, who was always singing and was therefore known as *Funcillo*, Neapolitan for chaffinch. 'I'm devoted to my family's tradition, for what it represents and for what it's done for me. I'm proud to continue my great-grandparents' work. But it took me some time to understand that,' Giuseppe Benvenuto explains. He runs the family's dried-fruit business, which has been there for more than seventy years. Giuseppe went halfway round the world and had more jobs than he could count before coming back home and reclaiming his direct link with the past. At the market the link is not expressed through archaeological stratification but continuity of use and explicit pride in your origins. 'The family stories have become a part of me. An appreciation of this job is something you're born with,' he adds.

Their words help me to connect the many distant points on this journey into the relationship between ancient and modern in Naples. It is a delicate interplay of cultural and social references, the importance of family and tradition and factors relating to the urban fabric that connects to a sense of belonging that Neapolitans seem to cultivate more than those in other parts of Italy. It is a unique situation but a fragile one that is under threat not just from mass tourism but also from the city's movement into the future, the way in which people in Naples experience cultural heritage compared with the past, with more respect but perhaps also more detachment. To many Neapolitans, artefacts in glass cases feel confined. I recall the words of Signora Anna, who is starting to struggle with the local authority's restrictions aimed at preserving the theatre. I think of the body of Naples itself, the statue whose original head the Neapolitans believed had been separated from the body and placed in Piazza Mercato. This was not the case – the head in question came from another find from a different era – but, despite that, it was associated with the cult of the body of Naples and considered a part of the city, like the relic of a saint. However, once it was replaced with a copy in the 1960s, its importance inexorably disappeared from the popular consciousness until it was largely forgotten. I wonder whether in future many elements of the complex relationship between ancient and modern in Naples might suffer the same fate.

I also imagine the opposite, that this unique connection could be one of the new blueprints for tourism and urban planning now being sought by so many cities in Italy and elsewhere. To an extent Naples has already developed an effective model for this: the metro-museum, an idea that had already been successfully developed in Athens and has found fertile ground in Naples. I see it for myself at my final appointment on this short journey, a visit to the building site of the Municipio metro station right underneath the Maschio Angioino, the city's iconic castle. This is Europe's largest archaeological dig, and I feel incredibly fortunate to be given access in the months before it opens. I walk among the quays of the Roman and Greek port embedded in the station's concrete, the

GALLERIA BORBONICA

Beneath Pizzofalcone hill it is possible to see a clear example of the continuity between past and present, and even more so of the stratification of Neapolitan history – sometimes in a literal sense. The Galleria Borbonica (Bourbon Tunnel) – which was built in the mid-19th century between the palace in what is now Piazza Plebiscito and Piazza della Vittoria in Chiaia on the orders of Ferdinand II – was designed as an escape route for the royal family. The excavations intersected with the tunnels and cisterns of a 16th-century aqueduct (built in its turn over the older Graeco-Roman aqueduct) and the chambers of the Carafa Quarries used to provide building materials for the construction of various buildings in the area and are currently home to a multi-storey car park. The tunnel was never completed because of difficulties caused by the geology of the hill but also the death of the king in 1859 and the arrival of Garibaldi soon after, so it was left abandoned until the Second World War, when some sections were repurposed as air-raid shelters. Then, up until the 1970s, it was used as a municipal pound, where all the items left over from destroyed or demolished buildings, evictions and confiscations were stored (including large numbers of cars and scooters), while other sections were used as illegal dumps. During the restoration works that were carried out between 2007 and 2010 by volunteers from Borbonica Sotterranea (the association that operates the site, which is now open to tourists), statues from various eras were discovered, including the funerary monument to Aurelio Padovani, founder of the Neapolitan fascist party. From the Roman practice of *damnatio memoriae* to modern-day cancel culture, many have tried, but in the labyrinths of Naples history has no intention of allowing itself to be erased.

Above: Leather workers at La Pignasecca market.
Below: The Porta Nolana market, also known as Ncopp' 'e mura, is an ancient fish market in the centre of Naples.

> 'The experimental approach to stations such as Museo and Università was extended to history when the line began to enter the historic centre.'

Angevin *palazzi* that emerge isolated where once there were gardens. I see the impressive extent of the fortifications built by the viceroys running alongside the moving walkway of the station, still surrounded by numerous crates of finds labelled with more or less cryptic writing on the wood. More than a metro station, it resembles the set of an Indiana Jones film.

When I visit the station it is still not finished, although it is already open, but the integration between past, present and future is already solid and evident. It leaves me speechless. As a Roman I'm used to the opposite narrative, the idea that archaeological discoveries are an impediment to the development of public services and progress in the city. Here, on the other hand, they are seen as an opportunity. 'Every impediment is a benefit, as philosopher Giambattista Vico put it,' points out Antonello De Risi, the chief engineer of the Neapolitan Metro Consortium, who accompanies me on the visit. He and Professor Ennio Cascetta were the masterminds behind this perfect combination but also the uniqueness of the metro-museums that have made Naples a global example. He has been working on the concept since the beginning of his career. The experimental approach to stations such as Museo and Università – which embraced the vision of architects and artists such as Studio Fuksas and Anish Kapoor – was extended to history when the line began to enter the historic centre. An innovative solution to the dilemma of what to do with archaeological finds on construction sites in historic cities such as Naples was provided – a way of transforming the problem represented by historical stratification into an opportunity. Municipio presents numerous solutions: one part of the station will become a museum housing finds from the excavations, while another will be a small archaeological park open to the public. 'It's the idea of an obligatory museum, which works really well because there aren't just tourists here. Above all you have a huge flow of commuters, who find themselves immersed in the city's past,' Roberto Calise tells me. Roberto is an old friend who has written a book on the subject. He loves the history of his city but has a shrewd perspective on its future, so I thought he would be an excellent guide for a visit balanced between the two. He says that a success like the metro-museum was possible only in Naples because of its unique capacity to marry different cultures and periods in the city's life but also the pride in the past that allowed administrations to spend so much on addressing the challenge posed by a vast excavation below sea level – almost all of the remains were dismantled and reassembled, and the tunnels were dug out after freezing the ground to avoid flooding. 'But they had to go to that much effort. The future of the city was at stake in recent years,' Robert concludes. He believes that the far-sightedness and scale of the metro project provided the greatest – and perhaps only – stimulus for the city's new urban renewal. An impetus that led to the development of a recipe for cohabitation between the past, present and the future of Naples in a way that could become a model for the rest of Italy and perhaps also of Europe more widely.

I leave Naples thinking about the confidence of Roberto Calise and Antonello De Risi's vision of urban development, Matteo Borriello and Mario Gelardi's hopes for a new brand of tourism that keeps the experiment in the Rione Sanità alive, the continual intersection of the work of enthusiasts such as Ivan Varriale and Carlo Leggieri with Neapolitan everyday life. I leave the construction sites and the centre behind and head for the station. Before entering the Piazza Garibaldi underpass, however, I allow myself a final moment of distraction at Porta Nolana, home to another of the city's historic markets. The traditional name for it pops into my head – Ncopp' 'e mura ('on top of the walls') – because the area was built where the Aragonese fortifications once stood. I look for remnants of the walls

Above left to right: A man and his dog in front of his house in the historic centre of Naples; refuse collectors taking a break in the historic centre; a dealer in second-hand goods reads the newspaper outside his store.

among the giant swordfish heads, tuna and mackerel and the cassava sold by the greengrocers specialising in the foods of the diverse communities that shop in the market. They seem invisible but are actually right in front of me: the walls were transformed into the buildings that contain the workers' homes and workshops. There are Aragonese towers with apartment buildings that appear to date from the post-Second World War period, corners of the old construction once topped with battlements that have now become an unauthorised balcony from which a curious child looks down at me. In the great debate on the fate of ancient walls, which some cities (the majority) have destroyed and others (Rome being one of very few) have preserved, Naples seems to have found a third way, by giving them a new lease of life. As a woman hangs out her washing over the old arrow slits, I leave the city recalling the words of the writer Adrian Wolfgang Martin, who, in his work *Janus von Neapel*, associates Naples with the figure of Janus, the two-faced Roman god who looks both forwards and backwards at the same time. Only now can I see how faithfully Martin's words capture the indivisible soul of Naples, and his are the last words in my mind as my train leaves: 'He embodies the enigma of man as a living, creative unity of complementary contrasts, each one the cause of the other.'

The Neapolitan Janus

A view of Castel dell'Ovo and Monte di Dio from Castel Sant'Elmo.

GOING TO NAPLES

CRISTIANO DE MAJO
Translated by Eleanor Chapman

Is Vomero part of Naples, and are the Vomeresi Neapolitans? That depends on your perspective.

67

'I'm going to Naples.'

This is what my paternal grandfather, Corrado, who was born and lived his whole life in Vomero, would say when announcing any sort of trip into the city centre. Despite technically living in Naples, by saying he was 'going to Naples', he meant the flat stretch of city between 'the railway' on Piazza Garibaldi and the coastal district of Mergellina, from the seafront to the slopes of the hill. Naples was the shopping thoroughfare of Via Toledo and the coast at Santa Lucia, the Quartieri Spagnoli and Forcella. Naples was the Montesanto Funicular, the ancient *decumanus* of Via dei Tribunali, the old city gate at Port'Alba, Via Foria, Pizzofalcone, Chiaia and La Torretta. Everything above Corso Vittorio Emanuele – the street halfway up the hill that runs through a large swathe of the city – on the other hand, was *not* Naples. Or maybe it was another Naples, added too recently to be assimilated into the city founded by the Greeks – or rather by Cumaeans of Greek origin – in the 8th century BCE.

The Vomeresi's self-perception of not truly belonging in Naples – and, in particular, the subtly racist corollary that, in the eyes of those from the centre, Vomeresi aren't real Neapolitans – was not only held by my grandfather and those of his generation. The idea that this hilltop district is a separate suburb is something that has been integral to its history since its initial development at the end of the 19th century, even if the ways of expressing it have changed and the distance from the centre feels perhaps less.

When I was younger, in the 1990s, a different expression was used. It still implied a degree of separation but to a lesser extent. If you had to go somewhere downhill you wouldn't say, as my grandfather did, 'I'm going to Naples' but rather 'I'm going down into Naples', a phrase which implied a divided city, with lower and upper parts. No one would ever actually say 'I'm going up to Naples', but 'up' was loosely, and with a broad margin of error, understood to mean either Vomero itself or, more generally, Camaldoli hill. 'Going down into Naples' only made sense for those of us who lived up the hill – a certain shop would be 'down in Naples', or at night we'd go 'down into Naples' to meet friends. I think it is safe to say that the sense of separation is even less acute today, in part because the neighbourhood's presence in the city has become more established, and in part because, when Vomero merged with its neighbour

CRISTIANO DE MAJO is a writer, journalist and teacher of creative writing. He is executive editor of the magazine *Rivista Studio* and has worked with *la Repubblica*, *Internazionale*, *Diario*, *IL* and as an editor at various publishing houses. He is the author of four books, the most recent being the memoir *Guarigione* (2014, 'Healing').

> 'Elsewhere, Vomero seemed to be like one of those areas in every town that everyone knows, like Notting Hill in London or Greenwich Village in New York, while in the centre of Naples Vomero was not even considered part of the city.'

Arenella, it became, with around 120,000 inhabitants, the most populated district in the city.

Naples' annexation of Vomero is perhaps not unrelated to the fact that in recent years several famous Neapolitans have come from there. Luigi de Magistris, for one, mayor of Naples from 2011 to 2021, was from Via Belvedere, and he built his electoral success in the ward that encompasses Vomero and Arenella. And then, of course, Oscar-winning director Paolo Sorrentino grew up in Via San Domenico, only a few hundred metres from de Magistris. Another important development was the opening of the first stage of the so-called *metropolitana collinare* (hillside metro) in 1993, which formed an underground connection that contributed to a levelling between the upper and lower sections of the city.

During my first year of university, tired of friendships that never extended beyond the area of my college – an institution specialising in sciences situated between Arenella and Upper Vomero – I started to hang out with a group of students from Chiaia. They had all come from the most important college in Naples, the Liceo Classico Umberto I. Intelligent, switched on and rich, they could easily have been tagged with the hackneyed label '*Napoli bene*' ('posh Naples'). One of the first things I noticed when we started hanging out was how alien I was as a Vomerese – worse, as someone from Upper Vomero – in their friendship group, which was strictly concentrated in Chiaia or, at a push, in the historic city centre. I don't want to make this out to be a typical Disneyesque story of a working-class boy trying to be accepted by the aristocracy. It was more subtle than that. I wasn't working class, and I wasn't going to any great lengths to be accepted, although I think I can safely say that I never truly was. There was prejudice against and jokes at the expense of Vomeresi from 'real' Neapolitans, something that still goes on – I had to deal with it recently in a spat on Twitter. I don't want to exaggerate how serious it was; I just want to try to explain that there was a peculiar and seemingly unparalleled dynamic between this part of the city in the centre of Naples, whatever its socioeconomic makeup, and Vomero, higher up geographically but middle class socially.

*

Later, when life took me elsewhere, as it does many Neapolitans, I realised how little this slightly teasing, somewhat derogatory perception of the neighbourhood corresponded to the picture of Vomero that people had elsewhere, in Rome or Milan, say. In the rest of Italy Vomero is one of the three or four best known districts of Naples – at least by name – along with the Quartieri Spagnoli, Posillipo and Chiaia. I also discovered that if when asked by someone from Rome or Milan the customary question '*Naples* Naples?' I answered,

'Yes, from Vomero,' they would look at me as if I came from a beautiful, enviable place. Elsewhere, Vomero seemed to be like one of those areas in every town that everyone knows, like Notting Hill in London or Greenwich Village in New York, while in the centre of Naples Vomero was not even considered part of the city. I have often wondered where this discrepancy comes from.

There certainly is a small part of Vomero that is rich, but beyond that, wider Vomero is decidedly middle class. It could even be said that Vomero is the only neighbourhood in Naples, perhaps only alongside Fuorigrotta, where you can still see signs of 'normal' life, liberated from the exceptionalism that devours and contaminates everything in Naples. A middle-class, Italian normality that in the rest of the city has been ground to dust between the top and the bottom.

Vomero's 'normality' has been unpopular with people who love Naples and feel Neapolitan precisely because of this exceptionalism. On the other hand, it made – and still makes – the residents of Vomero feel safe within their own neighbourhood. It is, literally, a comfort zone; some people feel almost a sense of unease or hardship when venturing into other parts of town. Vomero differs from other middle-class districts of Naples, such as Chiaia or Posillipo, in that it does not have its own rougher areas, a labyrinth of streets with their own rules and atmosphere. The middle-class homogeneity of Chiaia is 'contaminated' by the Quartieri Spagnoli on the one side and La Torretta on the other, while Posillipo is home not only to luxurious villas with steps leading down to private beaches but also to the fearsome streets of Casale, an economically deprived and vaguely criminal core within what could be described as 'the Beverley Hills of Naples'. In Vomero, however, there are only a few disparate pockets of deprivation left: around the Mercato di Antignano or Piazzetta Arenella, Via Belvedere and the Petraio and Pedamentina steps, old, by now almost entirely empty streets leading down into the city centre, over which the three funicular lines were built. Any remnants of the quintessential Naples – the very small, windowless, street-level *bassi* flats, the little shops selling Nativity scenes, shouting from the balconies, washing hanging out to dry – are too dispersed to represent a threat to Vomero's 'normality'. The residents are unaccustomed to the sort of proximity between social classes that for centuries has characterised the city, that proverbially exists not only within neighbourhoods but also inside buildings, with lower floors occupied by less affluent classes and upper floors by the better off. It is often said that in Naples you can turn a corner or wander on to a new street and find yourself in a completely different world, with all the risks that that involves. This doesn't happen in Vomero. In so far as it is possible to speak of homogeneity in Naples, it is the most socially and visually homogeneous district in the city.

*

In July 1995 the second stretch of the *metropolitana collinare* was opened, connecting stops at Vanvitelli and Colli Aminei, a neighbourhood in the north of the city between the Zona Ospedaliera and Capodimonte. This extended the line towards the highly feared northern suburbs of Scampia and Le Vele – the sail-shaped tower blocks made famous by the international hit TV

GOING UP ... GOING DOWN

In order to get 'down into Naples', and even more so for the uphill return journey, for over a century the people of Vomero have used the city's funiculars. These are perhaps its most characteristic means of transport, built to support the transformation of Vomero into a residential area in the late 19th century. The first to come into service – at the height of the Risanamento urban renewal project – was the Chiaia funicular in 1889, initially steam powered, then electrified in 1900. Prior to that, Vomero was reached via the Calata San Francesco, a long flight of steps that heads directly south (when going down) towards the sun and the island of Capri. It was already featured in some views of the city dating from the late 17th century. The Montesanto funicular followed the Chiaia line just two years later, in 1891, running alongside two other flights of steps, the Pedamentina di San Martino and the Scala di Montesanto. The Central funicular – now the busiest (and the longest), connecting Via Toledo to the heart of Vomero – was inaugurated during the fascist era, as was the last, the Mergellina, perhaps the most spectacular and certainly the steepest funicular, with a maximum gradient of 46 per cent. This last example, however, does not serve Vomero but ascends from the Mergellina district to Posillipo hill. Since 1976 the funiculars have been operated by ANM, the municipal public transport operator, which has undertaken several restoration projects. ANM also controls the other 'hectometric' public-transport systems travelling over short distances, which include four elevators and two escalators, highlighting the vertical development of the city. The four funiculars transport 55,000 people a day on average, but there are still a few inhabitants of Vomero who consider it an effort to go 'down into Naples'!

crime series *Gomorrah* – adding stops at Frullone, Chiaiano and Piscinola. Sleepy Vomero was thus put at risk of invasion by hordes of louts – vulgar and unruly, if not downright dangerous – and fear seeped through the residents, who were jealously protective of their comfort zone. At the behest of concerned Vomero community members, the Comitato dei Valori Collinari (Committee for Hill Values) was founded by engineer Gennaro Capodanno. Along with safeguarding the area's traditional craft workshops and cultural heritage, it also aimed to block the arrival of 'barbarians' in Vomero. The committee still exists, although today it deals with less ethically contentious and more mundane issues such as potholes. Meanwhile, in the city, 'hill values' has become a particularly ironic expression.

The idea of beleaguered Vomero citizens barricading themselves in their own little fortress to protect themselves from the onslaught of kids from Le Vele makes me think of a scene from a famous novel set in Naples, *Il resto di niente* ('The Remains of Nothing') by Enzo Striano, a piece of historical fiction first published in 1986, four years after the completion of the manuscript, and which only found success a year after the author's death. It was described by Adolfo Scotto di Luzio, in his 2008 work *Napoli dei molti tradimenti* ('Naples: A History of Betrayal'), as the novel that established 1799 as a 'key turning point in the autobiography of bourgeois Naples'. The plot focuses on Eleonora de Fonseca Pimentel, a Portuguese noblewoman who moved to Naples from Rome at the age of eleven with her family, later becoming one of the key figures in the Jacobin Revolution of 1799, which aimed to make Naples an outpost of the struggles that had taken place in

LAZZARI AND SCUGNIZZI

Lazzari, scugnizzi, guaglioni – three terms to describe Naples' underclass, a presence in every era of Neapolitan history, praised, despised and stereotyped: from the smiling figure stretched out in the sun embracing the joyful side of life to the barefoot urchin, an embodiment of poverty and degradation. In the 17th and 18th centuries the *lazzari* were organised into hierarchical structures, with elected leaders and elementary forms of mutual support (the famous revolutionary Masaniello was one of them). During the Bourbon era they even took on official roles maintaining public order, and in 1799 they fought in defence of the popular King Ferdinand IV, the 'Lazzarone king'. In 1848 they once again took sides, against the revolutionaries, but in 1860 they had become anti-Bourbon and enthusiastically welcomed Garibaldi. By then, however, according to some historians, there was an overlap between the *lazzari* and the Camorra. In the meantime, a new figure was on the rise, the *scugnizzo*, a term of dubious etymology that at first suggested a whiff of criminality. However, their reputation was polished through their active involvement in forcing the Germans out of the city following the Four Days of September 1943 when Italy signed an armistice with the Allies. This insurrection is commemorated with a 'Monument to the Scugnizzo' on the Riviera di Chiaia. In its various forms and meanings – from Renato Carosone's song 'Guaglione' to Pino Daniele's 'Lazzari felici' – the street urchin is omnipresent in the city's culture, a central figure in such events as the Piedigrotta Festival and a source of inspiration for Neapolitan artists, not infrequently *scugnizzi* themselves by vocation or by background, even when they're far from home, like Nino D'Angelo in the classic 1984 film *Uno scugnizzo a New York*.

France a decade before. The very end of the novel describes the failure of one of the first attempts to establish democratic government in Europe. The Neapolitan republicans, who had been bombarding the so-called *lazzari* – a term still occasionally used today to refer to a criminal underclass – from the fortified Castel Sant'Elmo in Vomero, see their advantageous situation being overturned, as the hilltop fortress overlooking the city is besieged:

> For the whole afternoon and evening, the enemy fire concentrated on Sant'Elmo. They were now firing explosive shells from the fortress, too. Some of them arrived spent, but others whirled in mid-air, whistling and smoking, then exploding with terrible flashes of purple and yellow and bursts of deadly shards. Many of the gunners were in pieces, dead; other patriots had fallen in the square ... The night started calmly. The gulf was gleaming, the ships had turned on all their lights. But there was movement on the hill. For some while, *lazzari*, *sanfedisti* and soldiers had been clambering up the moonlit steps of Petraio, bearing rifles, pistols, white-and-red standards and flaming torches. Everyone was watching from the battlements ... The assault was expected at dawn, but an hour after midnight cries arose from the teeming crowds under the fortress. They started to shoot. Clouds of smoke, whistling shells.

This 'betrayal' by the people of Naples who, instead of joining the struggle against the regime of Ferdinand IV and his wife Maria Carolina, rose up against their liberators, from that moment on

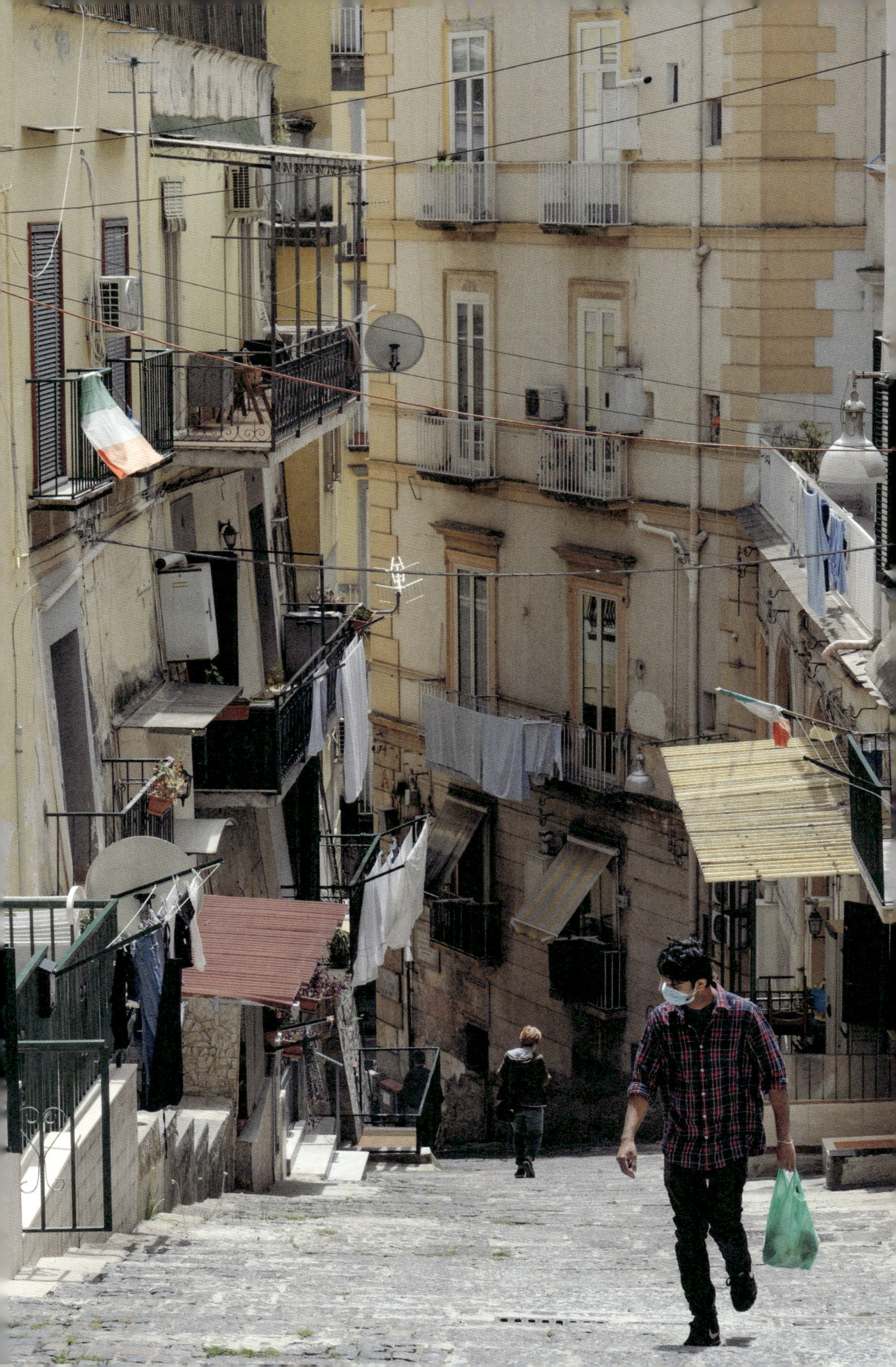

entered the city's DNA. The defeat of the revolutionary intellectuals at the hands of the *lazzari* came to be seen as foundational to many of Naples' ills – the bourgeoisie's lack of leadership on the one hand and the 'political' untrustworthiness of the proletariat on the other. There is no obvious relation here to the snobs at the end of the 20th century, frightened of being pickpocketed by hooligans from Scampia, but still, this fear of being toppled or invaded can be interpreted as symptomatic of the fragile ego of the city's narcissistic middle class.

*

I mentioned that Vomero is a sort of 'comfort zone', cushioned against all of Naples' social ills. On 11 June 1997, however, an event that remains seared in the city's memory tore violently through these protective layers: two cars carrying six heavily armed passengers drove from La Torretta, a seafront neighbourhood bordering Chiaia, to Salita Arenella, a busy street in Vomero. There, they opened fire – forty shots, it was later discovered – on two members of a rival gang, who were to be eliminated because of an issue relating to the control of business in the hills. The hitmen did strike their target, Salvatore Raimondi, but a woman also lay dead on the ground. Her name was Silvia Ruotolo, and she was thirty-nine years old. She had been picking up her five-year-old son Francesco from school, and her older daughter Alessandra, ten years old, had been watching from the balcony. Her mother was struck in the temple by a stray bullet, and she died on the spot. This accidental death at the hands of the Camorra caused great distress in Naples

Page 73: the Petraio Steps, a street of stairs connecting Corso Vittorio Emanuele with Upper Vomero. Walking around this area feels almost like you are in a small coastal village, but unfortunately there is no shortage of unregulated building work.
Left: A view of hilltop Vomero.

and remains traumatic to this day. The long, horrifying list of Camorra victims includes lawyers, entrepreneurs and people shot by accident or because they shared a name with the intended target. But it is hard to picture a victim further from Neapolitan criminality than Silvia Ruotolo – a mother struck dead as she was holding her son's hand on their way back from school, a 'normal' middle-class woman, the cousin of two well-known journalists, Guido and Sandro Ruotolo, the latter of whom had appeared on the popular news shows of left-wing journalist Michele Santoro. And this happened in Arenella – a fairly homogeneous, middle-class area between the pedestrianised shopping streets in the centre of Vomero and the other hillside districts of Rione Alto and the Zona Ospedaliera.

Troubled places need icons, Batman-style heroes, most often victims, whose parables can symbolise the hope for redemption – anti-Camorra priests, business owners who refuse to pay *il pizzo*, magistrates killed by car bombs. This is how it is in Calabria, in Sicily, and Campania is no different. Silvia Ruotolo, unsurprisingly, was ordained an 'accidental heroine', a tragic patron saint for those who could end up paying with their lives for the sickness of their city. Carlo Visconti, the judge who presided over the murder investigation, famously described the difficulty of obtaining witnesses – for a shooting that happened at rush hour – as related to a form of civilian *omertà*, or communities' participation in the Mafia's code of silence. On the other hand, her funeral, attended by vast crowds, went down in history as a demonstration of popular opposition to the Camorra.

In 2017, on the twentieth anniversary of Silvia Ruotolo's death, her cousin Sandro, the journalist, posted a photo of her on Instagram with the caption: 'This is my cousin, Silvia Ruotolo. Twenty years ago she was killed by the Camorra on her way home with her son, Francesco, who was five years old. There have been and still are many innocent victims of the Camorra, but Silvia's funeral was a watershed moment. Naples was outraged. Today Naples is a changed city, and that's because some of this outrage was channelled into action. It's not enough, but it would be a disservice not to acknowledge it. Some people did not truly do their duty, others still just stand by and watch. Twenty years ago it bothered me that the bourgeoisie said "That's got nothing do with us" and still today we must tell this bourgeoisie that we cannot be neutral, we have to take a stand for our land.'

Has Naples really changed over the last twenty years as Ruotolo claimed, and by what standards can we measure that? Where is the evidence for this 'action'? If we were to look at the city's reputation, how it is perceived from the outside, its appeal to Italian and international tourists, the answer to the first question would probably be yes. But if we were to look at criminal activity in the area, then the answer would have to be no. The Camorra has continued doing business and killing. After the death of Silvia Ruotolo, between the end of the

1990s and the first years of the 2000s, Naples experienced one of its most violent wars, the feud between the Di Lauro clan and the Scissionisti di Secondigliano, as depicted in *Gomorrah*. Then there were the *paranze dei bambini*, the 'baby gangs' (see 'Minor Saints' on page 33), and the *stesa* shootings, among other signs of the fatal power of criminality in the region. There was also the famous 'accidental death' of Annalisa Durante, a fourteen-year-old girl in Forcella. And what have the 'bourgeoisie', rallied by Ruotolo, done in the meantime? But, I might ask, what could they have done, especially against such firepower? The change Ruotolo had in mind was probably more political, represented by the figure of Luigi de Magistris, the popularly elected mayor, who, in an interesting coincidence, appointed Alessandra Clemente, Silvia Ruotolo's daughter, as a local council member. For many years, alongside her father, she had been heavily involved in civil efforts to combat organised crime, and at the end of his second term de Magistris put her forward as a potential mayoral candidate in the elections of October 2021, a candidacy that was later thwarted by the coalition between the Democratic Party and the Five Star Movement.

But even if not that much has really changed, Sandro Ruotolo still got to the heart of the complex position of the highly criticised Neapolitan middle class. What does 'taking a stand for our land' mean? What does it mean to be 'neutral'? In this context, at least in principle, it means that disengagement is not permitted: to be disengaged is to be complicit. It's more than simply colluding or participating in a particular structure of power. According

The Certosa di San Martino, a former monastery now a museum, in Vomero.

'It's more than simply colluding or participating in a particular structure of power. According to a certain line of reasoning, it is the duty of everyone living in Naples not only to bear witness to but to actively resist the cancer of criminality.'

PUB CENTRAL

As a city that jealously and proudly guards its cultural traditions, Naples is also, paradoxically, highly permeable to 'foreign' loans and influences. There is one obvious historical reason, relating to its domination by a succession of external powers over the centuries, the most recent – albeit not exactly comparable to the long periods of French or Spanish rule – being the 'domination' of the Americans, the city's saviours in the Second World War. Among the inexplicable phenomena, on the other hand, is the extremely high density of pubs in a neighbourhood like Vomero, often with the faux-authentic look of British and particularly Irish pubs, beginning with their signs written in Irish script. There must be a company in Naples specialising in pub furnishings that supplies everything you need, perhaps even suggesting an 'appropriate' name (the Penny Black, Beckett Pub, Murphy's Law and McCool's are just some of those that have sprung up). Legend has it that many years earlier the first pub to open in Vomero was Vecchia America in 1976, opposite the park in Via Ruoppolo – although, if truth be told, the vibe was more Tex-Mex than Dublin taproom. It was renowned for its delicious panini and for staying open practically all night to cater to clubbers coming home at dawn. But perhaps the real turning point was the opening of Napoli Centrale in 1984, a pub recreating the interior of a train carriage with furnishings bought directly from a railway company, a pub with an 'original concept', the popularity of which might have triggered the unstoppable wave of English, Irish and Scottish clones. (CdM)

Via Alessandro Scarlatti, a pedestrianised shopping street in Vomero.

to a certain line of reasoning, it is the duty of everyone living in Naples not only to bear witness to but to actively resist the cancer of criminality. It is, in short, a call for courage, fortitude or even direct action, as exemplified by, for instance, the extraordinary twenty-six-year-old investigative journalist Giancarlo Siani, who was killed – decidedly not accidentally – in 1985 for having got too close to the business of the Gionta clan based in Torre Annunziata. The execution took place beneath his parents' home in Piazza Leonardo, less than five hundred metres away from the tragically famous Salita Arenella (see 'Giancarlo Siani' on page 159).

But can we really expect the same passion and daring from the average citizen? This could be described as Vomero's great paradox – the idea of a normal life in a middle-class neighbourhood in a city where normality is impossible. Criminality is possible. Complicity with criminality is possible. You can be a hero, or you can honour the Mafia code of silence, but you cannot be 'normal'. This is partly because there is not really an economic system today that allows for the existence of a bourgeoisie in the true sense of the word and partly because a city in a state of emergency cannot accept the neutrality of those who would prefer to pretend that the emergency doesn't exist. And yet, walking around Vomero today, from Piazza Vanvitelli along the pedestrianised Via Scarlatti, seeing the shop windows, the bars and cafés with their outdoor tables, the old people sitting on benches watching passers-by, that's exactly how you'd describe it, 'normal'.

*

Personally, what I like about Vomero are its modern buildings, unexpected and underappreciated in a city that flaunts its history. There are the early-19th-century buildings and houses designed in Liberty style flanking Via Luca Giordano and the narrow side streets coming off it or those you can glimpse on Via Palizzi and Via Luigia Sanfelice. And then there are the modern apartment blocks, reminiscent of similar neighbourhoods in other Mediterranean cities (such as Kolonaki in Athens), buildings that were constructed and inhabited during the boom years of the 1950s and 1960s when the middle classes were growing and coming to live in the 'new' areas of the city – namely Vomero (especially Viale Michelangelo and Via Aniello Falcone) and the newer streets in Posillipo (such as Via Orazio or Via Petrarca).

Despite being noticeably underrepresented in the enormous literary output focusing on Naples, Vomero is the setting for one of the city's most important and celebrated novels, *Via Gemito* by Domenico Starnone (translated into English by Oonagh Stransky and published by Europa Editions in 2023 as *The House on Via Gemito*), which is set during the boom years and follows a lower-middle-class family who move from Ferrovia to the eponymous street that connects Via Cilea to Piazza Quattro Giornate. The family's hopes for happiness and normality are shattered by the ambitions and moods of the head of the household, a railway clerk who dreams of being a painter, inspired by the author's own father. Many people have drawn comparisons between the

Going to Naples 79

Strega Prize winner – and his wife, the writer and translator Anita Raja – with Elena Ferrante, and, indeed, if you walk up Via Gemito towards Piazza Quattro Giornate then carry straight on to Via Altamura, just a kilometre away from the setting of Starnone's novel, you end up at the opening scene of Elena Ferrante's latest book, *The Lying Life of Adults* (translated into English by Ann Goldstein and published by Europa Editions in 2020):

> Two years before leaving home my father said to my mother that I was very ugly. The sentence was uttered under his breath, in the apartment that my parents, newly married, had bought in Rione Alto, at the top of Via San Giacomo dei Capri.

I was even more surprised to find Vomero in one of the most acclaimed American novels of the last twenty years, Jennifer Egan's *A Visit from the Goon Squad* (Knopf 2010, USA / Corsair, 2011, UK), the 2011 Pulitzer Prize winner, a collection of interrelated stories set at different points in time. In one of these stories, two characters, Ted and Sasha, find themselves in Naples:

> Blowing smoke from the window of a taxi, Sasha harangued the driver in halting Italian as the car shrieked down alleys and the wrong way up one-way streets to the Vomero, an affluent neighborhood Ted had not seen. It was high on a hill. Reeling, he paid the driver and stood with Sasha in a gap between two buildings. The flat, sparkling city arrayed itself before them, lazily toeing the sea. Hockney, Ted thought. Diebenkorn. John Moore. In the distance, Mount

A view of the Gulf of Naples from Via Palizzi.

> Vesuvius reposed benignly. Ted pictured the slightly different version of Susan near him, taking it in.
> 'This is the best view in Naples,' Sasha said, challengingly, but Ted sensed her waiting, gauging his approval.
> 'It's a wonderful view,' he reassured her, and added, as they ambled along the leafy residential streets. 'This is the prettiest neighborhood I've seen in Naples.'

Putting the oversimplifications and stereotypes aside, in this passage the American novelist's outsider perspective manages to grasp the nature of the relationship between the two close but separate entities that are Naples and Vomero. It all lies in the distance expressed in 'the view' and the characters' discussion about where is best to enjoy it from. Even for people who live in Vomero and see it every day, the panorama over the city is always a revelation.

I have often wondered whether a landscape can influence the character of a place or the people who live there. In the case of Vomero, it is maybe the act of looking down on Naples from afar, of maintaining this distance, of being *above* the city and not *in* the city, that can explain, perhaps better than any sociological study, why Neapolitans from below regard those from above with suspicion, and why those from above, when below, have to overcome a vague sense of unease. If so, my grandfather wasn't entirely wrong when he said, 'I'm going to Naples.' ⬛

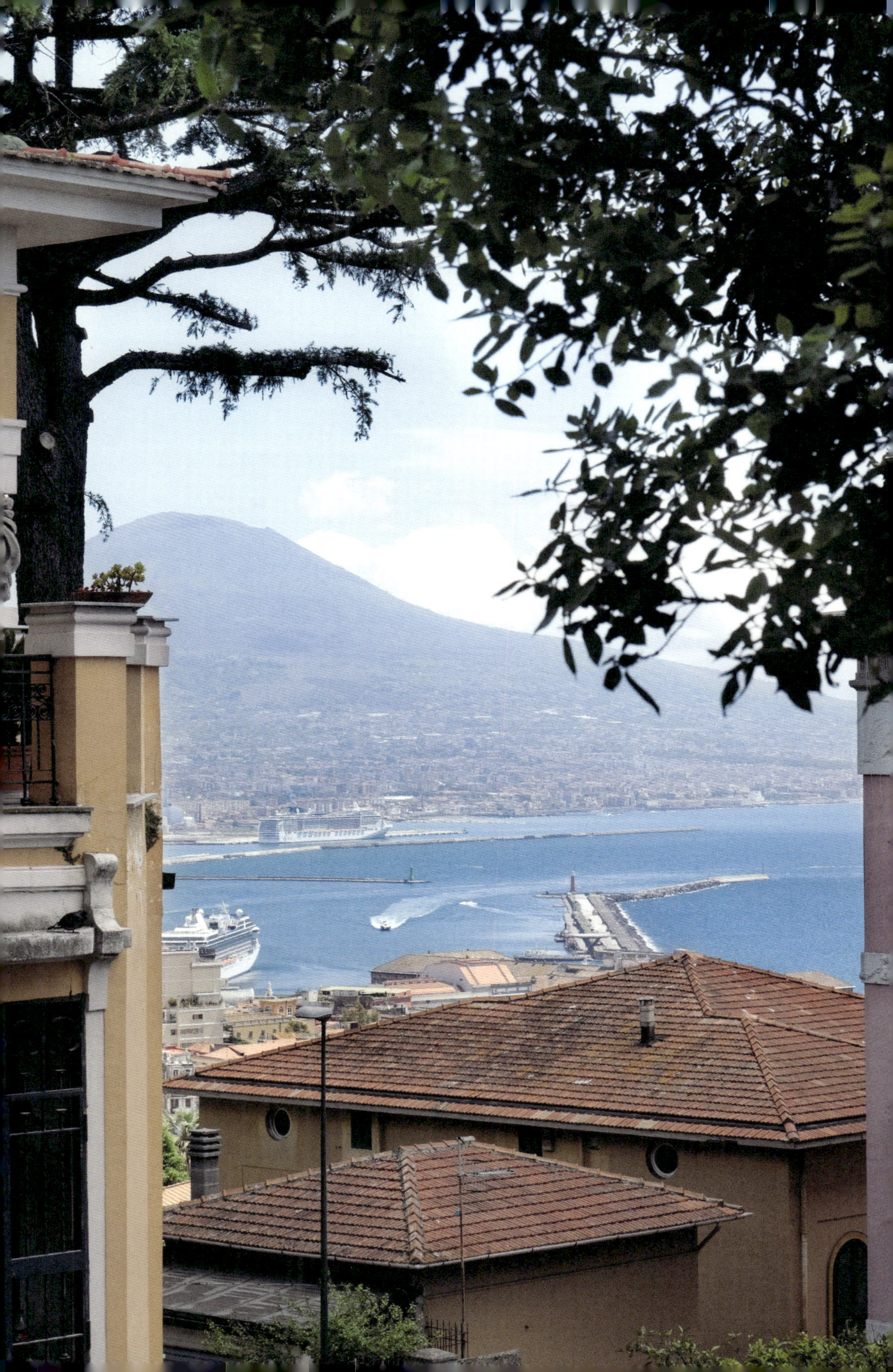

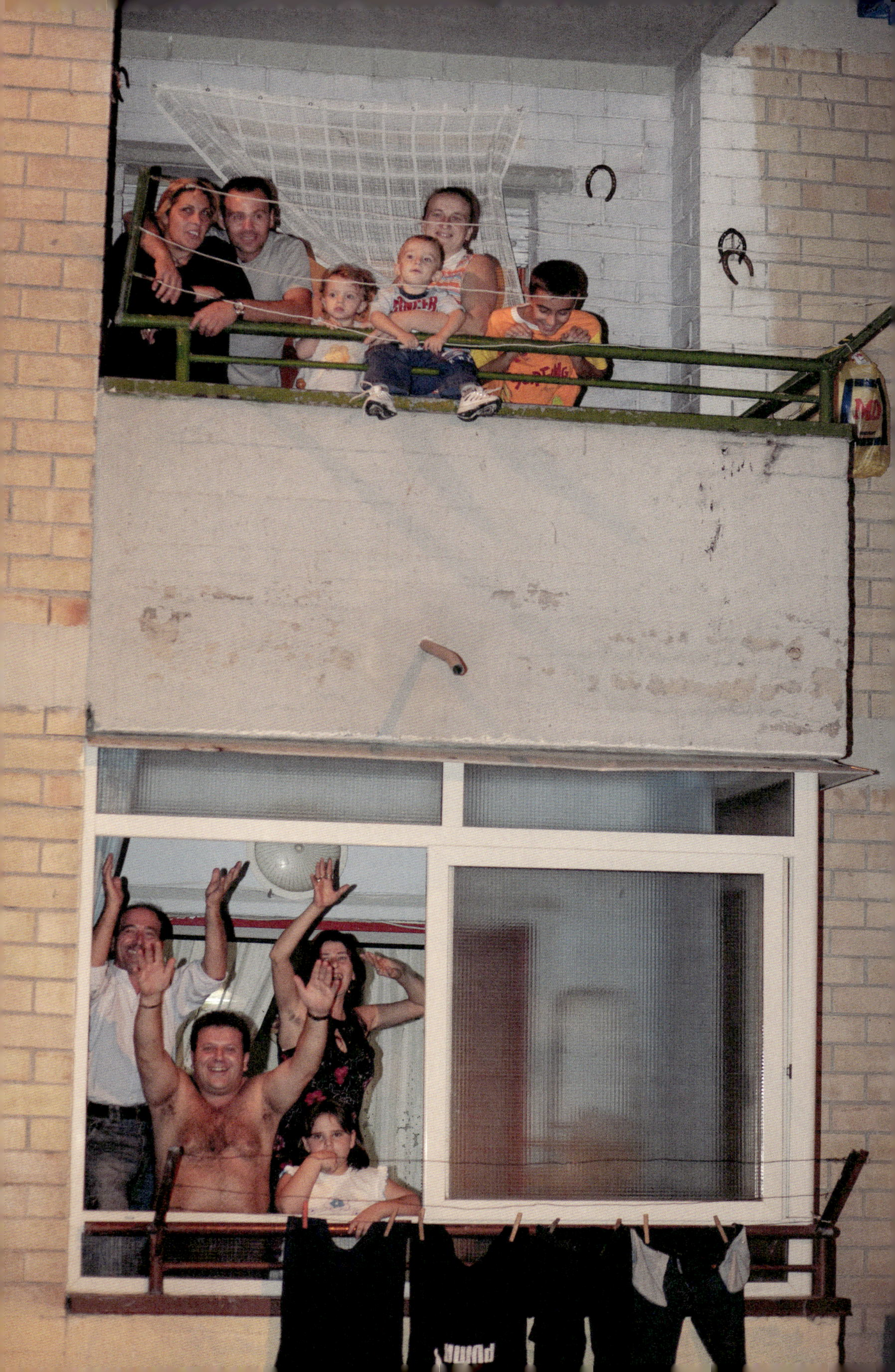

Nero a metà

The presence of US armed forces in the city since the Second World War has had a profound effect on the culture of Naples, making it a hybrid city musically, from jazz to the African American influences on the Neapolitan Power movement and up to today's rap and trap.

FRANCESCO ABAZIA
Translated by Alan Thawley

Residents of a block of flats in Afragola enjoying a concert by saxophonist Daniele Sepe and his band.

Nero a metà is probably one of the most important records in Italian musical history – it certainly is for the Neapolitan scene, because it definitively and unquestionably sealed the reputation of Pino Daniele, the artist that the entire city had learned to love and worship, dreaming that he would become its definitive voice. 'I put my whole self into those songs. Not that I hadn't into my previous work as well, but sometimes, for reasons that no one is able to explain, everything just falls into place in the right way at the right time. And that was what happened with that record,' Daniele said in an interview with *la Repubblica*. It was such an important album for Naples, but the most striking thing about it was its title: *Nero a metà* ('Half-Black') was a tribute to his friend Mario Musella, who had died not long before the record came out. Everyone regarded Musella as 'half-Black'; his mother was Neapolitan and his father an American soldier with Cherokee ancestry. And so, with the distinct lack of political correctness that characterised the 1970s and 1980s, he was known as the 'Redskin of Piscinola', Piscinola being one of the most populous parts of the now famous Area Nord, the northern suburbs known for deprivation and crime but one of those places that exists in quasi-anonymity: it doesn't have the sinister reputation of its neighbours, from Scampia to Secondigliano, and is perhaps also more anonymous than Marano or Miano. It was in the latter neighbourhood, at the Parco ICE SNEI, a vast, faceless housing complex, that Musella met another 'half-Black' artist – in fact, more than half. Gaetano (stage name James) Senese was Black, the son of an African American soldier from North Dakota, James Smith, who had left Gaetano's mother Anna at the end of the war.

This was not an unusual story in Naples, as the sociologist Luigi Caramiello wrote in his essay 'Il mito di Mario Musella' ('The Myth of Mario Musella'). At the end of the Second World War American soldiers found themselves on the streets handing out flour, chocolate and even music in the poorest districts of a starving, penniless city, which often had no other way to pay them back than in kind, with love. These were the same situations that Curzio Malaparte wrote about in *The Skin*, but instead of the drawing rooms of the upper bourgeoisie that only (white) officers could access, these stories were set both in the centre and on the outskirts of Naples, where African Americans – in an era when segregation was still in force in the

FRANCESCO ABAZIA is a Neapolitan author, proud to have been born in what is called the 'historic centre' in 1991. He works as head of editorial content at a creative media agency, nss magazine, and founded BrandNapoli, a movement that celebrates Neapolitan culture. He has written for numerous publications, including *Il Foglio*, *Esquire*, *Rivista Studio* and *Rolling Stone*.

'Senese and Musella were both introduced to music through the records their fathers had left behind in Naples or those sent to them from the USA.'

United States under the Jim Crow laws – were sent to pound the streets and mingle with the people. Obviously, it is not easy to reconstruct the line that divided those relationships between prostitution, abuse and love; all we know for sure is that not all war babies were born by accident, and many of them continued to maintain links, however distant, with the United States.

This was true to a degree for Senese and even more so for Musella. Both were introduced to music through the records their fathers had left behind in Naples or those sent to them from the USA. These were the first encounters with jazz (which had been banned by the fascist regime), rhythm and blues and soul, influences that would never leave. Jazz circulated on the frequencies of Radio Napoli, restarted by the American Giorgio Rehm on the Pizzofalcone promontory with the aim of introducing the locals to American music but above all to broadcast everyday propaganda, the sort of thing we would nowadays call 'exporting democracy'. Radio was just one of the channels that facilitated the spread of jazz; the other came about via the V-Disc (V for victory) record label established by Lieutenant Robert Vincent. The aim of that project was to supply soldiers stationed in Europe with the best music produced in the United States. The catalogues of RCA and Columbia Records were combined, taking advantage of the opportunity to unlock a market that was in serious difficulties at the time with funds provided by the government. The V-Disc records that arrived in Naples included Frank Sinatra but also Duke Ellington, Benny Goodman and John Coltrane. One day James Senese's mother came home with a Coltrane record under her arm and said to her son, 'See that. He looks like your dad.' Apparently, this was Senese's first encounter with the sax. In fact, Italian jazz was born in Naples thanks to V-Discs, just as the port of Bagnoli, with its NATO base, became the gateway to American music and, effectively, a record store. But American music in Italy was 'invented' in the city's Miano district.

Musella and Senese started travelling from Miano to visit their teacher in Piscinola – Pasquale Santoro, who became leader of the neighbourhood band after the Second World War – and shortly afterwards they got together with friends from Terzigno to form the group Gigi e i Suoi Aster, followed by I 4 Conny with Vito Russo, a musician from Aversa. It was only some time later that their band The Showmen arrived on the scene.

The Showmen was one of the most important collectives for the development of music in Italy – with an original line-up that also included Elio D'Anna (who went on to form the prog-rock outfit Osanna) and Franco Del Prete. Although they were mainly remembered by the wider Italian public for their participation in the Sanremo Music Festival, with their popular cover of 'Un'ora sola ti vorrei' and their hit 'Mi sei entrata nel cuore', the group were responsible for some of the

Saxophonist James Senese, a hugely important figure in Italian music and founder, with Franco del Prete, of Napoli Centrale, a notable avant-garde 1970s group known in particular for their contributions to fusion music.

BADMOUTHING NAPLES

In 2017 the Neapolitan authorities decided to set up an online portal, *Difendi la Città* (Defend the City), to counter stereotypes of the city and insults directed against its inhabitants commonly aired on TV, in the press, on social media and at football stadiums. Two years later it was bolstered by a watchdog of legal experts, intellectuals, sports personalities and other prominent figures with the aim of 'analysing, monitoring and studying phenomena of territorial discrimination targeting Naples and Neapolitans'. Reports from citizens flooded in, and in some cases the watchdog has taken an active role in bringing legal action against whoever has besmirched the city's name. The list is long and varied, starting with journalists – notably Vittorio Feltri ('Southern Italians are inferior'), Francesca Fagnani ('In Rome we're going back to young people shooting each other following the Neapolitan model') and Paolo Mieli, who fears the reaction to the 'red zone' for rapid evacuation around Vesuvius ('Naples has the potential for armed insurrection that other regions lack; we can imagine things along the lines of *Gomorrah*'), not to mention Enrico Mentana, guilty of saying that Naples '*also* excels' in some things. Many complaints relate to the pandemic, such as the backdrop to TV personality Massimo Giletti's programme showing the Gulf of Naples with Covid emojis erupting from Vesuvius, or Padua's minister of culture who said, 'We aren't in Naples here. We have sense of civic duty.' Regionalist comments at football matches have been illegal for years, something opposed by supporters of all stripes, who want to retain their right to insult others – Napoli fans included, who protested with a banner echoing slurs relating to the 1970s cholera epidemic and challenging the authorities to take them on.

most interesting musical experiments, not just in Naples but on the wider Italian and international scene. The Showmen were a prog-rock group before prog existed, 'ethnic' in the way that they managed to convey the concept of Neapolitanness profoundly and with immediacy. But right at the height of their success Musella decided to pursue a solo career, leaving Senese with the task of forming The Showmen 2, the band with which he cut 'Abbasso lo zio Tom' (1972) – in English 'Down with Uncle Tom' – a vitally important track for Neapolitan-American history, in which Senese conjured up a sort of 'double consciousness' on the part of the war babies that mirrored the African American consciousness theorised by W.E.B. Du Bois in his book of essays *The Souls of Black Folk*. The people represented by Senese had been forgotten in Naples – in an economic situation lagging far behind that in the USA – with the aggravating factor of having darker skin than the Neapolitans and therefore being forced to suffer their intrinsic racism, the legacy of an era in which anyone different was deemed almost universally dangerous. They were born Black – in fact, they were *nire nire comm'a che* (Black as anything), in the words of the post-war Neapolitan song 'Tammurriata nera'.

'That? That's a racist song. Pay attention, don't listen to the music, listen to the words: they're insulting a white woman who has a child with a Black man. The basic message is *'o guaglione è nu figlie 'e zoccola* [the boy is the son of a whore].' When he talks about 'Tammurriata nera' James Senese almost takes it personally. It was composed by Edoardo Nicolardi, son of the then editor of the Neapolitan newspaper *Il Mattino* and manager of the Loreto Mare hospital, one of the city's busiest, which serves as a natural bridge between the port and the bowels of the city. After attending the birth of a Black baby to a Neapolitan woman, he mentioned the episode to his son's father-in-law, who was none other than the great composer E.A. Mario, who wrote 'La canzone del Piave', and together they wrote 'Tammurriata nera', which became a major hit in 1974 thanks to Roberto De Simone's Nuova Compagnia del Canto Popolare. The song also conceals another American influence. One of the verses borrows from the lyrics of 'Pistol Packin' Mama', Al Dexter's hit, which has gone down in history as one of the most popular songs of the Second World War.

When thinking about the influences of American music in Naples, you do not necessarily have to look around the fringes; quite the reverse. Just think of a hit like 'Tu vuò fa' l'americano'. What was its inspiration if not to parody Neapolitans who had learned to speak that strange mixture of Neapolitan and American (leading to the creation of such terms as *sciuscià* for 'shoeshine')? The song helped to build the legend of Renato Carosone, who would soon be on his way to becoming the most popular Italian singer in the United States, even performing at New York's Carnegie Hall, blazing a trail for Peppino di Capri and a generation of artists who became a source of pride for Italian Americans. At the dawn of the 1970s Neapolitan – and Italian – music was mainly their preserve. Naples was a city that changed at impressive speed, following dizzying growth that transformed it into a sort of city region. The cholera epidemic of 1973 threatened to set it back, but the disease was eradicated thanks to the vaccines delivered by the United States Sixth Fleet, one of the largest in Europe, which is now stationed by Capodichino Airport. This is an example of how the USA altered the urban characteristics of the city and its hinterland, as did the presence of AFSOUTH, now the Allied Joint Force Command Naples, anchored off the coast by Lago di Patria.

Napoli Centrale, the eponymous 1975 debut of James Senese's group, was released during the decade of terrorist atrocities in Italy known as the Years of Lead, which coincided with the beginning of a renaissance of Neapolitan music under the banner of 'Neapolitan Power'. The movement informed music in the city for the next forty years, triggering an explosion of its cultural and human talent. These were the same years in which the communist administration, led by Maurizio Valenzi, promised miracles of public housing, convincing Neapolitans that as well as in the centre, they could also live in complexes like Le Vele di Scampia. These were the result of an old approach to social housing development, based on the idea that concentrating the poorest classes in concrete agglomerations could be a healthy solution for their development. In Naples, as in the Bronx, it backfired.

The name given to the movement was not chosen at random, as Francesco Festa points out in 'La potenza plebea della musica' ('The Plebeian Power of Music', published on the site alfabeta2 in 2015): 'In the same way [as Black Power], Neapolitan Power, in its own small way, was the affirmation of a diversity of languages, other forms of consciousness, challenging the stereotypes, to give new meaning to your own identity and to subordinate identities. *Nero a metà*, Pino Daniele's 1980 album, is perhaps the one that profoundly captures this process.' The idea was that Neapolitan Power could transport the city into the future, a

> 'Naples also worshipped Pino Daniele, the artist who completely rewrote the Neapolitan song, moving towards something completely new, which he termed "Tarumbò".'

city whose cultural magma was nothing like the postcard image (or, at the other extreme, the image of squalor) that the media usually conveyed. This was the period in which Neapolitan world music was born, and in which local cinema and theatre also altered the common perception of what Naples expressed in its music. The cabaret trio La Smorfia was formed by Massimo Troisi, Lello Arena and Enzo Decaro, who poked fun at typical Neapolitan ways. Then in 1982 we saw *No Thanks, Coffee Makes Me Nervous*, Lodovico Gasparini's film starring Lello Arena and Massimo Troisi, a sort of horror comedy that tried to capture the changes the city was undergoing and confirmed the artistic partnership between Troisi and Daniele. This was the same period that *neomelodica* music took shape, a musical style that was in some ways completely different from Neapolitan Power and also different from the music of Edoardo Bennato, who had started out from the Italsider steelworks in Bagnoli and won over the left-wing intelligentsia. *Neomelodica* was a revival of the traditional Neapolitan song that made stars of Nino D'Angelo then Gigi D'Alessio and right up to the more recent – but perhaps less highly regarded – exponents of the genre.

But at the same time Naples also worshipped Pino Daniele, the artist who completely rewrote the Neapolitan song, moving towards something completely new, which he termed 'Tarumbò', defining it as a mixture between tarantella and the blues. The most perfect example of the genre can be found in the song of the same name, on the 1982 album *Bella 'mbriana*, released during a period of pure creative ecstasy between 1979 and 1989 when he released a record nearly every year. In 'Tarumbò' Daniele develops a fusion of Naples and Alabama that also emerges on a linguistic level: the lyrics are from a Neapolitan popular song, interspersed with blues-inflected English and with a hot, experimental sound. Daniele came of age between the port and the city centre, in other words between the bars where the Americans performed and those of the historic centre, where he and the saxophonist Enzo Avitabile cut their teeth, at the same time as the Festival di Napoli was hitting the rocks and a whole new way of thinking about music was beginning to gain traction. And this space was occupied by Daniele, Tony Esposito (percussion), Tullio De Piscopo (drums), a whole generation of musicians who looked both to the USA and to Africa. A dimension in which there was space most importantly for what Tony Esposito described as 'voodoo', in other words 'that sense of ritual when on stage that goes beyond the notes'.

The war was only responsible for part of the musical link between Naples and the United States, however. The other part related more to the way Americans were drawn to the city and the surrounding area, as was the case with Shawn Phillips in Positano. Born in 1943 in Texas, Phillips was what the American music impresario Bill Graham called 'the best-kept secret in the music business'. He

Nero a metà

was the son of James Atlee Phillips, a successful writer of spy stories, whose constant search for subjects and inspiration meant that his son grew up travelling the world: from the UK, where he collaborated with arranger and composer Paul Buckmaster (who worked with the likes of David Bowie and Elton John), to India with the Beatles, encountering figures such as Joni Mitchell and Eric Clapton along the way. When he arrived in Positano, drawn by the beauty of the coastline, it was 1970, and Phillips was in the midst of his hippie period. He was tall and thin as a rake, with long blond hair. He immediately became the linchpin of the local artistic community, which also included Mark Harris and Tony Walmsley – who were later part of Napoli Centrale – but most importantly Jenny and Alan Sorrenti. 'One morning I left Naples with my guitar and backpack, heading for Positano. I was on the point of going through the mystical crisis that led to the creation of *Aria* [his 1972 debut record]. I had heard of Phillips as a charismatic guy who had become popular with the fishermen,' Alan Sorrenti recalled. His encounter with Phillips encouraged him to keep on experimenting and using his voice in a certain way, and in 1974 Sorrenti released his wonderful reinterpretation of 'Dicitencello vuje', a groundbreaking progressive version of one of the classics of traditional Neapolitan song. The young musician then left Italy, travelling to Nepal, Africa and Los Angeles, and it was in California that his life changed when he met some of the most innovative musicians of the time (including David Hungate of Toto) and started work on the record that marked the turning point of his career, *Figli delle stelle* (1977). A hit that heralded the arrival of disco in

Watching a Nino D'Angelo concert in the municipal park in Marano di Napoli.

Italy, the title track was also one of the first songs in that genre sung in Italian to be played in discos, and for a week it even knocked the Bee Gees' 'Stayin' Alive' off the top of the charts. And so Sorrenti had imported another piece of the USA into Italy, showing a different side of Naples, educated and refined, bohemian and bourgeois, the same side of the city that reappeared a few years later, three to be precise, in the song 'Ma quale idea'. Giuseppe Chierchia, who later became Pino D'Angiò, was born in Pompei in 1952 before leaving for the USA with his engineer father as part of the post-war brain drain. That was where the young Pino discovered rock 'n' roll and funk: Chubby Checker's 'Let's Twist Again' was his first single. Those riffs, the falsetto, the sampling of the bassline from McFadden and Whitehead's 'Ain't No Stoppin' Us Now' and the lyrical experimentations of Fred Buscaglione and Adriano Celentano in Italy contributed to the creation of the song that went down in history as the first example of Italian rap/funk, which was followed up by the less popular (but equally iconic) 'Okay okay' (1981). 'If Celentano's "Prisencolinensinainciusol" was the first rap in history, back when the Americans in the ghettoes didn't know what rap was, we can say that "Ma quale idea" was the second historic global rap,' D'Angiò once told *Avvenire*.

But in Naples, between the 1970s and 1990s, we saw the advent of not just a new style of music but also a new style of Camorra. In the post-war period Lucky Luciano (the father of organised crime in the USA), sent a few years earlier by the US to Palermo's Ucciardone prison, had become a part of the Neapolitan Camorra, helping it to take on an entirely new dimension, more international and horizontally structured, mostly through cigarette smuggling. In the following years the emergence of figures such as Raffaele Cutolo and then Carmine Alfieri helped to establish the narrative of the Camorra as we know it today, until the outbreak of the Scampia Feud, the breakaway of the Di Lauro clan and the success of the TV series *Gomorrah*. This was the point at which a number of places entered the public consciousness in Italy and further afield: Secondigliano, Scampia, the 167 (which took its name from Legge 167, passed in 1962, the law that paved the way for vast complexes to be built with the noble objective of providing housing for all the inhabitants of Secondigliano) and what became known as the Bronx, a neighbourhood to the south of Naples. Not by chance was it named after one of New York's most famous boroughs – one with which it shares various social and urban characteristics, first and foremost the madness of the public housing projects – although the Naples Bronx never offered the same level of 'exotic' fascination for filmmakers and other artists, at least, not until street rap came along.

'African American rappers often take Italian names; Italian criminality is something legendary to them. When we go somewhere outside Naples to play gigs, we have the feeling that everyone would like to be us, that we come from a reality that is genuinely criminal, not just messed up, as if this adds value to our words. It's incredible, but they would also like to be the product of a situation like that. But we don't care. Coming from where we come from just means we demand more truth from our art.' This was how Luchè, at the time one of the two minds behind Co'Sang, tried to explain their relationship with the United States and American rap to Roberto Saviano. It was 2006,

Nero a metà

AN AMERICAN IN NAPLES

It was the late 1990s, and the New York anthropologist Jason Pine was in Naples to study the gestures and dialect of its inhabitants when he heard about *neomelodica* for the first time. He became fascinated by the genre, the heir to the classic Neapolitan song, but viewed with suspicion by critics and the intelligentsia and inextricably linked to the Camorra, not so much in musical terms but socially, because it is sung in the vernacular of the working classes, and the performers have the same background as the audience. Pine spent thirteen years, from 1998 to 2011, as an infiltrator on the scene, studying it from an anthropological angle, his great dream being to meet a genuine *camorrista* up close. It operates as an underground economy, a mistrusting environment that uses what he calls 'self-folklorizing tactics' as a shield ('we sing to forget about our misfortunes', 'Vesuvius reminds us that we only have today, that's why we sing', etc.). The only way to get in there was to become one of them. Pine worked with a recording studio, shot videos and adverts, mixed with improbable singers and crime-boss impresarios, pirate-TV stations that broadcast from garages and private homes, attended weddings and public festivals, acquired a brazen, ambiguous persona to prove himself. He became a shrewd observer of this type of 'Neapolitan-ness', picking up thousands of nuances: mockery as a sign of affection, reciprocal lying as a form of connection, people's resentment of curiosity, frustrating inscrutability and aggressive affection, how much remains unsaid, the indiscreet questions to avoid and much more.

and Co'Sang had recently released *Chi more pe' mme*. Saviano was still being billed as the author of a '40,000-selling exposé', according to the subtitle of the interview published in *la Repubblica*'s *XL* magazine. Co'Sang was a rap duo originating between Marianella and Chiaiano, in what was soon to become the notorious Area Nord, although at the time few people had heard of it. Scampia, Secondigliano, the 167: places that featured almost exclusively in rap, offering a warts-and-all vision of the Neapolitan-style ghetto, which had so much in common with its American counterparts. It was no coincidence that Public Enemy's Chuck D called rap the 'CNN of the ghetto'.

Co'Sang's music was always very different from the rest of the rap doing the rounds in Italy. In contrast to its development in the United States, Italian rap had spread via different channels, coming to prominence through the politically infused *posse* phenomenon and spreading from the squatted community centres to the petit-bourgeois city centres. In Naples rap was pioneered by Speaker Cenzou in San Gaetano, in the heart of the historic centre, by Sha One in the Colli Aminei and, above all, by La Famiglia, who released their debut *41° parallelo* in 1998. Even in its title, the album referred to the connection between Naples and New York, two cities with a number of things in common – the 'new' element in their names, for one – but mostly the fact that they are both on the same latitude, which, according to legend, makes them practically identical. *41° parallelo* revolutionised Italian rap, precisely because of its extreme closeness to the American models of De La Soul and A Tribe Called Quest, New York collectives that actively promoted African Ameri-

Tourists visiting Largo degli Artisti in the Quartieri Spagnoli, which is dedicated to Maradona and to Neapolitan artists; in the background are paintings of the actors Totò and Massimo Troisi and singer Pino Daniele.

can culture. Hip-hop arrived in Naples through the work of Paolo Romano, aka Sha One, and once again the US forces were involved: in the 1980s MTV helped bring the new phenomenon of hip-hop to a wider audience, but not in Italy, where it was not yet broadcast except by Canale 21, a Neapolitan channel that was able to piggyback on the signal from the NATO base in Bagnoli. That was how Sha One first discovered rap. Along with Alberto Cretara – aka Polo, another of the OGs (original gangsters) of Neapolitan rap, who now actually lives in New York – he organised the first jams, from Notting Hill in Piazza Dante to Skillz Detector, one of the very first rap battles in Italy, and Officina 99, the squatted community centre that would later become the talismanic venue for another Neapolitan rap group, 99 Posse. All this is described in *Napolizm vol. 2*, a documentary made by Polo that followed on from the release of *Napolizm vol.1*, a collection of Neapolitan rap that Polo sold on the stalls of Mulberry Street in New York during the Feast of San Gennaro, the largest celebration of Naples' patron saint in the world after the Neapolitan event. Alongside legends of Neapolitan rap – such as Speaker Cenzou, 13 Bastardi and Clementino – the anthology also included Fuossera, Lucariello and Co'Sang.

Representing the Area Nord scene, the latter three had a different perception of rap from the experience in the centre of Naples. As Antonio Bove recalls in *Vai Mo: Storie di rap a Napoli e dintorni* (2016), Neapolitan rap, like much Italian rap, had working-class roots but

Nero a metà

did not come from the ghetto: 'Young members of the "middle proletariat" (not rich but not poor, basically, in the city where nobility and extreme poverty often coexist) raised more on TV schedules than cultural politics, of course, but who somehow had been provided with a higher level of education than the previous generation, which had actually opened out horizons that had up until then been restricted to the darkness of their own alleyway, and not just in a metaphorical sense.'

Co'Sang shared this same background: they were not criminals or drug dealers but were immersed in a situation that was too problematic to ignore. It is no surprise that the record that changed Luchè's life was *It Was Written* by Nas, a rapper from Queensbridge, a public housing development in Queens, who came from a relatively good family but was forced to grow up in a place where the social constructs are generated specifically to keep you close to delinquency. In this part of the world Scampia is not so very different from Queens.

The musical and cultural affinity between Neapolitan and New York rap, from the Bronx and Queens, also derives from the particular status of Neapolitans in Italy, something that still relates to that kind of double consciousness expressed years earlier by Senese. The phenomenon was explained by the rapper Lucariello – who had been introduced to American rap thanks to the military base at Lago di Patria – in an interview with *Internazionale*: 'In Italy gangsta rap can only be made in Naples, because we are the Black people of Italy. Everyone has a slightly racist attitude to us. And then there's the social factor. If you're born in certain neighbourhoods, your path is marked out.' Luchè and those of the second generation of street rappers, like Geolier or J Lord, have also drawn on this connection in their lyrics. And this is nothing new. As early as the 1990s the dub outfit Almamegretta derived a large part of their creative approach from the similarity between Neapolitans and African Americans. They had grown up on Black music and were inspired on their first album, *Figli di Annibale*, by the words of Malcolm X. Following trouble between Italians and African Americans in Brooklyn, he had said in a lecture, without any proper historical source to back him up, that: 'This is why you find many Italians dark – some of that Hannibal blood. No Italian will ever jump up in my face and start putting bad mouth on me, because I know his history. I tell him when you talk about me, you're talking about your pappy, your father. He knows his history, he knows how he got that color.' This perception, self-fuelled to a greater or lesser extent, persisted until Neapolitan rap entered its most brilliant phase. After the end of the Co'Sang era – the group broke up for good in 2012 – and the success of Clementino, Neapolitan rap went through a period of stagnation and reflection, trying to reconnect with the genre's latest evolution around the world and in Italy. In spite of Luchè's very early attempts, the Neapolitan scene – like its New York counterpart, which had always directly fuelled its development – found itself unprepared for the trap explosion until Geolier made his appearance. On *New York*, a record dedicated to the city where it was written and conceived, Geolier says: '*Si ric' n— me condann', pe' l'Italia nun so' bianc.*' ('If I say n— you condemn me, but to Italy I'm not white.') Once more, years later and in a cultural context profoundly different from the 1990s, the Neapolitan

LITTLE NAPOLI

Cultural cross-pollination between the United States and Naples has never been a one-way street: the huge flow of Italian migrants to America impacted the way of life in their new home and made a significant mark on music as well. Of the eleven million Italians who had emigrated by 1913, at least four million came from Naples and the surrounding area. Their presence was particularly apparent in New York, especially on Mulberry Street, which remains the heart of Little Italy to this day, even though the expression of Neapolitan identity there is now more than anything a tourist phenomenon. This is particularly noticeable at the annual Feast of San Gennaro, which has been held since 1926 and has become more of a secular festival (complete with meatball and cannoli competitions) than a religious procession. The exiles helped to perpetuate and develop the tradition of the Neapolitan song by bringing their feelings of nostalgia into the lyrics, creating new hybrids with American (and Latin) music, working in the record import-export *bisinisse* and burnishing the reputation of Naples thanks to stars such as the tenor Enrico Caruso – and also helped homesick Italians find solace in the New World. Recently, however, the Italian-American community, now fully integrated into US society, took offence at the scrapping of Columbus Day, which was transformed by compromise into a double celebration: Indigenous Peoples' Day and Italian Heritage Day. In Pittsburgh, meanwhile, there were protests against a plan to take down a statue of Columbus. The first Italian in North America is in danger of being cancelled.

double consciousness is again starting to emerge, although perhaps with less awareness or maturity. Nicola Siciliano, J Lord – who is of Ghanaian origin but was born and raised in Casoria dreaming of becoming Italy's answer to Jay-Z – Vale Lambo and Lele Blade all see the uniqueness of their identity as the key to success in a market that has in the meantime gone mainstream and swallowed up every other type of music. As was the case during the Neapolitan Power era, the new generation of rappers sing almost exclusively in Neapolitan dialect, which goes out on Italian radio like a foreign language – for some incomprehensible, for others just good to listen to – in the same way as when rap was a subculture flooding on to the encrypted Italian airwaves thanks to the programme *Yo! MTV Raps*. 'P Secondigliano', 'Mambo', 'Loco' and 'We we' are tracks that can be linked to the broader genre of trap – which arrived in Italy from the trap houses of Atlanta – but, unlike in the rest of Italy, was absorbed, chewed up and recontextualised within a culture that, starting with its language, makes the fusion of its own identity with American and Black identity a fundamental part of its narrative.

There is no single way in which American music, and in particular African American music, invented Neapolitan music. And any such assertion would be profoundly inaccurate, in any case, given the existence of an endless discography that goes beyond what the musician and writer Renato Marengo collected and promoted under the banner of 'Napule's Power'. But amid sirens, statues of liberty, minorities and neighbourhoods that share the same name, there is nothing that makes Naples and New York more similar than music. Not even San Gennaro.

Nero a metà

NAPULETANA

CRISTINA PORTOLANO is a comic artist and illustrator. Her books include *Quasi signorina* (2016), *Non so chi sei* (2017), *Io sono mare* (2018) and *Francis Bacon* (2019, which was published in English by Prestel in 2022), and other comics books both for adults and younger readers. She contributed illustrations to the internationally bestselling series *Good Night Stories for Rebel Girls* (Rebel Girls, 2016–22). She works with various publishers and *Internazionale Kids* magazine and teaches illustration at IAAD college of art and design in Bologna.

CRISTINA PORTOLANO

What does it mean to be Neapolitan but to leave? And what is it like to return to the place you call home and yet feel like an outsider? A colourful and personal journey along the streets of a city, stuck somewhere between past and present.

Translated by Jamie Richards

97

NAPULETANA

THE CALL...

... EVERYONE WHO HAS LEFT A PLACE THEY CALL HOME FEELS IT, PULLED BY SOME IRRESISTIBLE FORCE ...

... AND THEY FALL INTO AN ALTERNATE REALITY WHERE THEY NO LONGER SEE THAT PLACE OR ITS STREETS AS THEY ARE NOW BUT AS THEY WERE IN A FAMILIAR PAST.

YOU EVEN RUN INTO YOUR YOUNGER SELF...
THE FIRST NEAPOLITAN TAGGER
INFINITY SHOP
THE COMIC SHOP WHERE THE FOUNDERS OF NAPLES COMICON MET
99 POSSE 20/12 2001
VENUE WHERE NEW BANDS WOULD PERFORM
JAIL CLUB
MAMAMÚ
BRIAN THE BRAW
TEETH CRASHERS
VELVET
TANK GIRL
FRANK TELLINA
... BUT SHE DOESN'T RECOGNISE YOU.
HEY, WHAT'RE YOU LOOKIN' AT?
OH MY GOD, SHE ISN'T RIGHT THAT GIRL. WHO IS SHE?
C'MON, LET'S GO. OMBRI'S WAITING FOR US IN THE PIAZZA.
PROZAC+

YOU CROSS THE 17 KM OF THE CITY THAT WAS ONCE YOUR ENTIRE WORLD ...
SKA
LABORATORIO OCCUPATO
ZEAL
IS SHE FOLLOWING US? SHE REALLY LOOKS LIKE ME!
TRUE.

MURAL BY FELICE PIGNATARO
THE PANTHER
STUDENT PROTEST MOVEMENT AGAINST UNIVERSITY PRIVATISATION
99, CODICEZZ, 24 GRANA AND RFC ARE PLAYING AT THE CASTEL NUOVO TOMORROW.
NAH, I'M GOING TO GOTH NIGHT AT ROCKNET TO CATCH DJ FUFFY.

...AND REALISE JUST HOW SMALL IT IS.

VIA SAN SEBASTIANO, FAMOUS FOR ITS MUSIC SHOPS

DANTE & DESCARTES BOOKSHOP

NOW YOU CAN VISIT THE ENTIRE CITY IN HALF A DAY AND SEE HOW FAST-FOOD FRANCHISES HAVE MOVED IN WHERE MUSIC SHOPS USED TO BE.

CRISTINA WANTS TO LEAVE TOWN. SHE'S ABANDONING ME!

WHAT AM I SUPPOSED TO DO WITHOUT YOU?

WHAT DO YOU WANT TO DO THAT FOR? MY COUSIN WENT TO BOLOGNA AND CAME BACK ALMOST IMMEDIATELY.

ALL HE COULD THINK ABOUT WAS NAPLES. IT'S SO HARD TO LEAVE. WE HAVE IT GOOD HERE: THE FOOD, THE SUN, THE SEA.

LOVE IT OR LEAVE IT!

EVERYONE MOVES AROUND IN THEIR LIVES, SO HOW COME IF YOU'RE FROM NAPLES YOU'RE NOT TRAVELLING, YOU'RE EMIGRATING?

CRI, IS THAT YOU?
WHAT ARE YOU DOING BACK HERE? DIDN'T YOU MOVE AWAY? ALL GOOD WITH YOU?
HERE IT'S THE SAME OLD SAME OLD. LIKE WHEN WE WERE 15 BUT WITH LESS MUSIC AND FEWER THINGS TO DO. I FINISHED UNIVERSITY, BUT I STILL CAN'T FIND A JOB.
I DON'T DO DRUGS ANY MORE. TOO MANY FRIENDS DYING KIND OF PUT AN END TO ALL THAT. REMEMBER 2001?
YOU SHOULD COME OVER FOR COFFEE. HOW LONG ARE YOU AROUND?
I'M OFF TOMORROOOWWW...
OH, SHAME. OK. GOOD TO SEE YOU, THOUGH. SAFE TRAVELS.

NAPLES IS A CITY WITH TOO MUCH HISTORY AND TOO MUCH BAGGAGE OF ITS OWN...
PTUI!
... TO WORRY ABOUT YOURS.
THUMP!
THE CALL SOON TURNS INTO A FEELING OF INTOLERANCE AND REJECTION.
LIKE A FOREIGN BODY IN THE ENVIRONMENT IN WHICH YOU WERE RAISED AND TO WHICH YOU'LL BE TIED FOR EVER, EVEN IF YOU NO LONGER LIVE THERE.

Naples, the Sacred Ground

CARMEN BARBIERI
Translated by Ned Darlington

A caretaker from one of the numerous archconfraternities that manage the various tombs that house the remains of the deceased.

The cult of the dead is central to Neapolitan society, and the necropolis of Poggioreale is emblematic of this. Carmen Barbieri guides us through this veritable city of the dead that sprawls over 500,000 square metres, comprising ten cemeteries and many centuries of history.

Naples is a sacred burial ground. Different areas of the city compete with each other over the exact spot where the mythical siren Parthenope was buried, but Naples is a sacred burial ground that doesn't distinguish between myth and reality and hardly cares whether it is sitting on the tomb of a Sicilian princess or the carcass of a bird-fish. Someone died here, and that is enough for sacred-ground Naples, which makes no distinction between human and beast. Here people have ornithological features while animals only lack the ability to speak. A female died: her species is but a minor detail for a city with roots in the Greek Orient. The creature is dead – *chest'è*, so it is – and we live on top of it.

Swallowed up beneath this narrow stretch of holy ground, next to the hybrid body of a young virgin, lie many other corpses. Naples swallows itself – but can't stomach itself. Again and again, across the ages, for one reason or another, the city arches its back, sucks in its belly and sticks two fingers up its rear end. More recently, after drilling through deep layers of the urban subsoil during the construction of the new metro line and burrowing through strata of limestone and earth, skeletons of ages past are now rising to the surface. Incidentally, in Naples the concept of the past is perpetually frozen in time, so it is more accurate to say that nothing is past, it's all here *ncopp' 'o stommaco*, stuck in the gut. Death is always fresh when you dig it up.

A 1667 chronicle entitled *Parthenopes Morbosa Contagione Subactae* – written by Pasquale Giovan Pietro – and the writings of the canon Carlo Celano describe how in the mid-17th century a plague swept through Naples, breaking the barrier between the city buried below and that above ground. In Via Toledo those who still had the strength to walk would be treading on corpses. Below Via Toledo, the plague-ridden cadavers were thrown into the cesspit of the open-sewer canal nicknamed the 'Chiavicone' ('Little Sewer') along with their belongings to await the rainwater and be flushed out to sea. In June 1656 Naples recorded two thousand deaths each day from the plague. Pits were dug everywhere, and many ended up buried on the beach.

But Naples *chiagne e se scorda*, weeps and forgets all about it. The burial pits of churches and hospitals as well as the catacombs – essentially the entire city's subsoil – continued to fill up with corpses, one plague and cholera epidemic after another. Many of these

CARMEN BARBIERI is a Neapolitan writer and actress. Her stories have been published by various publications, including *minima&moralia* and *Corriere della Sera*, and in 2014 she was shortlisted for the Hystrio alla Vocazione award for young actors. In 2021 she published her first novel, *Cercando il mio nome* ('Searching for My Name').

> 'But Naples *chiagne e se scorda*, weeps and forgets all about it. The burial pits of churches and hospitals as well as the catacombs continued to fill up with corpses, one plague and cholera epidemic after another.'

places are particularly popular with tourists, from the well-known Fontanelle Cemetery to the catacombs of San Gennaro and San Gaudioso – where one can find the seats, or *cantarelle* in Neapolitan dialect (from the Greek *kantharos*, a kind of vessel), where the dead were propped up to drain body fluids during the first stages of decomposition.

It was the Bourbons who first tried to deal with the problem of undignified burials. In the mid-18th century the architect Ferdinando Fuga was commissioned to solve the issue of the poor: first, while they were still alive (the Bourbon Hospice for the Poor, built in 1751) and for after they were dead and in the process of putrefaction. In 1762, anticipating by forty-two years the Napoleonic Edict of Saint Cloud – in which it was decreed that the dead be interred outside the city and away from the living – the Florentine architect designed and built the 366-pit cemetery in Poggioreale at the foot of Leutrecco hill on the swampy eastern outskirts of the city, an area that was already the location for messy burial sites. The sectioning off of the dead of lower castes was thought of, outside the Kingdom of the Two Sicilies, as an exciting 'Enlightenment invention', applauded for having initiated a rational clearing out of the city's mass graves and restoring healthy air to places of healing and worship.

In the wake of the cholera outbreak that ravaged the city in 1837, the burial pits of the city's hospitals started to overflow, as did Fuga's meandering burial lanes, so Leonardo Laghezza was commissioned to design a new burial precinct to be sited on the same hill, of a more Romantic design, and this made way for the funerary monuments of noble families and illustrious individuals that contrasted with the profusion of anonymous tombs already there on the hillside. These terraced graves in the Poggioreale district expanded over time to accommodate the tombs of those who died from the 'Asiatic disease' in the second half of the 19th century.

More than a century after the erection of Poggioreale's mountain of graves, in 1877 the Tuscan writer Renato Fucini spent the month of May in Naples. He described his stay in an epistolary novel, *Napoli a occhio nudo* ('Naples to the Naked Eye'), a text that Neapolitans aren't sure whether to despise or tolerate because of Fucini's exoticising frankness in describing what he saw then and which remains unchanged in that vast necropolis where 'the spirit of a primitive independence reigns absolute'. On 22 May 1877 he visited the Cemetery of the 366 Fossae in which the municipality continued to dump seven thousand bodies each year, and he turned to look at the city and its inhabitants from the perspective of their burial practices: 'As an elderly man was being carried by the shoulders, his bearer lost his grip, and I saw the man's skull hit the slabs with that sinister sound that can never be forgotten nor confused with any other.

The Monumentale Cemetery in Naples is the size of a small town. As there is no public transport, and the roads that cross it are wide enough for cars and scooters, they are choked with traffic.

But this is nothing! Naples is far away; the satraps are at lunch, and this little noise will certainly not come to disturb their peaceful rest.'

But, contrary to Fucini's description, the living would soon start to sleep shoulder to shoulder with the dead, because on the hill in Poggioreale the dried-up corpses, piled one on top of the other in mass graves will stretch out and *si metteranno chiatti*, make themselves at home. By the beginning of the 20th century the illusion of keeping the realm of the living separate from that of the dead was well and truly shattered. Next to the Enlightenment invention also known as the Cemetery of Santa Maria del Popolo, other cemeteries were constructed, those of Santa del Trivio, Santa Maria del Pianto, the British Cemetery, the Monumentale, the Santa Maria della Pietà Cemetery (which locals still call the 'Nuovissimo', 'the Newest'), the Cemetery of Santa Maria del Riposo, two Jewish cemeteries and the Fondo Zevola, which together amount to a total area of 502,510 square metres. The cemetery divided up the city through intensive construction and made it impossible for the living – somewhat resigned and more often than not indifferent – to ignore the dead lying under their feet or above them. Poggioreale is among the largest cemeteries in Europe, officially numbering 6,448 private chapels and three hundred *congreghe* (areas of the cemetery designated for a specific group or association). It houses architectural works of considerable value and at the same time embodies a large part of the illegal property trade that defined the city during the second half of the 20th century – evidenced by a large display of funeral artefacts of questionable quality. 'We'll never know exactly how many people are buried,' explains one of the cemetery employees. 'A month ago, for example, yet another owner of a grave turned up who had built a private chapel on it – without permission, of course. He built himself a cathedral, but what are you gonna do? Do you have any idea how many people buy a plot and build a shrine on top of it? *A zeffun e a beverun*, more than you can shake a stick at!'

The *congreghe*, on the other hand, are the property of the Curia of Naples and, up until ten years ago, to join a *congrega* one had to pay an annual subscription of 1,000 lire in the early days rising to €50 in more recent times. The subscription makes the future deceased a fellow of those already registered in that mortuary condominium. Each *congrega* is assigned to a district of the city, or a church with strong popular attendance, or groups people according to their profession. The enrolment boom came along with all the other booms of the last century. By the end of 1960 the confraternities were signing up a thousand members a year for every *congrega*. Those less wealthy were especially keen on being buried in the *congrega* assigned to their neighbourhood in life. An appointee of the Curia wrote down the fees paid in a notebook, and, at the time of actual death, the subscriber was entitled to admission to the *congrega* and the family to a funeral at a price agreed upon with a funeral parlour linked to the confraternity. 'The situation has got a lot worse,' explains the caretaker of one of these edifices. 'Prices have risen too high, and people don't care as much as they used to. Now when someone dies, they go where there's space, but they have to pay an arm and a leg. Bear in mind, miss, that up to seven years ago €300 covered access to the cemetery, then you had to add the undertaker's fee and all the ancillary costs. Now between the municipality and the Curia alone it costs €800. People are cremating their relatives and taking them home.'

Many members of my family rest on the hill in Poggioreale, and over time I have also made friends with other departed souls that I have come across on my walks. Like Mrs Bice Vigo, who smiles at me from her photograph at the beginning of Viale dei Cipressi just as you enter the Monumentale Cemetery from Via Santa Maria del Pianto. Nothing is known of her, not even her date of birth or death, only that she had a round face and that she posed very naturally in front of the camera. These graves I like the most, the ones without dates. They keep me from making any self-referential cabals; they release the bodies buried below from the prison of time, mutely conveying the sense of an eternal return. Conversely, I dislike those where a grief-stricken relative has agreed to a gushing dedication carved at the expert suggestion of an engraver-cum-master of vapid melancholy rhetoric. These tend to be women's and children's graves – there is one such grave at the beginning of Viale della Scala Santa that I usually walk past on my way to what will probably be my own final resting place. In the city of the dead, the main roads are avenues with either sad or comforting names. Every edifice, large or small, has a number, just like a house. Given the vastness of the necropolis, people travel across it by car without hindrance. The fact that cars

> 'Whenever I returned to Naples during that time of masks and hand sanitisers, Poggioreale offered some sense of normality with the noise of the living flocking through the city of the dead.'

and motorbikes can enter the cemetery will now and again provoke diatribes in the local newspaper by the odd aspiring philosopher or art school poser championing public decency and the preservation of what is Europe's oldest cemetery complex. 'But what are works of art doing in the cemetery anyway?' scoffs Naples, as streams of traffic choke the walls surrounding those at eternal rest and cars shuffle and honk their way through the main gates, while unlicensed traffic workers help cars to park right next to the gravestones and along the walls leading to the *congreghe*. Meanwhile from the stalls stretched along the cemetery walls, convenient florists hawk their wares or belt out songs, like the red-faced Salvatorino, who sells flowers outside gate number five of the Nuovissimo Cemetery and drives you up the wall with his endless rendition of Natale Galletta's song 'Amanti'. The local police only step in on special occasions, when the noise of people, cars and mopeds reaches such a pitch that sending four uniformed individuals in among the crypts *s'adda fà*, just has to be done, as if it were part of some ceremonial protocol. But once such occasions are over the cemetery continues to receive visitors. Even during the Covid pandemic, those with private chapels – which is 45 per cent of those in the complex – were granted access to the cemetery, which meant that during the pandemic the place where I personally spent the most time stopped in traffic was at the traffic lights in Largo Santa Maria del Pianto. Whenever I returned to Naples during that time of masks and hand sanitisers, Poggioreale offered some sense of normality with the noise of the living flocking through the city of the dead.

When two people start dating, the true test to tell if it is serious is not the first family dinner together but the initiation ceremony of visiting the deceased relatives of your new love. You only become part of their family when their dead become yours as well. The lovers hold hands, walk together to the grave shedding a tear – as is required by the intimacy of the situation – and then it is up to the visiting boyfriend or girlfriend to perform the act of laying fresh flowers. Finally, if they've arrived by motorcycle, they climb back on and head off down the steep terraced slope of Santa Maria del Pianto, which provides alluring glimpses of the city's harbourside to which they will soon return. In the meantime they attempt to pledge themselves eternally to one another by kissing at the cemetery lookout point. Naples: it swears to itself the impossible, believes in it beyond any doubt and then, suddenly, doesn't believe in anything any more. I find no other explanation for the state of neglect that large sections of the cemetery complex are in, or for the fact that a boy I watched growing up brings a different girl every month to see his *mammà*'s grave. The exception to this decay is the panoramic area I just mentioned, thanks to the fact that the tenor

POGGIOREALE CEMETERY

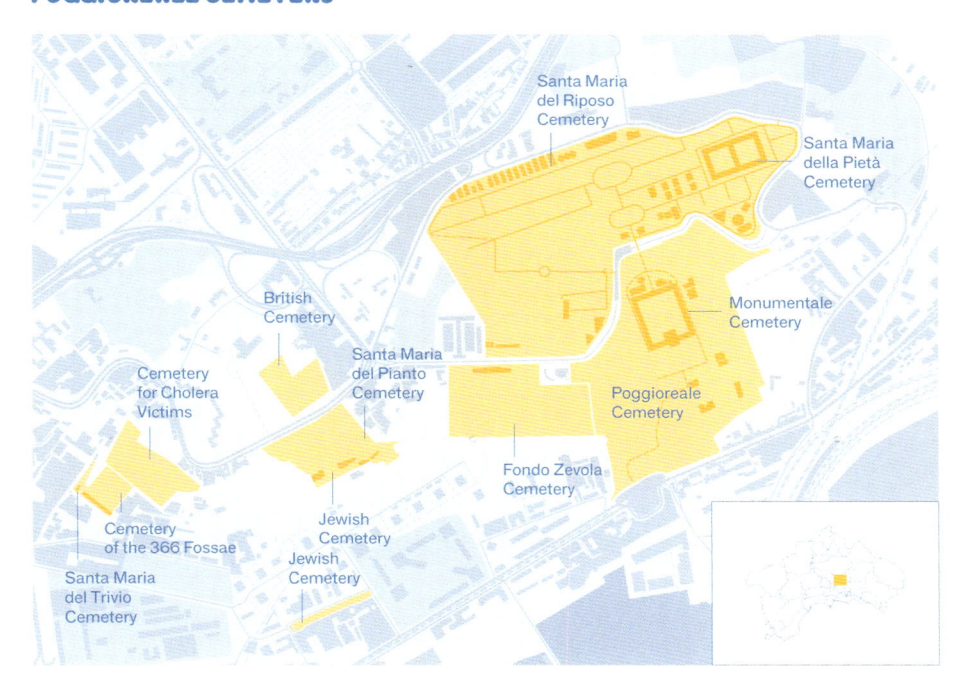

Enrico Caruso, the legendary comic Totò, the playwright Eduardo Scarpetta and his family and other not-yet-forgotten artists are buried there – even tourists come to cast an eye over them. Hence the regular pruning of the trees and plants, the cleaning of the volcanic-rock steps that make the arduous hillside easier for visitors to climb and a friendly caretaker who welcomes them at the entrance. It is the foundational part of the cemetery, the Monumentale, that is in the worst condition. It was conceived in 1838 as a villa and a park, with tree-lined avenues running up the slope from the main entrance, the one on Via Nuova Poggioreale, which is one of the principal and most obvious non-boundaries between the two cities. This is the section of the cemetery where, in close proximity, are gathered 'the illustrious men' who in this century have unequivocally fallen from grace. In 1899 the journalist and novelist Matilde Serao described it as an 'immense and flourishing stately garden' featuring 'groves of trees' providing shade to the chapels, tombstones and churches. Nowadays the vegetation is pushing the tombstones up, invading the chapel roofs, destroying the graves. There is no trace of the 'grand stately park' of the late 19th century, no trace of flowering plants, just undergrowth. And then all the tombs with defiled commemorative busts, the names with letters missing, the private chapels with smashed-in doors and the vandalised and desecrated altars. This is one of the places on which Naples easily turns its back, finding in the midst of the rampant vegetation the darkness needed for decay to settle in. The houses

Visiting a loved one at the Belvedere Cemetery.

of the dead are looted, the marble statues within raided and the mummified bodies – a practice carried out until the beginning of last century and reserved for a few artists and baronesses there – desecrated. Acts perpetrated by people working in the cemetery (according to others who also work there) with impunity, just like the unauthorised property market that the municipality, as usual, comes to address – theatrically – with the proverbial 'quarter-of-an-hour delay'. A recent case was the sale of some of the hundred aristocratic chapels in the upper monumental section. Sold by private individuals to entrepreneurs in the area, they were seized in 2015. The people who bought them carried out aggressive renovations that altered the funerary artefacts. These late-19th-century chapels have been gutted, their altars ripped out, refitted to make room for more bodies; concrete slabs are fitted into the undercrofts to await the remains of more poor souls to come. One of the cemetery's groundkeepers tells me, 'A lot of stuff has come in and out of here. First they made them finish things up and made them sell the spaces. They made the trade and then put their seal on. '*E mò, cu chi t'a vuo' piglià*, who are you gonna take it up with?' Those who were unfortunate enough to have a relative laid to rest in one of these chapels now under lock and key are only allowed access to the building on Saturdays and Sundays when an attendant removes the bolts from the doors. To all intents and purposes they have an innocent relative who, after death, has ended up a prisoner. There are over six hundred dead behind bars. On one of these chapels the municipality has carried out a kind of civil reclamation initiative by acquir-

PANDEMICS PAST AND PRESENT

During the seventh cholera pandemic, which by late 1972 had already affected fifty-nine countries, the first deaths from acute gastroenteritis were recorded in Campania in the summer of 1973. The epidemic of 1911 – which had claimed the lives of six thousand people in Naples and had been preceded by equally devastating epidemics in 1837 and 1884 – was still fresh in the collective memory, and panic quickly broke out. Neapolitans themselves were the ones loudly calling for a mass vaccination campaign – there were even violent protests and road blocks. The campaign achieved the amazing result of 80 per cent of the population being vaccinated over five days. The vaccine centres were set up in public buildings of all kinds and kept open twelve hours a day, administering doses to a highly disciplined population. Today we look back on that experience almost with envy. Covid-19 arrived at a time of growing scepticism regarding vaccines, and the mortality rate was much lower than that of cholera. During the first wave of the Covid-19 pandemic Campania was one of the least-affected regions in Italy, but, as time passed, rules designed to prevent the spread of the disease were increasingly ignored, a situation exacerbated by the difficulties faced by many people working on the black market, who were not eligible for state assistance. The vaccine campaign, as in other areas of southern Italy, went slowly, sometimes obstructed by distrust of vaccines and disinformation.

ing the unauthorised burial recesses and reselling the fifty available spaces by public tender, renaming the building the 'chapel of lawfulness'. The fight seems to be less about the illegal property trade than about the municipality having been bypassed by private citizens.

'The municipality is in crisis and wants to take money from the dead,' another cemetery worker tells me, explaining that after the scandal of these seized chapels, trading between private citizens has been forbidden by law, and among the changes introduced in the last fifteen years there is the one that concerns regular and legitimate owners of private chapels, who, if they have a dead person to be laid to rest in their property, must pay an entrance fee to the municipality that is calculated on the basis of the overall surface area of the building and the number of burial niches within it. 'Private property doesn't even pay off when you're dead!' he concludes. 'Do you want to know how much it cost a doctor on Via Medina to put his brother in the family chapel? He paid €30,000 just for the sub-concession rights because they have an enormous monument. I always tell my wife and children that when the time comes *ittateme proprio rint' 'a munnezza*, just leave me right outside with the rubbish.'

I ask an heir of one of the city's eight historic funeral parlours how it came to be this way, as we look into one of the monumental chapels and peer at a Honda Transalp motorbike parked inside. 'We see a lot of illegal activity here. Aside from the historical establishments that have been active for generations, there are others who've taken out licences without even fulfilling all the requirements to open a funeral parlour. Once there were too many of them the municipality tried to keep them under control with laws and regulations. But instead of solving the problem it now means there are people working with expired licences and then relying on third parties to foot the bills.' Another factor contributing to the crisis in the funeral sector pertains to those companies who don't declare all their activities to the tax authorities, thus allowing them to offer families lower prices, starting with the coffins that they import from Albania for a hundred euros apiece and on which they can charge extras that cannot be traced by the buyer but which still work out lower than a regular undertaker can offer. 'What are we up against?' I ask him. 'We're facing total extinction. The cemetery is doomed. We have already introduced the use of biodegradable urns. Along with the ashes, a plant or seeds of some tree of the relatives' choice are placed inside. The box can be buried freely in a private garden and wait for the plants to bloom over time. It is cheaper and takes away all the hassle of taxes and countertaxes. For the time being, however, most people opt for cremation and keeping the urn at home.'

In 1743 the actor, playwright and abbot Charles-Gabriel Porée wrote, in a letter opposing burials in church grounds, that the dead are dangerous to the living and that they must be removed from the city if the living are to continue loving them. To the living, according to the French clergyman, cohabiting with the dead is only cause for disgust. Again, in 1781 the architect Francesco Milizia argued in his *Principj di architettura civile* ('Principles of Civil Architecture') that the dead must be placed outside the city so as 'not to poison the living'. The documents produced during the Enlightenment in favour of separating the living from the dead emphasise the need to do so not only for reasons of health and hygiene but also for the mental wellbeing of living citizens, as if to say that it is healthy for the living to cut themselves off from the dead. As I read these three-hundred-year-old words again I wonder how different those of you who aren't from Naples might have become as human beings if you, too, had started planting loved ones like trees in unconsecrated ground and how much more you would suffer if the practice of keeping ashes in urns turned your homes into little mausoleums. This is a question I put to anyone who is not Neapolitan – since sacred-ground Naples has never, as I hope is now clear, given up on living with its dead. What *malaise* may result from this, I leave to your imagination.

Naples is a complex catacomb and a catacomb complex. This year I came of age: eighteen years since I stopped living there permanently. Yet I return often. I come down to it, like Erigone descending into the well to retrieve Icarius' corpse.

I was born there in 1984. A hundred years earlier the young engineer Guglielmo Melisurgo, an employee of the municipal technical and hygiene offices, personally descended into the city's underground and re-emerged with an account of a city of water that has existed there since the time of the ancient Cumaeans and which was formed of canals and basins, holes dug into the rock: veritable underground labyrinths. The area covered in this expedition, and the borders of which Melisurgo traced in his *Napoli sotterranea* ('Underground Naples'), goes from Sant'Antonio Abate to the district of Pizzofalcone, and from the Duchessa

Monumentale Cemetery is in a state of disrepair and dereliction, with bronzes and other valuable artefacts often plundered. Here, a coffin has been dumped in a quiet spot in the cemetery between two private chapels.

Naples, the Sacred Ground

THE FOUNDLING WHEEL

First introduced in Italy by Pope Innocent III in 1198, foundling wheels (*ruote degli esposti*) have over the centuries taken in thousands of children, often born as a result of adulterous relationships or into families unable to take care of them. The rotating mechanisms, usually made of wood, were installed in a hole in the wall of a church or monastery and divided into two parts, one facing inwards and the other outwards, so that people could place abandoned babies into the wheel to be given up to the charity of others and the protection of the Holy Virgin without being seen from within. The practice gave rise to the surname Esposito, which remains with its many, many variants – Espositi, Esposto, Esposti, D'Esposito, Degli Espositi, Degli Esposti and Sposti to name but a few – one of the most common in Italy, particularly in Campania and Naples. The habit of giving orphans a surname highlighting their origins – for which the first written evidence dates back to 1623, when a certain 'Fabritio, two years of age' was registered with the surname Esposito – was stopped in the early 19th century to tackle the discrimination that these individuals suffered into adulthood. The foundling wheel in Naples adjoining the Basilica della Santissima Annunziata Maggiore in Forcella, was established in the 14th century and operated until 1875, even though many newborns continued to be abandoned in the porch or on the steps of the basilica for many years afterwards, and its home for illegitimate children accepted orphans up until 1980.

> **'"Cemetery" has its roots in a Greek word, *koimeterion*, meaning "dormitory". In sacred-ground Naples the living sleep on mattresses made of water and anonymous bones.'**

to the Cavaiole and the Trinità areas, including a large part of the districts of Vicaria, San Giuseppe, San Carlo all'Arena, Stella, Avvocata, Montecalvario, San Ferdinando, San Lorenzo and the northernmost part of Pendino, Mercato, Porto and Chiaia. Aqueducts run through the rocky mass, he writes, 'on which a large part of the city rests'. 'Cemetery' also has its roots in a Greek word, *koimeterion*, meaning 'dormitory'. In sacred-ground Naples the living sleep on mattresses made of water and anonymous bones.

Every Neapolitan, writes Melisurgo, is the author of an 'underground tale'. I will borrow this expression of his to tell you one of my own. In the summer of 1933 my father's father was delivered to the church of the Santissima Annunziata Maggiore in the Pendino district of Forcella. The church was associated with an orphanage, and there was a foundling wheel through which unwanted children could be passed anonymously to be taken into care. Immediately after giving birth to him in the hospital within the same 14th-century complex as the church, his mother did not claim him. It was early afternoon, according to the register. In the arms of a nun, he was given the name Michele and was sent to a home in Genzano, near Rome, 217 kilometres from where he had been abandoned. (I was born on 17 February, in the second month of the solar calendar. The date of my coming into the world echoes those numbers.) As soon as he turned three years old the nuns took my grandfather back to the orphanage for a few days. The doors of the holy house opened every weekend to allow potential adopters to choose a child to take home with them – a kind of release from custody rather like that of the dead in the confiscated chapels in the Monumentale. On the first Saturday of his return to Naples Michele caught the eye of Maria Concetta Liguori, who wanted to adopt a little girl. But Michele clutched the woman's skirt in his fists, begging for a mother. Michele was three years and a few days old. Had he really taken a proper look at this 67-year-old woman? Maria Concetta tried to convince her husband, Carmine Barbieri, thirty-two years her junior, who was not much interested in the orphan's sex or, indeed, in his wife. Thus it was she who decided for Michele, and so the child moved two kilometres away from the orphanage of the Real Casa dei Figli della Madonna, near Via della Veterinaria in the San Carlo all'Arena district, not far from the hillside cemetery area. The move from one part of the city to another was only physical, as my father's father would remain stuck in the rooms of that illustrious orphanage for the rest of his life, consuming

The side entrance and office of the manager of the Cemetery of the 366 Fossae.

his own heart bit by bit, and very soon requiring electronic devices to prevent his heart from failing. Empty, like a desolate building, of love for the many children he would produce. Busy looking for plausible answers to a single, futile question 'Who was my mother?' Deaf to the needs of those around him, he would lead a feral life, unsure even as to what name to give the vital impulses he might do well to listen to. Because Mrs Liguori would die in 1944 after calling him Tanino, a popular nickname for Gaetano, for eight years and leaving him a flourishing business. The customers would then turn Tanino into Tonino until it grew into the respectable Don Antonio when the now adult boy took it upon himself to sink the family business.

Barbieri, therefore, is a borrowed surname, a snatched legacy that I have inherited and in which echo many quarrels and countless misunderstandings. My father, the eldest of seven children, was also born in the summer. He was baptised Carmine in honour of his father's adoptive father, an act of duty. Many more of those would follow, and the thread that bound Carmine the old man, Michele-Tanino-Tonino, and Carmine the young man came closer and closer to breaking.

The first memory I have of the cemetery in Poggioreale was in the spring of 1989. I was five years old, and with my parents I had to get to the Confraternity of the Guardian Angel. We didn't know where it was exactly, and we walked for more than two hours before we managed to find it. The caretaker of the *congrega* noticed our bewilderment and asked us who we were looking for. 'Carmine Barbieri,' said Carmine Barbieri. The caretaker consulted a register and then led the way down a flight of stairs, past a wall of tombstones and told us to look up at the ceiling. Carmine Barbieri was on the top right, in a dark corner that was difficult to reach even with a ladder. And there wasn't even a name on the marble.

It was the adopted son's final insult to his tyrant of a father, perhaps the only possible act of revenge against a man who had forced him into child labour and to sleep in a basement, who had locked his wife Maria Concetta away in an asylum just to be rid of her, who had buried her in a tomb and then made her disappear even from there. That was revenge for Michele, who could no longer even mourn his adoptive mother at the cemetery. My father, on the other hand, who, since he bore the same name, was the only grandson Carmine Barbieri had welcomed, had my great-grandfather's name and surname put on the tombstone at our own expense. It was like a signature on a list of disagreements between him and his father.

Aristocrats carry their genes with them; their ancestors continue to live around them, on them. I have been inside aristocrats' houses. They were empty of the living and full of the dead. The dead came out of the paintings, sideboards, coats of arms and banners. According to Michele, his real mother was a young noblewoman who had conceived him with a commoner and was therefore forced by her family to give him away. It is pure fantasy, one common to many orphans who, in trying to live with their fate, try to save their mothers from blame. But in sacred-ground Naples, which makes no distinction between myth and reality, a story need only be told more than three times for it to be true. When my father discovered that he was suffering from a melanoma, he rushed to buy an aristocratic

FONTANELLE CEMETERY

Fontanelle Cemetery, located in a former tuff quarry in the Rione Sanità, was used to house the bodies of those who were unable to afford a burial, notably the many victims of the plague of 1656 and the cholera epidemics of 1837 and 1884. But what made it famous is the chamber that contained the bones of the poorest citizens, where the rites of the *anime pezzentelle* ('poor abandoned souls') were celebrated. In exchange for protection, people would adopt and look after the skull of one of these abandoned souls, known as a *capuzzella*. The cult followed a very specific ritual, which involved cleaning the skull with water and adorning it with rosaries, flowers and candles in the hope that the soul would appear in a dream and grant a favour – in the form of numbers that the worshipper could play in the lottery – in exchange for prayers and intercessions to alleviate their suffering in Purgatory. If the favours were granted, the skull was honoured with a more fitting burial but never covered with stone, because the soul had to be free to communicate with the living. In the 1960s the cult started to cause concern among representatives of the Church, and on 29 July 1969 it was prohibited by decree from the Diocesan Court for the Causes of Saints, although the celebration of a monthly mass for souls in Purgatory was permitted as well as a procession in the cemetery every 2 November to commemorate the dead. Irrespective of the decision taken by the religious institutions, over the years the cemetery was forgotten about and abandoned; nowadays, however, it is a popular tourist destination.

chapel dating from 1896 – the municipal law preventing its direct sale between private individuals was still a long way off. He put a lot of money into restoring the building to keep it in its original state. He left the heraldic coats of arms of the two families over the entrance, and underneath he had our surname and my mother's surname engraved. For twenty years I have been trying to trace back through those faded coats of arms the married couple who had given rise to that dynasty. Only recently have I managed to identify two possible leads: two surnames present in Naples since the mid-17th century, but one previously established in Sicily and the other in Basilicata. I believe that, aside from securing a place 'for himself and his family', Carmine the younger wanted to reclaim his father's lost nobility. But Michele had the terrible habit of not listening to other people's stories, least of all his eldest son's. That's how it works in sacred-ground Naples. Everyone has their own underground tale and does not necessarily have eyes and ears for other people's. Every time I return I immerse myself in its perpetual state of paralysed darkness, the aura of a metropolis that can't ever sleep soundly, troubled by its dead, by the voices that inhabit its underground and its northeastern hillside. By the stories of the many who swim at the surface wearing the time-honoured outfit of our tradition: the denial of guilt.

Cages of Metal and Cages of Paper

PIERO SORRENTINO
Translated by Will Schutt

The writer Piero Sorrentino guides us through the two greatest economic and ecological rifts in Naples, in San Giovanni a Teduccio and Bagnoli, both once major industrial hubs. Between them they exemplify the importance – and the difficulties – of redeveloping the old industrial areas of the city.

The Gianturco Industrial Zone.

One winter's morning in 1802 the French pastry chef Nicolas Appert placed the leftovers of his supper of the night before – a gluey, unappetising mess of peas and ragout – in an empty bottle of champagne, sealed it with a cork and boiled it in a bain-marie for fifteen minutes. Then he let it sit. When the glass was cold again, Appert placed the bottle in a cupboard for two or three weeks. Later, on a particularly cold evening, as only winter evenings in Paris can be, he opened the cupboard, uncorked the bottle and tasted its contents, first having had a sniff, then heating it up in a pan and having a chew. It was good. There, in that French kitchen, thanks to the intuition of a chef who had no knowledge of microbiology yet was sure that heat impeded or at least drastically slowed down the decomposition process, one of the most groundbreaking food-preservation techniques in history was born.

Appert initially opened a small shop in the city where Parisians flocked to buy 'appertised' asparagus, artichokes and beans. In 1810 no less a figure than Napoleon bought into the idea, rewarding the chef with a satchel of hard cash and the promise of cushy government posts, for the pastry chef's intuition had solved the serious problem of preserving food for troops going on campaign. For Appert, a bright and glorious future under the protective wing of the empire appeared on the horizon. Too bad that a few years later, on 18 June 1815, Napoleon was defeated at Waterloo, and Appert died poor – but not until the Englishman Peter Durand had pinched his idea and patented a system of preserving food in flat, rectangular tin cans that were far more practical for transporting than fragile and bulky glass bottles.

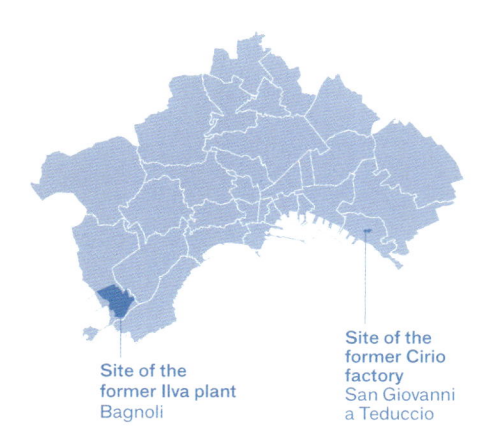

In 1824 the French edition of an anonymously authored book, *The Art of Preserving Food*, began to circulate in Italy. The book illustrated Appert's method, describing its qualities and merits as well as how it evolved in Britain through the use of tin-plated cans. The book eventually fell into the hands of Francesco Cirio, a twenty-year-old from Nizza Monferrato, Piedmont, who, sniffing an opportunity, rushed off to Turin to start reselling preserves made from vegetables that he would buy cheap in wholesale markets at closing time. In 1856 he opened the first Cirio factory where tinned peas were mass produced. When, a few years later, the Piedmontese unified Italy, the doors to the south swung open.

Site of the former Ilva plant
Bagnoli

Site of the former Cirio factory
San Giovanni a Teduccio

PIERO SORRENTINO is a Neapolitan writer and radio host. He made his literary debut in 2007 with the anthology *Voi siete qui* ('You Are Here'), and his stories have been published in a number of other collections. A journalist for the daily newspaper *Il Mattino*, he is also writer and host of the programme *Zazà*, broadcast on Rai Radio 3. His first novel, *Un cuore tuo malgrado* ('A Heart Against Your Will'), was published in 2019.

THE 1980 EARTHQUAKE

With a magnitude of 6.9, the Irpinia earthquake of 1980 was the most powerful to hit Italy in the post-war period, claiming 2,914 victims. The worst-affected provinces were Avellino, Potenza and Salerno, with 362,000 buildings damaged in 687 municipalities, three of which were razed to the ground. The quakes, which were felt all over Italy, were focused on a particularly poor area of the southern Apennines, shining a light on its underdevelopment but also on the vulnerability of buildings that failed to comply with anti-seismic regulations and contributed to the extremely serious housing crisis, with 280,000 evacuees and twenty thousand homes lost. Emergency solutions were implemented, such as the use of makeshift camps, schools, trains and boats to provide accommodation for the homeless. (The chaos and the difficulties experienced by the authorities in coming to their aid opened people's eyes to the need for a civil protection service, the Protezione Civile.) Many waited for housing for years, decades even – some are still waiting and continue to live in 'temporary' prefabricated homes made from timber and plywood. The earthquake created serious problems in Naples as well, where another fifty thousand were added to the pre-existing fifteen thousand homeless. It was a defining moment, one that enabled the Camorra to get its hands on the huge sums of money (64 trillion lira; €34 billion) handed out to fund the reconstruction, to work with companies (many from the north) and politicians, to expand into provinces where it was not previously established and to significantly raise its game. At a time when Campania was already undergoing a process of deindustrialisation, construction fuelled by public money became the only resource.

The Cirio factory in San Giovanni a Teduccio, on the eastern outskirts of Naples, began to produce small, red, rectangular cans bearing elegant silver lettering: 'Cirio General Food Preserve Company – Concentrated Tomato Extract – Headquartered in San Giovanni a Teduccio (Naples)'. Was the young Cirio a visionary? Sure, although he wasn't the first to perceive the enormous potential of San Giovanni a Teduccio: the Romans built a villa there, somewhere for the daughter of Emperor Theodosius to hold wild parties and endless banquets; later, in the 13th century, the French established slaughterhouses, tanneries and mills to the east of Naples.

One of the city's many outlying neighbourhoods, San Giovanni a Teduccio is located smack in the middle of a vast area that forms a kind of barrier between the city centre and the hinterlands of Caserta and Nolano, the Agro Nocerino-Sarnese and the Sorrento coast. If you look at satellite images of the area to the east of Naples, the whole place appears to be a gigantic basin that functions as an axis around which a key part of the entire city's urban plan revolves, mostly because it marks the point where the city opens out to the sea, its most important artery. Here begins what almost a century later the writer Anna Maria Ortese called 'the involuntary city', given the impoverished state of the Palazzo dei Granili, the Old Royal Granary, which, by the beginning of the 1950s, was so clear, so dramatic, so lacking in opportunity and beyond repair that anyone who happened upon it froze, drained of will. But the hard times described by Ortese were still in the future when, from the end of the 19th century until the outbreak of the First World War, Cirio – and with him

San Giovanni a Teduccio, the site of the first Apple Academy app-development centre in Europe.

industrialists such as Del Gàizo, Bevilacqua, Curcio, Vela, Paudice, Santarsiero – built plant after plant in the area, making Campania the Italian region with the greatest number of businesses, industry professionals and workers. The east was an incredible social and urban experiment in cohabitation between farmers and workers, where those who tilled the land lived elbow to elbow with the housing that sprouted up around the mechanical, textile, pharmaceutical and steel factories to which workers rode on efficient trams powered by electricity generated by the Enel coal plant in Vigliena.

It was Law no. 2892 of 1885, concerning the renewal and redevelopment of the city of Naples following the previous year's cholera epidemic, that elected to make the area the city's industrial suburb. Broadly speaking, the plan was to demolish those old neighbourhoods most affected by the epidemic and replace them with a state-of-the-art industrial district. The massive project would profoundly change the layout of that part of the urban landscape. Later, Mussolini took an interest, and during the twenty years of fascist government he established national oil refineries connected to the port's petroleum dock, 'the regime's gateway to the Mediterranean colonies', as historians call it. It seemed like the dawn of a golden age for the area, but it turned out to be the start of its decline. By the end of the

Second World War the eastern suburbs were in a mess, with the port destroyed and neighbourhoods heavily bombed. This is where the housing emergency described by Ortese begins, where the unrestrained property speculation that blights the area to this day kicks off. This is where the world of peasants and labourers dies and another world – grim, shadowy, dark – emerges, turning the eastern hinterland into an ecological and health death trap. It's no coincidence that it was among the areas hardest hit by the cholera epidemic in the summer of 1973.

And this is where I come from. From those 1970s, from that cityscape – specifically Poggioreale, which lies only a few metres away in that sprawl of neighbourhoods (it's almost impossible to tell where one begins and the other ends) – from that tangle of off-ramps, from that skyline of empty warehouses and metal towers, of piled-up shipping containers and rusty buildings. The large iron depots, surrounded by a never-ending chain of steel peaks and boarded-up warehouses. One of the most vivid memories of my childhood dates to the night of 21 December 1985, when a fire at the Agip depot between Gianturco and San Giovanni caused the explosion of twenty-five fuel tanks. I was seven years old. I was woken up by probably the most powerful explosion I've ever heard: five dead, 165 injured, 2,600 displaced, 100 billion lire in damages. This is where I come from, and it's the area to which, one pleasantly sunny April morning, I'm returning.

I arrive in San Giovanni by scooter after travelling down the long stretch of metalled road (in a manner of speaking, given all the potholes) that runs from Via Galileo Ferraris to Via delle Repubbliche Marinare. All along the road, the blackened bins that prostitutes use as braziers to keep warm at night act like milestones, ticking off the route to Corso Protopisani, where the old Cirio factory has now been replaced by Apple's Developer Academy.

'From tomatoes to apples,' says Pietro Nunziante, greeting me with a joke. An architect and industrial design researcher at the University of Naples Federico II, Pietro represents the heart and soul of the academy, where, until a couple of years ago, he taught design. In the astonishing morning light the colours of the impeccably designed university campus are arrayed under a blue sky; shades of turquoise and grey and the bright green of trees and the matching square basalt façades of the buildings that make up the area have a disorientating, incongruous effect. Am I in Berlin? Is this London? Every centimetre, every square metre of this space is perfectly placed, exactly where it should be, and has a function. Even the old brick chimney of the Cirio plant has been repurposed as a vent for the campus's cooling system. Tall as a sundial, it creates a shadow separating the two large wings of the university: L for laboratories, C for classrooms. Apple came to San Giovanni in 2016 when it opened its first academy for app developers. Money from the European Regional Development Fund (ERDF) well spent by the university. Other companies followed suit, including Cisco, Capgemini and Ferrovie dello Stato. Every year the nine-month programme draws 378 students from thirty-six countries across the world. No special skills or qualifications required, just an entrance exam. Pass it, and you're in. In the span of four or five years the San Giovanni campus has blossomed into an ecosystem of academies for digital transformation. The most important European initiative that the Cupertino company has ever embarked on is here. Strolling through the soundproofed rooms I look for evidence of the classrooms and student laboratories but to no avail. 'You're standing in them,' says Pietro. There are no teachers' desks, the idea being to put everyone on a level footing. They call it 'campfire style', where it's all about teamwork: tables arranged in peer-facing groups constitute a small hive of activity with no barriers or divisions. Spaces and educational innovation go hand in hand. For each lab there is a 'collaborative' area flanked by another room where students learn how to present their projects and the progress of the apps they're designing to industry experts. After the thousandth sharp turn taken across the classrooms, through the windows overlooking the surrounding area appear the large eyes of Maradona, staring at us from a gigantic mural made by the artist Jorit on one of two large buildings designed by Pietro Barucci in Taverna del Ferro, an area of San Giovanni known as the Bronx, which emerged out of a pair of major public housing works in the wake of the earthquake of 1980. (The other led to the creation of the Pazzigno district.) That was followed by a void – a political, economic, cultural, productive and social void – for forty years. For this reason the university chose not to build cafeterias or dormitories for their student body; they want to make a positive impact on the neighbourhood. Students leave college to grab a sandwich at the corner deli and find apartments or rooms to rent by knocking on doors or checking the to-let ads. In a world like this the experiment might seem risky, but the effect

THEY CALL IT THE BRONX

Naples' Bronx – officially called Taverna del Ferro – is a pair of huge apartment blocks built in San Giovanni a Teduccio in response to the major housing crisis caused by the 1980 earthquake. Some of the housing complexes in Naples that suffer the most problems today were built in the 1980s to house the thousands of evacuated families. As well as Taverna del Ferro, the period saw the construction of the Rione Salicelle in Afragola and Parco Verde in Caivano, the neighbourhood with the highest rate of juvenile delinquency linked to organised crime in the city. These were buildings designed for a short lifespan, but they are still standing after almost forty years, having undergone very little maintenance – none at all in some cases – and in poor condition in terms of safety, hygiene and health. These days in Taverna del Ferro approximately a thousand people occupy the 360 flats, of which around forty are occupied illegally. Nothing came of the demolition plan in the 1990s, which also included Le Vele di Scampia, and serious interventions require funds measured in the millions of euros. In September 2020 €570,000 was allocated for the most urgent maintenance jobs, which began in February 2021 with improvements to the stairways in the two complexes. So the bitterness of certain residents was entirely understandable when in 2018 the artist Jorit created his vast murals of Maradona, Che Guevara (fun fact: this is the largest image of Che in the world) and Niccolò, an autistic child. For those living in leaky homes built from poor quality and sometimes toxic materials, they were viewed as a mere lick of paint on a situation which by that point was one of unbearable decline.

has been felt, even at the level of infrastructure. If a stop was added to Line 2 of the metro, from Gianturco to San Giovanni, it's thanks to the academy. The entire area stands to benefit, but it is a long process, set to grow over the years. The surrounding landscape is all cranes, excavators and cement mixers; there are new buildings under construction, and a plan is afoot to open the campus gardens along three sides, which will enable locals to access the park's tree-lined paths and use the space to walk or exercise.

Pietro takes me to the roof, and once up there a strange thing happens. The bird's-eye view is astounding, with the light flooding the whole city and melting into the blue of the sea, and nothing – not even the profusion of urban ruins, not even the illegal buildings that have eaten up these areas or the natural disorder lurking ten or fifteen metres below us – detracts from the perfect, placid flight of seagulls over the eastern dock, about which there's now talk of bolstering its role as a container terminal. You could say the whole strategy for this part of the city lies there, all perfectly encapsulated by the project to expand the eastern dock. Revitalise the historic Miglio d'Oro ('Golden Mile') and the marvellous Vesuvian villas? Re-establish the connection between the city and its coastline? Where does one start when the port is an actual physical border and not only has no intention of ceding space but plans to expand? San Giovanni and the entire east of the city risk being further suffocated if the so-called waterfront becomes – is increasingly at risk of becoming – a gigantic storage facility.

Naples isn't Hamburg and it isn't Rotterdam, yet there are plans, and the money to finance them, to modernise the freight yard from the port to the Nola Interport, plans that have been made public and developed but never realised. The fate of this whole area of the city rests on this ongoing and thorny negotiation over the port. From their point of view, the logic is, at the end of the day, flawless: the shipowners make money, and the industry reps become interlocutors that the city's politicians and administrators can't do without. But the port remains as tightly clenched as a clam and won't grant the city an inch to access the coast, redevelop the area and allow the plan to move forward, even if it is in keeping with the entire city fabric that extends around it so densely.

Of all the neighbourhoods in the city, San Giovanni a Teduccio (plus Barra, Ponticelli and every other travel-to-work location in this area) is at the centre of the most promising and well-organised Neapolitan system of trade and commerce. In addition to the Apple Academy there is the National Railway Museum in Pietrarsa, the studios of Teatro di San Carlo in Vigliena, the university departments and buildings, the metro and the Circumvesuviana train from Naples to Sorrento, industrial buildings to reclaim, urban fabric and spaces to modernise, infrastructure to upgrade.

*

'The university chose not to build cafeterias or dormitories for their student body; students leave college to grab a sandwich at the corner deli.'

The same is true of Bagnoli, only there heroic people who kept believing something would soon change were in short supply. Because one thing is certain: just under twenty kilometres from San Giovanni, from the east to the west of the city, the most enervating experiment in empty promises that present-day Italy can boast has been going on for decades. San Giovanni may be confined to a metal prison, impervious yet concrete, but Bagnoli is trapped in an imperceptible and barbaric paper cage, buried under an enormous pile of texts, documents, stamped papers, certificates, appeals, seizures, feasibility studies and, more than anything, failures, failures, failures. A plan for a future that is forever postponed and never becomes the present.

To get a good idea of what Bagnoli could become for Naples you have to take a step back and observe it from a distance. Ignore the news for a moment and focus on nature. And to see, to take in, in its entirety, the former Ilva plant – the state-sponsored steel company gets its name from the Latin name for Elba, the island from where the iron that fuelled the blast furnaces built at the end of the 19th century was brought – one of the best vantage points is still the Parco Virgiliano at the top of Posillipo hill.

There it is, the plant, extending over an area that seems to leave the city behind and flow towards the sea across a landscape that is part green and part blue, lying along the bay that stretches from Miseno to Nisida. It is early afternoon on a day in late spring, so nearly summer as to vaunt an intensity of light that looms over a graveyard of industrial works, over the curved, gleaming, sheet-metal rooftops with nothing beneath them, like empty, purposeless shells now that the giant tortoise that lived there has gone. Instead of white smoke from the chimneys, clouds hover over the water, and the combined effect of the motion of the waves and the veil of vapour that seems to swirl around Nisida makes it hard to gauge distances, with the rust-coloured blast furnace and the red warehouse appearing to stretch over almost the entire two hundred hectares of a void that people have been trying to fill for thirty years. With the closure of the 'hot area' and the last iron casting on 20 October 1990, the Bagnoli plant became the perfect model for how urban deindustrialisation can fail spectacularly, a case study in what not to do and the shining example of how in one fell swoop the political mill can turn everyone against each other in a wearying competition to see who can waste the most time, as local administrators, national politicians, technicians, committees, lobbies and pressure groups continue to vie for control. The one enduring question hovering over the area is simply: what should we do with this place that was once home to Ilva? 'Give it back to the city,' is the answer. OK, but how? There are countless examples of industrial areas that have put the past behind them and have been

Opposite: The Port of Naples.
Pages 130–1: Relaxing on the shore at San Giovanni a Teduccio with the old industrial buildings in the background.

restored to their cities, and each time it was a powerful idea that propelled them in that direction. In Duisburg a large natural park was built over the remains of a steelworks; in Bilbao the Guggenheim; in Essen, in Germany's Ruhr, brought back from the brink by the steel industry, even the 'shit stream' – the hardly affectionate nickname that residents once used to refer to the river Emscher – was revived, a waterway into which, for more than 160 years, everything imaginable had been dumped, becoming a paradigm of smart ecology for the 21st century.

'I'm selling Bagnoli to whoever's buying / Green hills, blue sea / Will the highest bidder step forward,' sings Edoardo Bennato. There have been so many projects to revitalise the former industrial area of Bagnoli and so many reasons why they failed to come to fruition that there isn't room to list them all here. Amid all this, it must be said that residents and neighbourhood boards represent an extremely precious social capital, the one glimmer of hope in an otherwise very bleak situation. Dario Oropallo, activist of Bagnoli's Osservatorio Popolare, emits waves of enthusiasm and optimism that until now I'd never encountered in anyone involved in the matter. 'The tools for

Cages of Metal and Cages of Paper

IRON CITY

Throughout the 20th century, on the western outskirts of Naples, Bagnoli was home to the Ilva steelworks (known as Italsider from 1961), a symbol of Campanian industry established in 1905. When it opened it employed 1,200 workers, and the complex grew significantly during the First World War and continued to expand during the fascist era. It also survived the attacks of the retreating Germans in 1943 and was reactivated the following year. In the period following the Second World War the Bagnoli plant remained a central pillar of industrial production, gaining emblematic status because of its size (at its peak in 1977 it occupied two million square metres and employed eight thousand people), its industrial relations and trade union disputes and its contribution to economic growth in the south of Italy. But it was in the 1970s that reduced demand for steel and international competition, as well as strategic errors, bureaucratic obstacles and Italsider's decision to invest in its Taranto site, led to a long decline at Bagnoli that culminated in the decision in 1989 – just seven years after the facilities had been renovated and made more sustainable – to dismantle the structure. The closure of Bagnoli had such an impact on life in Naples that it inspired numerous artists: Ermanno Rea's 2002 novel *La dismissione* was made into a film by Gianni Amelio in 2006, entitled *The Missing Star*, but it also provided the subject matter for Edoardo Bennato's songs 'Zen' and 'Vendo Bagnoli'. The plant is still waiting to be redeveloped.

Above: Vigliena, a former industrial area in San Giovanni a Teduccio.
Opposite: Decommissioned works adjacent to the port.

mobilisation are innumerable, but we can't continue to operate by knocking heads. The presence of a local support team that can monitor what's going on is fundamental, and we have to involve as many citizens as possible in that.' For now, what's 'going on' is that Invitalia, the national development agency owned by the Ministry of Economy and Finance, is in charge of the administration of the area. It took over after the management company for Bagnoli's urban transformation – a group supported by public funding (90 per cent from the municipality of Naples, 2.5 per cent from the province and 7.5 per cent from Campania) – went bankrupt in 2014, following, in turn, the bankruptcy of Bagnoli S.p.A. and the failure of two reclamation and regeneration projects spearheaded by the Ministry of the Environment and Protection of Land and Sea in 2003 and 2007.

From Posillipo you can make out the tents belonging to the operation undertaking the removal and reclamation of asbestos between Coroglio and Cavalleggeri, close to Via Cattolica, near the former Battisti barracks. The area was handed over to the contractor in July 2020 and covers a total of sixteen hectares, with 150,000 cubic metres of asbestos to be cleaned up. The land is being rehabilitated and the excavations made good, and after that they will have to deal with transporting and disposing of the waste. The Osservatorio Popolare and other committees fought for the installation of seven air-quality control units, which can be monitored online in real time. When the level of air pollution is exceeded, the operations are put on hold. This is a small concrete example of what Dario means when he says that ultimately 'it's better to work together than fight'. In other times, in times of bitter struggle and endless barricades, any activist who uttered these words would at the very least have been accused of 'conspiring with the enemy', as they say in wartime. Instead, who knows, maybe this firm but not radical way of thinking could create the right conditions to finally build something rather than nothing.

Of course, the causes for conflict have not gone away; they never will. The next front after decontamination, so to speak, will be the debate – already quite fierce – over the removal of the so-called landfill, the sandbank created at the beginning of the 1960s to meet the plant's expansion needs. I found old photos, wide-angle shots taken with a lousy camera, of the warehouses wreathed in whitish fumes. Expansion was necessary, but there was one big problem: the sea. How do you build on the sea? You fill it. And how do you deal with water? The managers at the time had an idea: reshape the coastline. It wasn't too complicated. They already had all the materials they needed: blast-furnace slag, a by-product of the cast-iron production process, mixed with cement and tuff. The job lasted twenty-four months, from 1962 to 1964, during which numerous houses in the area were demolished for rubble. In the end they found themselves with 1.2 million cubic metres of materials and ninety thousand tonnes of boulders with which they assembled a gigantic parallelepiped of tuff, cement and volcanic ash. And there's your landfill, an area covering approximately 157,000 square metres. It is also – a minor detail overlooked in those intoxicating times of industrial progress when nobody thought of nitpicking about environmental issues – a gigantic ecological timebomb composed of polycyclic aromatic hydrocarbons (PAHs) and heavy metals (arsenic, zinc, vanadium, lead, tin). Do they remove it? Keep it? The state thought it ought to be eliminated. There is a law from November 1996 – no. 582 – that explicitly says so, and that law was bolstered by another in 2000. According to Francesco Floro Flores, the government's special commissioner, the operation will cost €141 million, but the neighbourhood committees, he adds, 'might get the notion to leave it be'. A notion. Who knows if they will?

Meanwhile, as I cross the city, leaving the Virgiliano behind and passing in front of the Pausilypon Archaeological Park on my way to the Ilva plant, I phone Guglielmo Santoro, president of the former Ilva workers' association in Bagnoli, who mentions an academic study of the landfill which found that removing it could create marine currents capable of wiping out the beach in Coroglio. 'In my opinion it's better to keep it,' he says. 'According to core samples the beach where it's located is, paradoxically, the least polluted in the whole area.' And the money? The money is there for now, yes, but not for long and not for everything. Apparently it will last a couple more years, then another €700 million will be needed, which might come from the development and cohesion fund (not to mention the deluge of money from the national recovery-and-resilience plan). However much it costs, just as with San Giovanni a Teduccio and the eastern outskirts of the city, in Bagnoli the question is not so much what to spend the money on but how and for whom. If politicians choose not to oppose lines of absolute autonomy and remain in dialogue with the territory – forgetting for a moment local potentates, small power groups and local and national lobbies – something might well get built, finally. And just as for the east one can't imagine a project that doesn't run from the port to the Miglio d'Oro, it's unthinkable not to couple the fate of Bagnoli with that of the Phlegraean Fields and with tourism and infrastructure networks in general – in short, with issues concerning the entire layout of this city. So that's how things stand, with the desire for something on an international scale in a city that often feels provincial.

From Coroglio I pass down Via Bagnoli with its series of murals created over the years on the perimeter wall separating the road from what remains of the factory. It's the closest thing to Berlin's East Side Gallery that you will find here in this city. I park my scooter and walk around for a while, taking in the aroma of wood and tree resin and the shade under the trees until, as the sun burns through the clouds, I stop near the giant AGL chimney – the elaborate brick-and-concrete structure can be seen from every part of the neighbourhood – and fetch a book from my backpack.

Ermanno Rea's *La dismissione* ('The Divestment') opens with a question: 'What do you have in you now that the millennium is no longer so new?'

What does the city of Naples have in it now that the millennium is no longer so new? Whatever it does with its old industrial areas is what it has in it. That might be a good answer.

Opposite: A view of the old Italsider and Cementir plants from Posillipo.
Below: The former Cirio canning factory in San Giovanni a Teduccio.

NAPOLISPHERE

PEPPE FIORE
Translated by Ned Darlington

Since the success of *Gomorrah*, the television and film industries in Italy are increasingly choosing the capital of Campania for their stories and their locations.

Taking a break on set at Le Vele di Scampia during filming for the movie *Gomorrah*, directed by Matteo Garrone.

The year 2021 marked twenty years since I had left Naples to go to university in Rome. I am now, *quantitatively* speaking, more Roman than Neapolitan, and in some ways this is the fulfilment of my destiny. Over the last twenty years Naples and I have always kept an eye on each other from a distance. The city has had little or no part to play in my work, except for the insidious label 'Neapolitan writer/screenwriter', which is almost impossible to shake off. And from afar I have witnessed the exodus of my high-school friends and the counter-exodus of recent years, generated variously by the cultural revival – whether real or preconceived – of the administration of Luigi de Magistris (the former prosecutor-turned-mayor of Italy's most chaotic city), by the tourist industry or by a child to be raised close to the sea and to their grandparents. In the meantime I continued to feel a sense of mutual distrust between myself and the city, the same distrust I felt when I lived there as a boy and which later made me into the atypical Neapolitan I became as an adult. Naples felt too complex, too dark and opaque, which is why I left as soon as I could. But in all these years a kind of unresolved question remained suspended, frozen between us, which is why when, between 2018 and 2019, I was to write a film set in Naples, I hoped it would be an opportunity for us to be reconciled. At last, after nearly twenty years, I was returning, not as an expatriate grudgingly being sent home for the public holidays but with an assignment that forced me to negotiate with the city on the level that was closest to the truth for me, that of narrative creation, and, moreover, with total artistic security since the director, Francesco Lettieri, is a brother with whom I have shared projects, tastes and visions for years.

So in the summer of 2018 here I was back in my childhood home – the large, silent and empty house of my parents, who were away on holiday – to work on a screenplay with Francesco. The subject, a classic coming-of-age story set around a fictional Neapolitan ultras club, had been preselected by a major production company with a promptness that was almost miraculous. Of course, there was Francesco's renown, earned through years of dedicated service and the fact that the subject was well written, but there was also something else. There was, to put it bluntly, the sense that a project set in Naples would automatically be fast-tracked to being commissioned.

PEPPE FIORE is an author and screenwriter who has published two collections of short stories and four novels, the most recent being *Gli Innamorati* (2023, 'The Lovers'). He has co-written two films with Francesco Lettieri, *Ultras* and *Lovely Boy,* and has worked on numerous TV series, including as head writer on the Sky series *Il re*, which won the prestigious Nastro d'Argento award for best crime show in 2024. He created *Piedone*, a reboot of the classic 1970s cop comedy set in contemporary Naples, which was aired in 2024 on Sky.

Michela Andreozzi about to shoot a scene on the set of the Naples-set TV series *La squadra*.

That Naples has in recent years been very much in vogue in cinema and TV was something I knew. What I didn't know was just *how* in vogue it was. When I was on location – Francesco and I on a motorbike in the August heat, between the neighbourhood of Pianura, the Phlegraean Fields and the Centro Direzionale business district (see 'The Centro Direzionale' on page 182) – my first concern was to pick locations that had not already been seen in other films or series. No easy task. Just as it was not easy to write the dynamics of our ultra football fanatics – who do what all football fanatics in the world do: chant, mass, organise and fight – more than once we found ourselves discarding certain narrative solutions because they were 'too *Gomorrah*-like'. The truth is that in our twenty years of long-distance relations, the city had become infused with cinema, and the result is that writing even a minimally informed narrative about Naples today is a very different task from even just ten years ago. First of all, it is much more densely cross-referential, because now Naples is not simply a movie-making city. In today's Naples, the city and the city's film-making industry work in tandem.

To get an idea of the scale of this, in the last five years roughly a thousand productions have been shot, including films, TV shows and TV commercials, a huge number, and that makes Naples the number one film set in Italy. 'As of 2017, we have financed 281 works,

Napolisphere 139

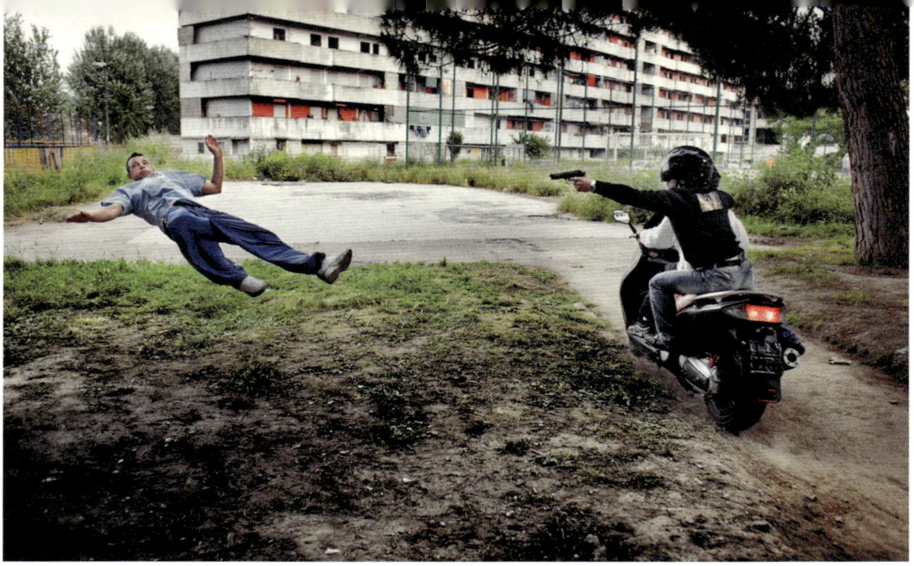

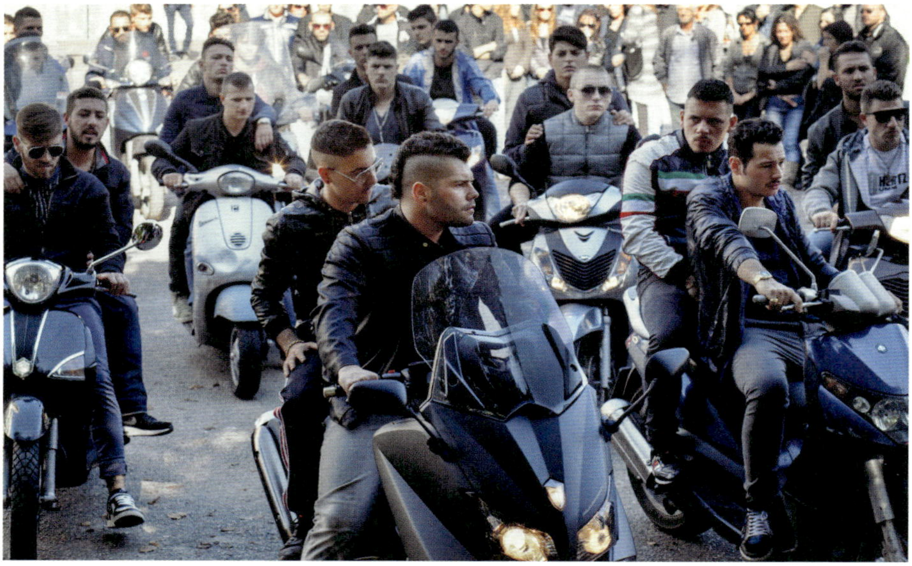

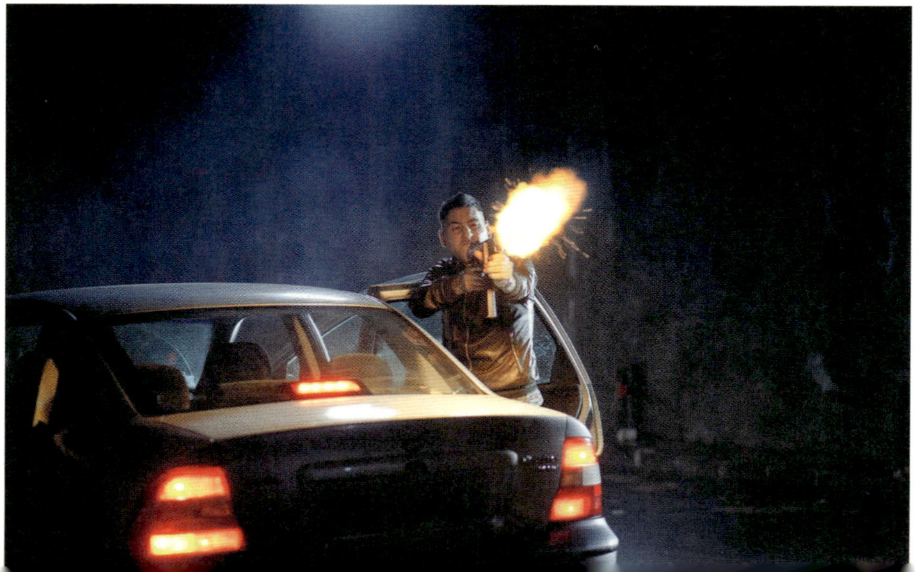

> 'The impact, or presumed impact, of *Gomorrah* has been much discussed and debated. For those in the film industry in Naples there is before *Gomorrah* and after *Gomorrah*.'

including feature films, documentaries, shorts and series. Eighty for awards, festivals, reviews and film education projects. Around thirty theatres have been financed per year.' (Maurizio Gemma, Campania Regional Film Commission) In the wake of leading examples such as Apulia, Piedmont and Trentino, and with the support of Campania president Vincenzo de Luca's regional audiovisual law – which has streamlined procedures and made the processes of accessing EU funds easier – Campania, and Naples in particular, has in recent years positioned itself as a magnet for large productions. But is it really all down to politics and film commissioning? 'Naples owes its flourishing cinema industry to authors who have been burrowing into the minds of their audiences for years. Let's not make the mistake of thinking that it's the industry that influences authors. It is the authors, assuming they are strong enough, who deeply shake the mechanisms of perception. At some point it becomes inevitable for politics and the industry to adapt.' (Edoardo De Angelis, film director)

It is a fact that, even before the landmark show *My Brilliant Friend*, the 1990s had seen the rise of young artists such as Paolo Sorrentino, Antonio Capuano, Mario Martone and Pappi Corsicato – as well as long-running series such as the soap opera *Un posto al sole* and the crime drama *La squadra*. Even before that there was, and always had been, an inexhaustible pool of talent – 'I remember a person in charge of the Solinas Prize [for screenwriting] who had thought of making a separate category just for Neapolitan screenplays' (Nicola Giuliano, producer) – a pool with, moreover, a precise territorial character. 'In Naples there is traditionally a market for theatrical and musical entertainment that is more lively and demanding than elsewhere. Generally, Campania is a region that is its own audience and that chooses talent by paying for a ticket. This results in tremendous competition to come out on top. It has allowed various waves of actors to forge themselves and raise their profile in a heterogeneous mix of avant-garde and pop productions.' (Luciano Stella, producer)

Beneath every attempt to restructure a cultural system there are proportionally complex concatenations, tensions and flaws that run through the years before they start an earthquake. In our case, the earthquake was a TV series called *Gomorrah* (2014–21), the production that put Naples in the international limelight like never before. '*Gomorrah* tapped into a typically Neapolitan narrative without ever being conventional and featured locations in Naples that are truly international. It showed everyone that Naples is one of the most contemporary cities in the world.' (Fortunato Cerlino, actor, writer and director)

The impact, or presumed impact, of *Gomorrah* on the collective imagination

Stills from the film *Gomorrah* and the series of the same name.

has been much discussed and debated. Here, I'll just say that for those involved in the film industry in Naples there is before *Gomorrah* and after *Gomorrah*. '*Gomorrah* has been the greatest training ground for film crews ever seen in Naples. Skilful foremen coming from Rome picked local people. Those who started the first season of *Gomorrah* as handyworkers are now best boys. If six years ago we had three good electricians in Naples, now we have twelve.' (Walter de Majo and Alessandro Elia, producers)

At the same time it is as if Naples had found a peculiar way to make films. 'It is clear that all Italian cinematography was born in Rome, but Naples assimilated Roman cinematography, infused it with street smarts and reintroduced it to the profession. The Neapolitan filmmaker has this appeal that no one outside has – our *cazzimma*, our grit in doing what it takes to make things work makes us ultra-professionals.' (Ezio Pierattini, stage manager)

Gomorrah and its boundless territorial pull – magnified by the show's five seasons – have helped to organise a widespread yet elusive kind of knowledge already ingrained in generations of showbusiness professionals in Naples – even going so far as to create entirely new paradigms that did not exist previously. 'I'm a volunteer assistant in the Poggioreale district. I took a guy who'd had a rough life, one who had a gambling habit, a pizza maker who had lost his job. We start roping off the locations forty-eight hours before the shoot. When the production vehicles arrive we help them park. During every shoot security needs to be in place. Guys like him do a really great job. It's the often-discussed option that the government should provide.' (Peppe Cioffi, security)

On a deeper level, every time one talks about *Gomorrah* with someone who is familiar with its context, there's an implicit understanding that concerns the way the city's underground society understood that the film industry was an opportunity, and it answered the call. 'In '87, to shoot in the Scampia district of Secondigliano you first had to talk to the local boss. *Gomorrah* created a new dynamic: the producers made the territory responsible. *Gomorrah* was a game-changer because it came saying: *I come into your home to tell a story about it. I'm not asking your permission to shoot, but I'm giving you work, and you'll be with me*. The trouble Matteo Garrone ran into with his film [version of] *Gomorrah* [2008] would be unthinkable today.' (Raffaele Cortile, location manager) 'When productions come to Naples they are bringing work, and when they go to a place they systematically involve local people. Handyworkers, extras ... so-called ordinary folk watch for these productions because they give them the chance to earn a day's wage. It's become a normal thing.' (Peppe Cioffi) The obvious flip side is that a city that soaks everything up stops being amazed after a while, even by the movies. 'It used to be fun when the movie trucks came to the neighbourhood. Today everyone is used to seeing a shoot – and when you walk around you hear, "What a drag,

Angeloni's trucks are here." There is no longer the wonder of before, the magic of the set.' (Ezio Pierattini)

After *Gomorrah*, which had been filmed in Scampia, the movie industry started regularly using tough neighbourhoods as locations. Castel Volturno was one. In 2008 the Camorra had massacred six innocent African immigrants and a convicted criminal suspected of being an informer in Baia Verde, a part of Castel Volturno. 'Castel Volturno was the kingdom of the Casalesi clan. The massacre of these immigrants changed the course of history: the state reacted and decapitated a clan that had ruled every aspect of people's lives. With the disappearance of the Casalesi the area found itself free of mafia dynamics, and it just so happened that such directors as Matteo Garrone and Edoardo de Angelis captured the narrative potential of these places. Nowadays, Castel Volturno is a permanent film set. In recent years an average of three films have been shot there annually. There are thirty young people working in movies on a permanent basis, professionals that started from nothing. Some are working to become the new Matteo Garrone. Campania has four or five such places. The next one for me is the Cilento region.' (Raffaele Cortile)

The film industry shepherded people into leading law-abiding lives. Much has been said about this, but if it is true, it is also cynically true that for people who do Francesco's work or mine, *Gomorrah* is problematic primarily because not only has it transformed Naples – and especially the hinterland – into a galaxy of *Gomorrah* locations (fifty-eight episodes means a lot of location work) but it has also drained the pool of actors, many of them excellent, whom we end

ANTONIO CAPUANO

Even though he didn't make his debut as a director until the age of fifty-one, Antonio Capuano is regarded as a master film-maker. Loved by the critics and often ignored by the distributors, he has a reputation as a misunderstood genius. After many years' experience working as a set designer, in 1991 he released his explosive *Vito and the Others*, winning the Critics' Week prize and the Silver Ribbon at the Venice Film Festival. He was immediately compared with Pasolini for his almost documentary-style approach to a story of degradation and juvenile criminality, but his work has proved impossible to categorise. In fact, it is its very variety that characterises it: he made films offering social criticism on uncomfortable subjects – such as paedophilia in the Church in *Sacred Silence* (1996), set in the Rione Sanità, or *Dark Love* (2010), in which the rape of a well-to-do girl by a group of boys from the Quartieri Spagnoli explores the distance between the two sides of the city – but alternated them with comedies including *Polvere di Napoli* (1998) and *Achille Tarallo* (2018). The former, besides paying tribute to Vittorio De Sica's *The Gold of Naples*, also marked the screenwriting debut of the future Oscar-winner Paolo Sorrentino, who credited Capuano as being his guiding light. Of the Neapolitan *nouvelle vague* that emerged between the 1990s and 2000s, Capuano was the most unpredictable, coherent and independent of the dictates of the market. Although he has cast some famous actors, he admits to preferring young non-professional actors who actually live and breathe a character rather than playing one, such as Marco Grieco, who plays Marco, who worked in a deli in real life as well as in *Bagnoli Jungle* (2015).

A scene from Matteo Garrone's *Gomorrah*; in the background is Le Vele di Scampia.

up discarding during casting because they are too closely associated with the series.

Or, at least, that is what our biases lead us to think, because it is possible that that might be much less of a problem than we believe. 'People who work in movies overestimate people's memory of places. When the audience is really invested in the story they don't start thinking about where they've seen this place before. I have always been sceptical as to whether there is any great value in choosing locations on the basis that they are unfamiliar to viewers. As for the alleged "*Gomorrah* style", I think things are oversimplified, not only by authors but also by critics and journalists. I reject this sort of obsessive need to always find a reference to compare everything to.' (Nicola Giuliano)

Indeed, anyone who has experienced the movie and TV industries on the creative side has come up against the *reference* obsession. When presenting a project, trying to convince a broadcaster or justifying a character or a scene to whichever doubting commissioning editor one happens to face, the first instinct is always to cling to something that already exists – 'Our protagonist is kind of Walter White from *Breaking Bad*, a bit Vic Mackey from *The Shield*, something like the guy from *Peaky Blinders*.' Personally, I suspect that this is a toll that cinema has to pay for a degree of gravitas to be afforded to what is essentially an ephemeral industry: something as intangible as the idea of a film or series needs noble forebears to justify the huge amount of money it will cost – along with all the interests at play and the inevitable squabbling.

But *Gomorrah* style aside, it is a fact that the series has focused a huge amount of attention on the city of Naples. A string of case studies prove it: from an exquisitely postmodern production such as *Love and Bullets*, directed by the very Roman Manetti brothers, which has racked up prestigious David di Donatello Awards, or Ferzan Özpetek's film *Naples in Veils* (both 2017), or the Rai-produced biopic *Carosello Carosone* (2021), written by the two Roman screenwriters Francesca Serafini and Giordano Meacci and directed by Lucio Pellegrini from Turin, and then the truly global phenomenon that is Elena Ferrante's *My Brilliant Friend* (2018–). Naples, which has always been a culturally prolific but self-sufficient city, has become a powerful magnet for talent from outside Naples. Of course, there are logistical and political reasons for this, but in terms of the collective imagination it is as if the world has only just realised that Naples is a treasure trove, an encyclopaedia of meanings on which even non-Neapolitans can draw freely. 'It is a polyphonic city. A world city that can be narrated from any perspective. If you want to tell a story about the bourgeoisie, you can do it in Naples; if you want to tell a story about common folk, you can; if you want to do a comedy, you can. It is a layered, interwoven city, where the territories favoured by different social classes converge and encounter one another like nowhere else in Italy. In Rome, between the contrasting areas of Prati and Centocelle there is an hour's drive; if you want to write a detective story you have to choose between five different police precincts. In Naples, however, in Via Toledo, up one end of the road you have one world

NAPOLI NOIR

A recently coined joke says that in Naples there are more police inspectors in books than there are on the streets. It makes you smile, but if you have a passion for crime novels, looking at the shelves in a bookshop and your own reading, you realise that it actually rings true. Everywhere you turn there are Neapolitan investigators, men and women, ready to solve mysteries big and small. But why should that be? What is the source of this desire to investigate the dark corners of the 'City of the Sun'? In the mid-19th century the journalist Francesco Mastriani wrote *Il mio cadavere* ('My Corpse'). Set in Naples, it is regarded as the first true example of a noir crime novel in Italy, but its author is now only remembered in place names – a very short alleyway, a school, a plaque – otherwise the city seems to have forgotten him. While the idea of Naples as the country's crime-fiction capital is quite recent, the narrative goal of shedding light on mysteries and crimes has never diminished, from Matilde Serao, author of *Il delitto di via Chiatamone* ('The Crime of Via Chiatamone') and *The Severed Hand* to Attilio Veraldi's *The Payoff* and Giuseppe Ferrandino's *Pericle il nero* ('Pericles the Black Man'). Naples is not part of the geography of Italian crime fiction, it is the starting point. And it is still forging ahead, through the work of Maurizio de Giovanni – creator of the likes of Commissario Ricciardi, the Bastards of Pizzofalcone, Mina Settembre and Sara Morozzi – Diana Lama, Patrizia Rinaldi and Sara Bilotti. But while crime and intrigue abound both on the pages of novels and in real life, the ability to solve such puzzles seems to reside solely in the writers' imaginations. (Raffaella R. Ferré)

Napolisphere 145

and down the other end another. And each district contains its opposite: hilltop Vomero has the Petraio, Chiaia has the Quartieri Spagnoli; and these worlds don't exclude each other. This makes everything extremely fertile from a narrative point of view.' (Maurizio de Giovanni, bestselling writer) A polyphonic city and, what is more, mysteriously inexhaustible. 'I really enjoy the location-scouting process. For me it feels organic and exciting. In Naples the incredible thing is that you always find new places if you're looking for them.' (Francesca Amitrano, director of photography)

It is precisely the kind of large multimedia 'factory' that is Maurizio de Giovanni's work – notably *The Bastards of Pizzofalcone* and *Inspector Ricciardi* series – that has proved how extremely adaptable Naples the encyclopaedia is: a system that can speak to audiences of different tiers, and potentially very large ones at that. But the producers of the dramas inspired by de Giovanni's novels are not Neapolitan. Even the production company of our little film about football ultras, although born in Naples in the 1990s, after ten years moved to Rome and then found itself in Los Angeles with the Academy Awards for Paolo Sorrentino's *The Great Beauty*. And, of course, *Gomorrah* is produced by a leading Rome-based company. Historically, Romans are the head writers – the director Stefano Sollima, for example, who created the gritty, realistic style of the show. In short, Naples' growth is not perfectly proportional to the enormous success of its cinema and TV brand. The big productions tend to remain Rome-centric, as they always have been. 'There are but a few high-profile assets in the Naples area, and to have international visibility you have to move to Rome. In Naples

The writer and screenwriter Peppe Fiore and the director Francesco Lettieri.

there's still a deeply Neapolitan mentality, which can create uncomfortable situations. I can't work on a set where the extras are paid €30 instead of the legal minimum of €80 just "because we are in Naples". And it is not unusual to get calls from Naples with proposals like "We can make this film for €150,000 because we're all friends," which means they pay pennies. The result is productions that cannot compete, because you can tell when a film costs €150,000 to make.' (Fortunato Cerlino) This is a fact, and indeed, for those who work or aim to work in cinema in Naples, it is a major hurdle. The saving grace is that a region's strength can also be measured by its responsiveness and ability to go back to the prototype, to refine the craftsmanship and not simply focus on large-scale mass production, something that has been undeniably flourishing in recent years.

'We aim to make ultra-independent cinema. If I make a film like *Veleno* or *Là-bas* – which nobody cared about before because it features the Africans from Castel Volturno – I can now do it for very little money, and I know that I will find distribution for it. They are films that embrace causes. I understand that the globalised world moves in a different direction. But I wouldn't call what is happening in Naples nowadays a renaissance, rather a small resistance.' (Gaetano Di Vaio, producer) 'My fringe status as an independent filmmaker who is very attached not only to the city but to my own neighbourhood, where all my stories are set, protected me in the end from being too bound to the audience

'But the point is, if we were never Alitalia to begin with, let's aim to be EasyJet from the off. Let's not imitate what we've never been.'

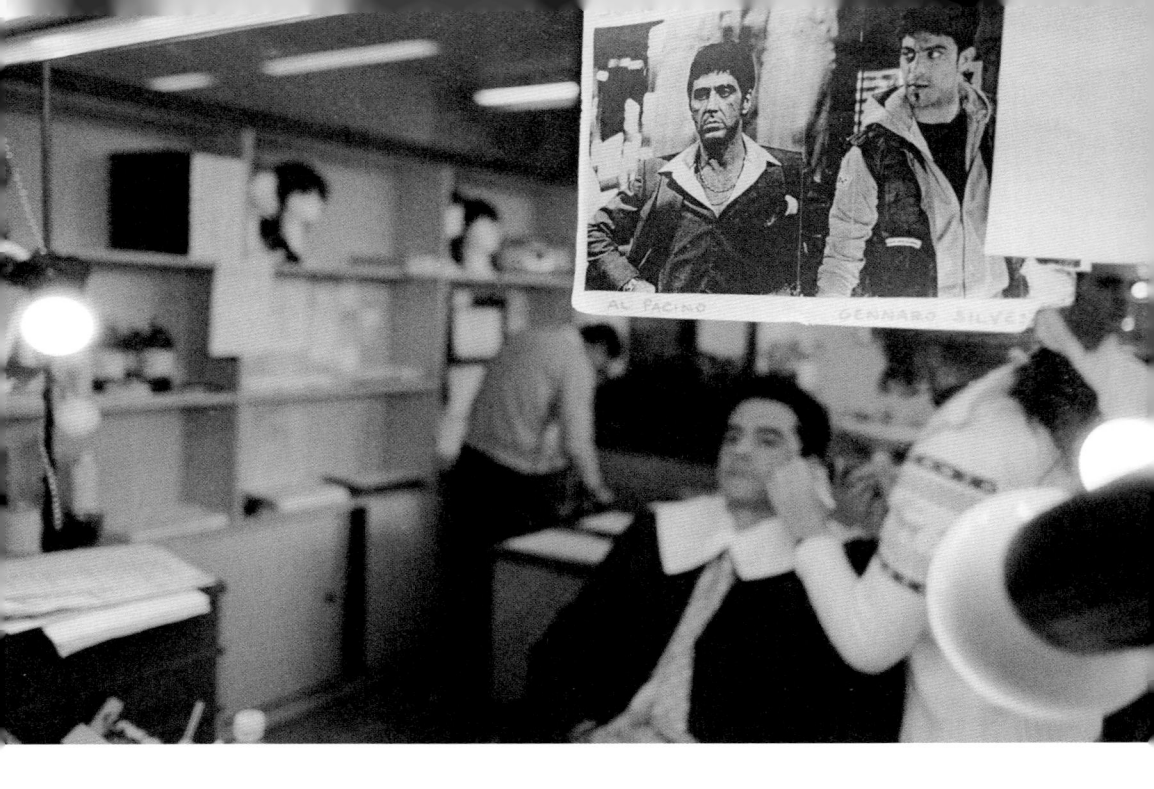

On the set of *La squadra*, a Rai 3 production, in Naples. Actor Andrea Marrocco is in makeup with a photo of the American actor Al Pacino stuck to the mirror.

and to the movie theatres. That's why I decided to stay in Naples. I'm trying not to get trapped and remain as free as possible'. (Edgardo Pistone, director)

A ghost has haunted the Naples movie scene in recent years, and its name is Turin, a model – created by the Film Commission Torino Piemonte – that was exemplary in the early 2000s but which failed to become a real system. This is why today, when talking about development prospects, two issues are bound to rear their heads. The first concerns which business strategies politics should choose to support the system. 'The challenge is to find which direction to grow in. I think that with the current budget flow, the audiovisual sector can grow locally. But the point is, if we were never Alitalia to begin with, let's aim to be EasyJet from the off. Let's not imitate what we've never been. The company I represent made a film that won, among other things, the European Film Award for animation. And today people from outside Italy ask, "How did you manage to create such smooth animation?" All with open-source software! If a department of digital animation and VFX were founded, Naples and Campania could become important and globally competitive attractors.' (Luciano Stella) In this sense, the role of politics is also to consolidate the local fabric of productivity. 'The region has given the film commission an excellent opportunity to intervene through a system of calls for tenders profiled specifically on our production needs. Productions in Rome don't put out €20,000 tenders. They serve the many small companies in Campania and promote the territory.' (Walter de Majo, Alessandro Elia)

The other issue is training, which has historically been lacking in the area. 'We are working on the creation of a cinema

AGOSTINO FERRENTE

The desire to make documentaries ever closer to reality led Agostino Ferrente to create two of the most touching works of recent years about Naples, while involving the subjects of his films in the process of making them. *Intervista a mia madre* (2000, 'Interview with My Mother'), co-directed with Giovanni Piperno, showed boys and girls around ten years old interviewing their own mothers. Fascinated by their stories, Ferrente returned two years later to teach them how to handle the camera as well. He kept up the relationship, and once he had found the money, went back to work. The result was the splendid film *Le cose belle* ('The Beautiful Things'), again co-directed with Piperno and released in 2014, in which the scenes shot in 1999 – poignant flashbacks to the protagonists' childhoods – are juxtaposed with their adult lives to see what remains of their childhood dreams. Back then Enzo used to sing Neapolitan songs in restaurants accompanied by his father on guitar, but we next see him selling mobile-phone contracts door to door. After the release of the film Ferrente explained that Enzo had stopped singing years earlier but had started again after seeing himself in the cinema. In *Selfie* (2019) the director decided to get even closer to his characters, leaving them to play the role of camera operator using their phones. Alessandro, an apprentice barista, and Pietro, an aspiring barber, give us a window into their lives in the Rione Traiano, where their friend Davide Bifolco was accidentally killed by a policeman in 2014. The protagonists of the two films share a certain level of fatalism and disillusionment but also the desire to make an honest living without succumbing to the siren calls of criminality.

hub, which in addition to being a business incubator will host the two-year master's degree course in cinema and TV from the Naples Academy of Fine Arts. We need to stimulate the growth of a new generation of authors. I think of films like *The Intouchables* or *The Dinner Game*. Navel-gazing does no one any good. I love American cinema: the market is there to be conquered, not hated.' (Maurizio Gemma) Bearing in mind that often the problems lie not with those in charge of the execution but with those in power, 'What Naples needs is bold producers. If the producers aren't bold then we'll never have good directors and writers. Naples needs this, but we as human beings need it more. Whether we get to see something beautiful depends on you, the producers.' (Francesca Amitrano)

Memories of my two weeks of writing in Naples in the summer of 2018 merge with the long, drowsy afternoons reading scripts at Francesco's house in the beautiful seaside town of Pozzuoli, birthplace of Sofia Loren – he is also returning from exile after years in Rome and starting a family in Naples. Bathing in the ocean at Bacoli and canoeing at Gaiola Island next to Posillipo, the fish dinners at Cape Miseno and at Naples' Pignasecca market, eating off plastic plates while surrounded by American tourists. How strange my parents' house felt without my parents there, and the evenings drinking at the Perditempo, the bar behind Piazza Bellini. The feeling of being a real summer tourist in Naples for the first time. Also for the

A scene from the film *Gomorrah* that didn't make it to the final cut, shot at a real construction site.

first time touching on a certain sincerity that had always eluded me until then: the gentrified and Barcelona-fied city of the EasyJet and Airbnb generation, after all much less dark and threatening and much more inclusive than it had seemed to me up until I was eighteen when I decided to abandon it. Who knows if it had always been this way or whether it had become like this in the twenty years of our long-distance relationship? Perhaps also thanks to cinema and TV, or perhaps because it was the most suited to the polymorphic zeitgeist of those years.

'The Neapolitan *type* is a deception. Neapolitans always aspire to a universal kind of expression. Socially, Naples has also been an esoteric and alchemical city, a city in a privileged position to question the meaning of being human within the cosmos. When you go through an era like ours, an era fraught with profound fractures of meaning and unparalleled collapse – of twin towers or of economic systems – it is precisely at moments such as this that some shops open their doors again. So it is no surprise that Naples now offers itself as a destination of choice for experimentation. Naples has this peculiar quality. Here you can be an alchemist of the lowest kind, looking to turn stone into gold, or you can be like the serious alchemists who dealt with the soul. Naples is a unique kind of laboratory for this.' (Fortunato Cerlino)

I am glad Francesco started his family in Naples, as, along with my own family, it is an incentive for me to go back more often. I cannot say whether this means I am reconciled with the city, but it is something. Our film about the ultras was released in March 2020, the first week of the Covid lockdown and the week Francesco's first child was born. A year and a half after our writing adventures the spectre of the equation 'Ultras = Camorra' would promptly enter through the back door in YouTube comment sections and social media clips about the film. Amen. Deep down this is what we had expected. What we had not expected was the onslaught of written threats from *real* Neapolitan football fans, who launched into us for a couple of weeks: against the film, against the platform that streamed it and, of course, against the director. There was the bleak paradox that, just as Francesco became a father, he would receive anonymous threats sprayed on the walls of the city. But we also had proof of something we had long suspected but now understood to be real: separating Naples in its flesh, blood and tuff from the *narrated* Naples there was now only a fine membrane, one that has never been so penetrable. In Naples cinema communicates with reality, and reality, when prompted, reacts, sometimes ferociously. How much of this is instinctive, embedded in the theatrical DNA of the city and its past and how much is the fruit of the polymorphic, chaotic Napolisphere of the present day? How much of this will remain for the benefit of the novels, films and drama series that have yet to be written and filmed?

'We were here when there were no resources. We resisted joining the diaspora towards regions that gave financial help when ours did not. We are still here, and the stories we tell are always at the centre of our struggle. The river of money that floods the city does not upset us much because, even if one day it dries up, we will still be here.' (Edoardo De Angelis)

Author's note
Gaetano Di Vaio died in a scooter accident on 22 May 2024. His death is a huge loss for the cinema community in Naples and throughout Italy.

TRISTAR
tel. 081 - 599 02 65
ECCO IL TUO QUOTIDIANO
LA TV DELLA CAMPANIA
ottochannel.tv
ROMA
QUOTIDIANO D'INFORMAZIONE FONDATO NEL 1862
SAN GENNARO, SALVA NAPOLI
L'ANALISI
Un monito condiviso che viene da lontano
LA RIFLESSIONE
La rovente omelia contro crisi e degrado
Il cardinale Sepe: «Il male che fanno i camorristi uccide la possibilità del futuro»
primo piano alle pagine 2, 3, 4 e 5
ABBONATI AL ROMA ONLINE
SU WWW.ILROMA.NET
UN NUOVO SITO PIÙ BELLO E PIÙ RICCO
CON UN SOLO ABBONAMENTO ACCEDI ALL'AREA PREMIUM DEL SITO INTERNET
CON GLI ULTIMI AGGIORNAMENTI, LEGGI L'EDIZIONE QUOTIDIANA DEL "ROMA" CAMPANIA,
DEL "ROMA" BASILICATA E DEL "GOLFO", ACCEDI ALL'ARCHIVIO STORICO DEL "ROMA"

A View of the City Through Its Newspapers

In the past fifteen years Naples has witnessed the birth of *Fanpage* and *NapoliMonitor*, two often diverging entities that nevertheless share the desire for journalistic experimentation and the ambition to achieve national relevance. It is all in the rich tradition of Neapolitan publishing, which comprises both long-running newspapers of its own and the local desks of national newspapers.

RAFFAELLA R. FERRÉ
Translated by Claudio Cambon

A hoarding advertising the Neapolitan newspaper *Roma* in the Centro Direzionale.

You don't need to catch a glimpse of it from the train window on the approach to the central station. You don't need to see its streets, squares and monuments for yourself. You can even spare yourself the traffic clogging its roads. You can leave the sea where it is, an immobile blue strip on a postcard shimmering with sun and light, which nevertheless almost always speaks of the dark shadow of some misfortune on the reverse side of the card. You can read about it, but let's be clear: there's no need to remember or to be able to point out on a map the neighbourhood where these troubles take place. Actually, it's better to keep well away from all that. It's a matter of perspective. Just like an alleyway that offers you a glimpse of the gulf below and Vesuvius further off in the distance, a page from a newspaper allows you to get to grips with an essential trait of this city: Naples is news that travels everywhere and that everyone knows about – but never well enough.

Perhaps that is what the singer-songwriter Pino Daniele meant at the end of his song 'Napule è': with its 'thousand colours and fears', the city is known the world over, but the world doesn't know the truth. So let us begin by admitting that we don't really know the city, not completely, not even those of us who write about Naples and put the news together, and this lack of knowledge is a point of honour for us. Anyone who talks about, comments on or writes the news stories about the city believing that they don't need answers or that they already have them to hand is making a mistake, and the city will be sure to point that out to them, proving them wrong every time. For example, take a sinkhole that opens up on a morning like any other, without anything in particular to distinguish it from any other sinkhole. This happened in May 2021 in the Rione Sanità, in a very beautiful, lively part of the historic centre that is off the tourist trail – even more so during Covid. A hole in the ground opened up. Some fifty people were evacuated. Fortunately there were no casualties. There were articles, agency dispatches, photographs and videos, but what happened was not simply a fact, a misfortune, a problem or a news item. It was history,

---

RAFFAELLA R. FERRÉ is a Naples-based writer specialising in long-form pieces, essays on social phenomena and crime. She contributes to *Valigia Blu*, *The Vision* and *Il Mattino*, for which she writes the weekly column 'Di riffa o di Raffa', and her work has appeared in publications such as *Vice* and *Fanpage*. As well as being a journalist, she also writes fiction. In 2015 she taught a writing course at Poggioreale prison focusing on inmates' personal life stories. She holds a degree in communication studies and wrote an experimental thesis on the history of Naples in the 1980s.

> 'Reading *Cronache di Napoli* feels like reading a transcription of a police radio report on the day's crime news, especially when those activities involve the Camorra.'

and it was history repeating itself. In the first half of 2021 there were six such episodes in six different places, and some 160 sinkholes have been documented since 2011. Even before this, the (actual) collapse of a street marked the start of the (imaginary) narrative of a novel that I believe says everything that needs to be said about Naples, *Malacqua*, by the journalist Nicola Pugliese. It was first published by Einaudi in 1977 and again more recently by Neapolitan publisher Tullio Pironti. Two issues arise here: the first is about the care that the body public takes of Naples' subsoil, which has always been known to be brittle and prone to runoff, especially after rains that are as brief as they are intense; the second concerns the pile of news about it that has been around for decades but which does not seem to foster a greater awareness of the subject among residents, administrators or politicians.

In Naples the sudden event thus becomes a constant, day in and day out, page after page. Details vary, there is a surfeit of evidence, questions remain, but there is always something more to ask. It is in this state of a slight nervous breakdown that the relationship between the city and its journalists is based. This ongoing, reciprocal relationship surprises me each and every time. It begins when a journalist goes out – or should go out – into the streets, and the streets open up, keep opening up, literally and figuratively, unearthing voices, events and stories with which to fill a newspaper.

There are many newspapers in Naples, and there used to be more. When I arrived in Naples in the early 2000s, almost everyone I knew worked for one small daily paper that no longer exists and which trained so many young people who dreamed of becoming journalists. The history of *La Verità-Napolipiù* is known by a few in the general public but remembered by those who worked there, often with a brief flush of pride, for being the first paper to offer a free phone line to its readers to report news items as they happened, to talk about the musical phenomenon of *neomelodica*, to follow the activities of the grassroots protest and advocacy group the Disoccupati Organizzati (Organised Unemployed) and to provide real-time news about crimes as they unfolded rather than relying on news-agency updates received in the comfort of their offices without any need to actually visit a crime scene. These were street journalists – *Cronisti di strada*, as they were called in the 2007 docuseries by director Gianfranco Pannone – who sought to investigate the city through their own eyes. Two such were Arnaldo Capezzuto of *Napolipiù* – who was repeatedly threatened by the Camorra for his work on the case of Annalisa Durante, the fourteen-year-old killed during a shootout between two rival clans in Forcella – and Giancarlo Palombi, who investigated drug trafficking for *Cronache di Napoli*, a local paper with offices in Marcianise in the nearby province of Caserta. Reading this paper feels like reading a transcription of a police radio report on the day's crime news, especially when those activities involve the Camorra. At the newsstand your eyes always fall on the front page, which is mostly filled with mugshots of people who have been convicted, arrested or killed and who are, in any case, affiliated. There, among the local leaflets and magazines of varying degrees of glossiness, you find the Naples editions of nationally distributed papers such as *la Repubblica* and *Corriere della Sera*.

*

Repubblica Napoli turned twenty in April 2020, during the first countrywide lockdown. Ottavio Ragone, editor-in-chief, wrote on the occasion of the anniversary that the paper 'pursues a certain idea of Naples as being neither provincial nor a snobby salon of courtiers at the service of whichever petty nobleman of the moment but rather as a European city that is open and alive, which has the same cultural energy as London, Paris or Berlin. Investigations, the struggle to report, a passion for telling stories and for writing well. Good movies, theatre, art, the creative spirit of our Naples.' The *Corriere del Mezzogiorno* is just a little older. It turned twenty in 2017, which it celebrated with an event held at the National Archaeological Museum: 'Liberty, credibility, and curiosity are in our DNA,' wrote editor Enzo d'Errico. 'Today, as when this newspaper was founded, what matters is providing facts with an independent voice, finding the right balance between the excellent work done in the past and the need to offer a new perspective.' The traditional core of Neapolitan journalism instead lies in other names and other pages, those of *Roma* and *Il Mattino*, who have to slug it out with these competitors and the new web-based outlets that are making headway in talking not just about Naples from Naples but also about Italy and the wider world.

'I have never wanted nor known how to be anything other than a faithful, humble chronicler of my own memory,' wrote Matilde Serao, the founder, together with her husband Edoardo Scarfoglio, of *Il Mattino* in March 1892. *Roma* was born thirty years before that, in August 1862. The histories of these two daily papers wound their way for many years along the city's streets and stories, experiencing the 20th century

NAPLES' NEWSPAPERS AND WHERE TO FIND THEM

Roma ③ ◆2
- T   Regional newspaper
- F   Pietro Sterbini and Diodato Lioy
- Y   1862; closed in 1981, revived in 1990–3 and again in 1996
- P   Nuovo Giornale Roma, Soc. Coop. (a cooperative belonging to the newspaper's employees)
- E   Pasquale Clemente
- C   5,100 copies (2020, SOURCE: AGCOM)

Il Mattino ② ◆5
- T   National newspaper
- F   Edoardo Scarfoglio and Matilde Serao
- Y   1892
- P   Caltagirone Editore
- E   Roberto Napoletano
- C   36,244 copies (2020, SOURCE: AGCOM)
- R   9.6 million (Q1 2021, SOURCE: COMSCORE)

Fanpage 2
- T   Online national media outlet
- F   Gianluca Cozzolino
- Y   2011
- P   Ciaopeople S.r.l.
- E   Francesco Cancellato
- R   31.6 million (Q1 2021, SOURCE: COMSCORE)

la Repubblica Napoli 1 1
- T   Local edition of a national paper
- Y   1990
- P   Gedi Gruppo Editoriale
- E   Ottavio Ragone
- C   c.15,000 copies (2021, SOURCE: AUDIPRESS)

NapoliMonitor 3
- T   Online local media outlet
- F   Luca Rossomando
- Y   2006
- P   Monitor Edizioni
- E   Riccardo Orioles

Napolipiù (formerly *La Verità*) 5
- T   Regional newspaper
- F   Giorgio Gradogna
- Y   1997, as *La Verità*; it changed its name to *Napolipiù* in 2002 and shut down in 2008

Corriere del Mezzogiorno 4 4
- T   Local edition of a national paper
- Y   1997
- P   RCS MediaGroup
- E   Enzo d'Errico
- C   10,538 copies (2020, SOURCE: AGCOM)

KEY:
● = FORMER LOCATION
◆ = CURRENT LOCATION
T = TYPE
F = FOUNDER
Y = YEAR FOUNDED
P = PUBLISHER
E = EDITOR
R = INDIVIDUAL MONTHLY READERS
C = CIRCULATION

A View of the City Through Its Newspapers

The former editor-in-chief of *Il Mattino*, Federico Monga, in his office during preparation of the newspaper's front page. The paper has recently moved its headquarters, leaving its historic home in Via Chiatamone, where it had been since 1892.

often in the same way – as, for example, in October 1943, when the disembarking Allies suspended both papers for cooperating with the fascist regime – but always achieving high levels of distribution and sales. *Roma*'s golden age was in the 1950s and 1960s under the ownership of the shipowner and mayor of Naples Achille Lauro, who moved it to the right politically. But in 1981 the oldest newspaper in southern Italy shut down, just as *Il Mattino* was setting new circulation records. The reporting on 1980s Naples in the pages of this daily newspaper was perhaps best summed up by the writer Erri De Luca when he described the city as 'a mix of the excellent and the atrocious'. There was the earthquake in Irpinia, which prompted the paper's famous headline demanding aid for the affected population, a gigantic '*Fate presto*' ('Hurry Up') splashed across the front page, which Andy Warhol then used to make a series of iconic silkscreen prints. There were musicians such as Pino Daniele and Edoardo Bennato, actor-directors including Massimo Troisi and Luciano De Crescenzo, philosophers for a new world who were nevertheless very much rooted in being Neapolitan. There was the left-wing mayor Maurizio Valenzi, a communist, and the disappearance of workers and factories with the lengthy process of shutting down the Italsider steelworks in Bagnoli in the suburbs west of the city. There were the so-called 'viceroys' of the city, from Gava to Pomicino – Christian Democrat politicians from Naples who were major figures at a national level – and there was heroin and the trauma of thirty thousand addicts, an 'army of pain', as per the headline of a June 1983 article. There was Raffaele Cutolo's 'New Organised Camorra', the restructuring of this organised-crime group that gave it a quasi-corporate structure and a set of regulations. And then there were the national football championships won by Maradona's Napoli. *Il Mattino* wrote about all this, and during that time, under the stewardship of editor Roberto Ciuni, it reorganised itself into departments whose various correspondents worked in the outskirts of the city and the further reaches of the province.

Torre Annunziata, a city some twenty kilometres to the south of Naples, was covered by a young man in love with his job who believed in his usefulness and whom the Camorra gunned down in September 1985, just a few days after his twenty-sixth birthday. His name was Giancarlo Siani. As I write this, I feel I am running the risk of shifting the focus of my words from his profile – his hair curling over his glasses, his odd green car, a Citroën Méhari, which was exhibited at the PAN (Palace of Fine Arts of Naples) – to his professional status. Today we would describe him as a precarious worker; at the time, though, the word was *abusivo*, unauthorised, which meant a journalist who, although working in an editorial capacity with all the responsibilities that that entailed, was neither publicly nor contractually recognised nor remunerated as such. Such journalists write and work, hoping for better prospects. *L'abusivo* is also the title of a wonderful 2001 novel by Antonio Franchini that interweaves three narrative threads pulled apart in real life and brought back together on paper. The stories we tell ourselves are often knots we tie to keep the hole in the knitted jersey of our youth from unravelling

GIANCARLO SIANI

Giancarlo Siani was born in Naples in 1959 to a middle-class family in Vomero. He studied sociology at the University of Naples Federico II and began working for Neapolitan newspapers, writing mainly about marginalisation and economic and social problems and how they created the circumstances that gave organised crime a ready supply of labour. He was also politically active in the Radical Party, and, together with other young journalists, he founded the Democratic Movement for the Right to Information. He wrote for the *Osservatorio sulla Camorra* and then became the Torre Annunziata correspondent at *Il Mattino*. When he wrote about the Camorra he didn't limit himself to reporting facts and crimes; he also tried to understand the inner workings of organised crime in the context of the reconstruction after the 1980 Irpinia earthquake. The article that signed his death warrant was published on 10 June 1985. In it he revealed the back story of the arrest of Valentino Gionta, the Torre Annunziata mafia boss who had formed an alliance with Totò Riina's Cosa Nostra and Raffaele Cutolo's New Organised Camorra. This was the result of a tip-off to the *carabinieri* by members of the Nuvoletta clan, who were also allied with Cutolo but who were bothered by the Gionta clan's expansion. Three months after this disclosure, which portrayed the Nuvoletta clan as snitches collaborating with the police, Siani was killed in front of his home, just a few steps away from Piazza Leonardo in the Arenella district. In the late 1990s the murder trial concluded with life sentences for those who ordered and carried out the crime, but, in a book published in 2014, journalist Roberto Paolo cast doubts on the outcome, leading to investigations being reopened.

further. Franchini wrote: 'Giancarlo is a *guaglione* [a young guy from Naples],' quoting a colleague who had said: 'A benevolent characterisation meaning someone who embodies a boy's lack of responsibility but also his lack of calculation and his light-heartedness ... I had thought that there was no more desirable condition than to be a *guaglione* for ever.' Giancarlo Siani would remain just that, being recognised posthumously as a professional journalist only on the thirty-fifth anniversary of his death, smiling at several generations in old Polaroids, when he was portrayed by the actor Libero De Rienzo in Marco Risi's 2009 film *Fort Apache Naples* and by Yari Gugliucci in Maurizio Fiume's *I Will Follow You* (2003). His story is well known to Italians right across the country, and his name is on a radio station, street signs, press rooms, schools, even the new offices of *Il Mattino*. But when I think of him I always end up imagining him striding briskly along a street I have also walked down hundreds of times, Via Chiatamone, which was, until just a few years ago, the heart of Neapolitan journalism.

*

It lies between Chiaia – a well-to-do neighbourhood of beautiful buildings, luxury shops and cafés (known as *baretti*) – and Santa Lucia, the historic neighbourhood that faces the timeless Isolotto di Megaride, the islet on which the Castel dell'Ovo stands. Via Chiatamone – formerly a broad, scenic street, now a narrow lane of honking cars emerging from a half-kilometre-long tunnel – was once home to the editorial offices of both *Roma* and *Il Mattino*, which were located just a few street numbers apart from one another. Just a kilometre to the west are the Naples offices of *la Repubblica*, and two kilometres to the east are those of the *Corriere del Mezzogiorno*. The relationship between the city and its newspapers seemed to converge and settle in an area facing the sea, leaving so much of the city at the edge of the page – or, perhaps, just out of the editors' lines of sight. For many people, young journalists in particular, these offices remained a dream that lay just beyond reach and were thus constantly subject to waiting, watching and trying again. Anyone who wanted and attempted to write full time for a daily paper in the 2000s did so within an area of two square kilometres. But, as all these newspapers added web addresses to their physical addresses, in some cases offering dedicated online content, Via Chiatamone began to empty out. *Il Mattino* and *Roma* moved, the former to one of the towers in the new Centro Direzionale business district designed by Kenzo Tange – which for some remains unfinished and for others is transcendent – and the latter, after a courageous strike by the employees who formed a cooperative to save the paper, to Via Generale Orsini in the same building in which *Fanpage* has its head offices.

And what is *Fanpage*? Many have asked this question, at first somewhat patronisingly and then with increasing apprehension but always with great curiosity. Just when the economic crisis began to shake print media to its core, the web and social media rose to the challenge in the form of a completely online newspaper – *Fanpage* was registered in 2011 – that was able to find users and subscribers willing to take part in a two-way conversation. In a city known for its entrenched unemployment rates and its emigration to points

Members of the *Fanpage* editorial board.

BLOODY MONEY

It's a mark of good journalism when a prosecutor's office decides to include all the material from a news investigation in its own investigative case file. This is what happened to *Fanpage*, whose video reportage 'Bloody money' was used by the Naples Prosecutor's Office to shed light on the waste-disposal business in Campania. In 2021 the official investigations led to preliminary measures being taken against seventeen individuals accused of bribery, money laundering, environmental pollution and the fraudulent transfer of funds. 'Bloody money' was initiated by Nunzio Perrella, a former Camorra boss who had infiltrated the waste-disposal business. Using more than six hundred hours of footage shot over six months with a hidden camera, *Fanpage* managed to reveal the links between the worlds of organised crime, politics, business and waste management. The seven episodes – which were published in early 2018 on YouMedia, the paper's video platform – range from the regions of Campania to the Veneto, clearly documenting conversations and the exchanges of bribes at a narrative pace akin to that of a TV series, the details of which were often shocking. There was no shortage of controversy over Perrella being seen as an agent provocateur, such that the then editor of *Fanpage*, Francesco Piccinini, and the journalist Sacha Biazzo, author of 'Bloody money', were investigated for incitement to bribery, a case that was later dismissed. Another sign that this was top-flight journalism came from the Camorra itself. During one intercepted call, investigators listened to the boss of a clan wish death on *Fanpage*'s journalists for having caused a big deal of his to collapse.

A View of the City Through Its Newspapers

> '*Fanpage* is the most read newspaper in Italy, with 150 million social interactions in 2020 – the year in which it also exceeded one billion video views.'

north in Italy and Europe, *Fanpage* had almost one hundred employees and freelances working at its three offices in 2021, thereby signalling a trend in the opposite direction; the city was no longer a place to leave behind to look for work and opportunities elsewhere. People arrive in the city, pitching up in an area that the publisher Gianluca Cozzolino calls 'Santa Lucia Valley' in reference to the part of northern California that serves as a worldwide centre of digital innovation and social media. But this is Naples, facing the sea. In this ancient place with its legendary panorama, somewhere that has symbolised the city in hundreds of paintings, which was filmed by the Lumière brothers themselves and described in classic songs such as 'Santa Maria Luntana' by E.A. Mario (about how ships left from here for the Americas), the view from *Fanpage*'s balconies is a fantastic photo-op for anyone visiting the editorial offices, be they politicians, writers or singers. Reliably the most read newspaper in Italy and one of its primary media outlets, with 150 million social interactions in 2020 – the year in which it also exceeded one billion video views – *Fanpage* is a veritable broadcast network whose editor for eight years was Francesco Piccinini, born in Naples in 1981, and who already had an international career behind him. His role was crucial in investigations, from 'Cella zero' ('Cell Zero'), about the systemic violence inside Poggioreale prison, to 'Bloody money', an investigation into the entanglement of businesses and politicians in the world of waste management. In the spring of 2021 Piccinini left his position, although he remains within the editorial group at the helm of a new project. With the support of co-editor Adriano Biondi, who has worked at *Fanpage* since it was founded, Francesco Cancellato is now editor-in-chief. He arrived in 2019, 'in awe of its legendary aura as the Italian BuzzFeed'.

'I live thirty kilometres outside Milan, probably the furthest point from any coast in Italy,' he tells me. 'I live in a state of anti-sea, and that's my home. But I fell in love with Naples. It is utterly different from what I had experienced in Lombardy and the Po Valley. *Fanpage* is the best answer to all the clichés about the south of the country: the inefficiency, the incompetence, a land that lets its young people leave. Of course, ours might just prove to be simply an exception, but knowing how to attract individuals, talent and skills to a place that usually lets them slip away has deconstructed the old publishing model based in Milan, Turin and Rome.' According to Cancellato, Naples is proof that you can foster a new, positive business culture and that the area's material conditions, the value of its human capital and the importance of its society yield more opportunities than obstacles. He explains that, in picking an editor who was not from Naples, the publisher made a courageous choice. 'It would have been easy to keep thinking of *Fanpage* as the Neapolitan newspaper out to win all of Italy over, but instead we are evolving and growing. We are growing our Rome and Milan offices and, who knows, we might even open others. Naples will remain central and fundamental to our identity, but it will no longer be by itself.

'I did not write an editorial guide for my team because I believe that intentions should be measured on the basis of the facts,' continues Cancellato, 'and I don't think we need a manifesto set in stone. The aim of *Fanpage* is to innovate and change while continuing to focus on investigative journalism. We are lucky to have an independent publisher, which is somewhat unusual in Italy, but this freedom is a responsibility, something that you can't let lie or just keep in your pocket; if you don't use it, you're wasting it.' And to those who call them the 'kids' in journalism, the new editor, just forty years old, doesn't take that as much of a put-down. 'Actually, it's more of a put-down for those who use the expression, because they aren't young, even if we are compared to them. If we consider how old it is, *Fanpage* is a child that has grown up to become an influential voice in a short time, both in terms of its numbers and as a forum for innovation. We have included video, social media and search engine optimisation in our journalism across Italy, which has influenced the debate considerably, so, in a way, we are the "kids" who had the guts to do what everyone else, the grownups in journalism, weren't able to do. On the other hand, I understand that some people might see what we do as slightly less serious; we are a publication with a somewhat unusual name and lacking in pretention. But I would never want *Fanpage* to grow old the way others have grown old. We must remain innovative, a training ground for young journalists who had doors closed in their faces elsewhere but who are often very good.'

*

Another site of journalistic experimentation, in many ways the opposite of *Fanpage* but driven by the same relentless desire to exercise its freedom, is *NapoliMonitor*, a small corner in the landscape of the city's journalism. 'It was founded in 2006 as a printed monthly magazine, but over time it has taken on different forms,' Luca Rossomando, a member of the editorial team, wrote in an email to me. 'Currently it is an information website, a publishing house and a printed semi-annual magazine called *Lo stato delle città* ('The State of the Cities'). Naples is our starting point, but we have never thought of ourselves as just a local information outlet. The goal has always been to use the city as a prism through which to talk about major issues that concern every city in Italy and across the world. From our inaugural issue onwards, we have sought contributions to further this ambition, and we have had editorial offices in other cities across Italy for years now. None of us is formally trained as a journalist, even though some of us have been writing for newspapers for more than twenty years. We are educators, teachers, designers, artists, independent researchers and scholars, but, above all, we are political advocates in various settings and cities. These attributes influence our work.' The perspective adopted to disseminate facts does seem removed from reporting; this is about remembering and reasoning through a process of committed, educated reflection.

Above: Roberto Paolo, the deputy editor of *Roma*.
Opposite: A newspaper archive.

The long, staggered view from the Quartieri Spagnoli where its offices are located expresses a commitment. 'Of course, since we have been operating in a particular field for the last fifteen years, that of publishing and journalism, we have tried to define and establish a style that pays close attention to how we tell the story, to the images, the graphic design and especially to the lives of the people we write about – and provide opportunities for young people who approach our work to test themselves and grow through comparison. This is, in fact, contrary to the practices of the current information system, which we consider to be one of the main causes of oppression in our societies. In this regard, the local-media landscape is completely aligned with the national one, both in terms of sloppiness of form, trivialisation of content, conformity of messaging and the deterioration of working conditions and the exploitation of precarious labour.'

NapoliMonitor's approach seems to emphasise their marginal position, attempting to turn it into a strength and a carefully considered stance. 'Riccardo Orioles is our editor-in-chief. It is a merely formal role to observe media laws, because, as I said before, none of us is officially a journalist. But it's also a personal decision, because Riccardo, who was Giuseppe Fava's deputy at *I Siciliani* when Fava was killed, set some of us "on the right path" when he was editor-in-chief of *Avvenimenti* in Rome. One of the lessons he taught us was that if you don't like the newspapers that are out there, get together with your friends and make one that you do like. And that's why we're here.'

*

Here is Naples. Like a Caravaggio painting the city switches from darkest shadow to warmest light in a single movement – in this case a click of a mouse or the turn of a page. Perhaps, I tell myself, it would be enough to demarcate the border that runs between the two halves so that we can remember this for the future. That the city doesn't change for this reason. That the city goes ahead or breaks down regardless. That light and shadow both pass and that writing is a way to stop ourselves, others and this setting, just for a moment. I don't know whether Neapolitan newspapers generate a greater sense of awareness and memory among the city's denizens or whether they simply yield a prism of perspectives that are all very willing but often at odds with one another and which never manage to offer a comprehensive view of the present. I'm not even sure whether or not gathering and reporting the news from Chiaia, Santa Lucia, the Quartieri Spagnoli, the port or the business district changes how journalists approach their profession. What I do know as a reader of newspapers, as a woman who sometimes writes for newspapers, as a citizen, as someone who asks questions, is that day after day I go through the very big news that is this city: Naples exists.

Author's note
This essay was written in 2021. As of 2024 *Fanpage* remains the top all-digital Italian newspaper, and in May of that year the total community/fan base had reached thirty-seven million (46 per cent men, 54 per cent women, mostly in the age range of twenty-five to forty-four). The professional journalists working there, whether in-house or contributors, number more than a hundred, including the writer Roberto Saviano. *NapoliMonitor* has been joined by *MonitorItalia*, and *Lo stato delle città* is still being published on a semi-annual basis. Nicola Pugliese's novel *Malacqua* has been published in a new Italian edition by Bompiani. There have been more sinkholes in Naples. In early 2024 some appeared in Vomero – including in Via Morghen, Via Solimena and Via Pietro Castellino – and the issue of underground instability is now once again a matter of public debate in the city.

A View of the City Through Its Newspapers

Blue Voices

GIANNI MONTIERI
Translated by Claudio Cambon

Following Maradona's death in 2020, many fans left offerings in memory of their hero, as here in front of the Curva B section of the San Paolo Stadium, later renamed the Diego Armando Maradona Stadium.

The communal and visceral attachment to the city's football team brings Neapolitans together, but it also drives them apart, especially in an era when being a fan is increasingly an individual act lived in front of a television screen rather than collectively at a stadium. Between nostalgia and madness, however, the passion for Napoli remains special.

She sits on a folding chair close to the entrance of the Convent of Santa Chiara, a small table in front of her. On the table are two decks of cards, face down. I can't tell what kind they are, but I'm guessing they're tarot cards. She must be about seventy. Her name is Flora. She has short, resplendently grey hair. It's just a few minutes before 3 p.m. on a Sunday in spring. Napoli are about to play. The game is the reason I have come to see Flora. Via Santa Chiara also happens to be one of the places I like to go when I come back home to Naples. The streets, the surrounding squares, the three Roman roads running like stripes across the old city, the handful of old shops that are hanging in there, still eking out a living, the secondhand-book carts, the smell of coffee the way it's supposed to be, these and so many other little things, like the sound of footsteps that get lost amid the noise of the heart of the city, all say home to me. It's as if, between Via Benedetto Croce, Piazza San Domenico Maggiore, Piazza Miraglia and Via dei Tribunali I were to find a much beloved sofa or armchair in front of a building where a friend used to live. The lower part of the street is in shadow now, but the sun still strikes the upper floors of the apartment buildings facing Flora.

Also in shadow is the most recent version of the Gothic façade of this structure, reconstructed after the bombings in 1943. This extraordinarily beautiful and melancholy place forms part of Naples' history of religion, art and song. The few travellers to be seen are the first to have returned. After so many pandemic lockdowns some of them filled their pull-along cases with courage and came to town.

Flora sees me and says, 'I'm not reading cards today.' I respond that I know that, and I approach, telling her that I'm here for the match. She smiles at me. 'What's the matter? Don't you have a television?' Waving her hand she gestures to me to sit as she unfolds another chair to her right. 'I was told that when Napoli play you sit here or on other streets in the city centre listening to the voices that spill out of the windows, that you remain perfectly silent, and that when the match is over you pack everything up and leave. I wanted to know why.' She bursts out laughing. 'And who's been talking about me? Are you a journalist?' I shake my head. 'I'm a poet.' 'Even worse. I have nothing to say, but you can sit here next to me if you want to. The match starts in two minutes. I must tell you, though, don't make comments, don't cheer, don't talk, don't move.' I nod my

GIANNI MONTIERI is a poet who writes for *Doppiozero*, *minima&moralia* and *HuffPost*. In his work for *L'Ultimo Uomo*, *Rivista Undici* and *Il Napolista* he seeks to intersect literature with sports writing. He is also the artistic coordinator of the Festival dei Matti (the 'Mad People's Festival') in Venice.

Napoli fans on their way to a match.

head to say yes, and then, just like Flora, I look up at the buildings in front of us.

We are in front of number ten. There is scaffolding, but through the open windows you can clearly hear the voices of the pay TV commentators. Napoli vs. Cagliari is about to start. Flora remains motionless for several minutes, and then her ears seem to prick up, as if she were a dog sniffing the air. But she's searching for sounds, not smells. I can't hear much. I recognise the commentators' voices and make out a few of their words emerging from the homes. I can't hear the sound of the fans at the stadium, which would usually guide me. Every now and then someone passes by and looks at us. A little boy says to his friend, 'Flora's back.' Flora raises her right hand as if to try to stop something. 'He's offside.' From that moment on she doesn't stop, taking me with her to an imaginary stadium where she helps me experience, just with ears and imagination, one of the most incredible games I can ever remember. Flora moves her hands constantly. 'Penalty,' she says. 'Corner.' 'It's too quiet. Someone's down, and the referee is showing a yellow card.' 'Pass the ball,' she says in the faintest voice. I get distracted watching the street. Flora looks at me contemptuously and places her hands on the table. 'Goal. We've scored.' At one point she tells me that a couple of seventy-year-olds live on the second floor of the building ahead of us, two retired professors. 'They watch the match in two separate rooms, and it's really like there are *two* games.' No one listening in for that hour and a half would ever think that they were watching the same match and supporting the same team.

Flora says that hearing the game from other people's homes is a kind of musical score of the city. You don't just

Blue Voices

169

> 'I get up to leave and say goodbye, but then I turn and ask, "How did you feel when Maradona died?" She moves her hands as if to dismiss me. "That is a private matter."'

understand the game and what's happening on the pitch, you learn about people's reactions. You understand their tensions, their states of mind. It takes her less than ten minutes to work out whether an apartment has changed hands, whether someone has gone on holiday or died. She reminds me of a story by Salvatore Di Giacomo set in the late 19th century in which a German teacher named Otto Richter sits under certain windows in Chiaia from which Beethoven's music emerges. I ask her when this all began. 'Thirty years ago a doctor told me that going to the stadium was bad for my heart, and I decided that watching the matches at home would be unbearable. I began going out right before kick-off, and I came up with these fake tarot cards just so I could listen to Napoli play out of people's windows.' She told me that the pandemic changed everything, even her listening, so she had to find a different way of understanding sounds, working remotely. Without the chorus of spectators at the stadium, every rant coming from the apartments is amplified, and you can get confused between the sound of a chair falling to the floor as someone jumps up suddenly to celebrate a goal and when it happens for something not related to football. The match is over, she tells me. 'One all. You can double-check. It was a draw. The coach lost the match. He got scared.' I'm astonished, but I know that I won't need to look at my phone for confirmation. I ask her if supporting the same team keeps people together. She stands up, and I notice that she is taller than I had imagined. 'You are indeed a poet, naive. There aren't two people in all of Naples who will answer you the same way. No one supports Napoli the same way as anyone else, just as happiness and disappointment vary from one person to the next, from this street to Mezzocannone.' I get up to leave and say goodbye, but then I turn and ask, 'How did you feel when Maradona died?' She moves her hands as if to dismiss me. 'That is a private matter. Have a good evening.'

This morning I met up with Francesco, one of my best friends, he, too, an ardent Napoli fan. We have often remarked to one another that because we were born before the 1980 earthquake we are bound by all the fault lines and the rifts, by belonging to this ground that sits on tuff and on empty space, by that inner trembling that our bodies experienced during those awful days, so much so that we have held on to it somewhere inside ourselves. We tell each other that we are children of that quaking and of our passions. And one of them, which so many people share, is for football and for Napoli.

Francesco and I have a tradition. Every time I come back we take a long walk that starts in Vomero and ends in the historic centre. We'll talk about anything and everything as I look around

Opposite top: A donkey, a symbol of Naples, dressed for the occasion.
Opposite bottom: Watching a match glued to the television.

NAPOLI
FEDELTA NAPOLETANA
MARADONA 10
MARADONA
EL PIBE DE ORO
NON DIMENTICA

like a child seeing the fairground rides for the first time after the end of winter. When you walk down into the city it opens up and meets you. It's almost as if the sea rises up to grab you. The conversation often turns to Napoli and to how the season is going. We dislike the same players, the ones who only know how to do one thing and who can't play without looking at their feet. Those who never look up are fated only ever to see a few square metres of the field. We start at Via Luca Giordano and begin our descent across Piazza degli Artisti and Via Tino da Camino, which brings us to Piazza Medaglie d'Oro. Francesco has ties to two parts of the city: he was born in Via dei Tribunali and lives in Vomero. I want to find out from him whether the ways in which people support the team varies according to which neighbourhood they live in. He raises his head to admire the buildings in the square and smiles, but he doesn't answer right away. I follow his gaze. Hanging over a balcony is a faded Napoli flag flapping in the breeze. We keep walking. He tells me distractedly that he has begun to listen to his old New Order records again. It takes time, and I grant him this. I tell him that it's been a while since I heard Pino Daniele's song 'Libertà', a piece of which we are both very fond. 'The streets were empty, and we were stuck at home. It's a song that can make you afraid and then make you cry – as always – although for other reasons.' I put my hand on his shoulder, as if in agreement. We continue along Via Menzinger and enter Piazza dell'Immacolata. Maradona's face is painted on a wall – actually, no, it's a small poster. 'Brother, they've proliferated,' and we laugh. We go along Salita Arenella. Francesco stops and tells me that there surely are many ways of supporting your

ULTRAS

The immense passion for Napoli has formed the subject of two of the most interesting films about hardcore Italian football fans, the ultras. The first is the seminal work by the director Vincenzo Marra, *Estranei alla massa* (2001, 'Strangers to the Masses'), which told the story of the lives of seven members of the legendary 'football firm' Fedayn (founded in 1979), known to be the hardest of them all, committed fans who sit in the Curva B section of the stadium. The portrait that emerged was far, far from the image of the violent ultra. On the contrary, the salesperson, the lighting technician, the video game repairman, the photographer and his assistant, the timberyard employee and the greengrocer were average people who shared a love for their team, and the documentary became a vehicle to show a cross section of city life. Francesco Lettieri – known for his legendary music videos for the rapper Liberato and himself a fan who sits in the Curva on match days – cites it as one of the inspirations for his Netflix debut *Ultras* (2020; discussed further in 'Napolisphere' on page 137), a story set among an imaginary firm called Apache that comprises three generations of fans: the core of middle-aged guys, keepers of the flame; the younger generation elbowing its way in; and the young children who are trying to get noticed. Lettieri's perspective is not judgemental either, but this did not shield him from attack from the world of the ultras, who expressed their hostility in graffiti that appeared on the walls of the city. Criticism also came from the mother of Ciro Esposito, the Napoli fan ambushed and killed in 2014 by AS Roma fans, who saw direct references in the film to her son's story, something Lettieri denies.

team, but that, like me, he doesn't think the variations are down to differences in ways of rejoicing, criticising or celebrating, even though these do exist. In such cases the differences aren't between one part of town and another but between one person and the next. He says something that Flora would later confirm for me. I tell him that in my opinion, perhaps up until 2002–3, support was a collective act. People were fans together, they went to the stadium together and at Fuorigrotta people would embrace anyone, even total strangers. It didn't matter whether they were from Vasto or Posillipo, because you didn't know. We supported together, pure and simple. People would discuss matches over the following days, as they do now, but the shared sense of belonging was stronger. Whether you were from Soccavo, Porta Capuana or Piazza Vittoria, it mattered less. You were my brother and friend because you were a Napoli fan. It was that simple. 'I agree,' Francesco says. We turn left on to Via Salvator Rosa. He remembers an anecdote that our mutual friend Bernardo had related some time ago. The episode dates back to 14 May 2016, during the Napoli–Frosinone match.

In the twenty-sixth minute of the second half Higuaín scored for the thirty-sixth time that season, setting a new record for goals scored in Serie A. Bernardo explained that all of Via Salvator Rosa erupted as if Napoli had won the championship again, adding, 'That was the moment when football once again became about the pure skill of the athlete and Neapolitans stopped thinking about statistics and rankings. Everyone gave in to the emotion of the moment and celebrated it as if it were a championship title.'

We smile. Bernardo is younger than us, and fortunately he still has a romantic vein running through him as well as a healthy streak of melancholy. Already before the pandemic, being a fan had become an individual affair. Younger generations go less often to the stadium, and why should they if they think watching football on television is better? You can replay a goal hundreds of times and re-enact it in a matter of minutes on your PlayStation. Football is no longer a means of aggregation, nor is the stadium a place where you learn to grow, to measure yourself against what is foreign to you, different from you. As I

Fans celebrate in Forcella and Piazza Municipio.

complete this thought we have to make a decision: either head towards Salita Tarsia or take a detour along Corso Vittorio Emanuele and make our descent further along. Francesco heads towards Tarsia. He decides. At the spot where we find ourselves, on the May night of the first championship a thousand lifetimes ago, a kid lay down on the ground and began to yell in Neapolitan dialect, '*Mo' pozze pure murì*,' 'Now I can die.' It was really hard to get him up off the floor. Before we get to Largo Tarsia we turn again to get a coffee at La Pignasecca. There's no way of explaining just how fiercely the heart of Napoli beats in these streets. An old man smokes a cigarette as he leans against the wall. I ask him if he's from the area, and he answers with a nod of the head to say, 'I live *here*.' And perhaps I was imagining it, but he didn't point to the door, instead to a photograph of Antonio Juliano, the legendary Napoli captain, stuck to the wall next to the doorbell.

We have our coffee, and then I ask Francesco if he feels like cutting across the Quartieri Spagnoli to walk along a short stretch of Via Emanuele de Deo, home to one of the best known (and most beautiful) murals dedicated to Diego Armando Maradona. The Quartieri Spagnoli is a city within the city, and it seems like a stadium among all the houses. Every metre of every wall, doorway, window, shop door bears – or flaunts – something about being a Napoli fan. Blue prevails here. The mural on Via Emanuele de Deo dates to

1990, the year that Napoli won its second championship. It's by Mario Filardi, a kid from the Quartieri Spagnoli who was in love with Napoli and *El pibe de oro*, the 'Golden Boy'. Filardi died in 2010. The mural, which had begun to fade over time, was restored in 2016 by Salvatore Jovine, a Neapolitan craftsman, and retouched in 2017 by the Argentinian artist Francisco Bosoletti. I always find being here moving because Filardi made it seem as if Maradona is running out of the building, as if this were his home, thus reiterating the feeling that he was (and is) family to anyone from Naples. He belongs to Naples the way Vesuvius does, like the emptiness on which everything sits and orients itself, like the darkness that surrounds you in the underground city. We came here the day Maradona died, we were in front of the stadium, everywhere, on every street, people experiencing a moment of collective emotion. I remind Francesco that in the hours after his death we wrote (and received) messages and phone calls as if they were condolences. 'That's how it was,' he says. 'We were his friends, his relatives, but we were also the little kids who had the privilege of seeing him play week in and week out in our formative years.' It took Filardi two nights and three days to complete the mural. He was twenty-three years old at the time. I wish I'd met him. Perhaps on some occasion on the stadium steps we'd hugged one another as strangers.

Once at the Teatro Mercadante, as we were watching a show starring Lina Sastri, we felt the ground begin to shake, as if an earthquake were beginning to strike. In a few seconds it became clear to everyone, even those who were on stage, that Napoli had scored. I think it

Blue Voices

175

was Cavani or Lavezzi who scored the goal, but who it was isn't important. What mattered was the fact that no event in this city could distance itself from the outcome of the match. In the hour and a half in which the teams face one another, a kind of invisible fabric awakens and conditions what happens outside the stadium. I remember that even Lina Sastri stopped on stage for a second, and then, reassured, resumed her set.

    I walk in front of the theatre and cross Piazza del Municipio. I am on my way to meet Vittorio, one of the founders of the Blue Lions, a historic Napoli ultras group who sit in the Curva A section of the stadium. I have known him for several years. Our shared passion led to our meeting. He is one of the biggest experts on the history of Napoli fandom, and in some ways he's better than an almanac. He is waiting for me in front of the Royal Palace. We scheduled this meeting here because, in faraway 1982, right on the steps of Piazza del Plebiscito, a series of encounters took place, veritable open-air meetings that changed the way the city supported football. We haven't seen each other for almost two years. Even before asking each other how we're doing we begin by commenting on the outcome of the Napoli–Cagliari match that had taken place a few days earlier and dropped us down to fifth place. Our chances of qualifying for the Europe-wide Champions League were once again looking bleak. I ask him if he, like me, was experiencing this season as a

A mural by Mario Filardi in the Quartieri Spagnoli depicting Maradona. In the distance Vesuvius can be seen.

grey area in which, between the team's highs and its lows, nothing really seems to be going on. Vittorio shakes his head and smiles. 'What you say is true. I also believe that to some degree, but unfortunately reality hits me when I think of our midfield and its deficiencies, and that's when I have to admit that things are happening anyway, even during this unusual season.' I burst out laughing. Vittorio has the same taste in football players as me. We head towards the porticoes of this majestic square, its charm intact. I stop for a second. A few years ago, right in the middle of this square, I took a picture of my dad's shadow next to mine. It was our last picture together. My father died just a few months before Maradona. A few days before he passed he told me over the phone, 'I never thought I would see Napoli beat Juventus again before I die.'

Vittorio asks me if everything is all right. I lie and say yes. His story begins in 1981 with the rise of new groups of organised support, including, among others, the Boys Fighters and the Hells' Angels, which Vittorio and some of his friends founded. The Quartieri Spagnoli gave birth to the Magic Warriors. Several youngsters from Pallonetto di Santa Lucia, known as the Gioventù Azzurra (Blue Youth), moved from Curva B in the stadium to Curva A. That was the first step towards a real schism between Napoli fans. Vittorio explains that everything arose after a long period of frustration at being a fan as people saw it at the time. 'But changing meant being united,' my friend adds. So meetings happened on these steps between groups from Santa Lucia and the Quartieri Spagnoli. The piazza sits exactly between them, a kind of easy border along which a transition could be envisioned. Furthermore, Barone, one of the

'YOU DON'T KNOW WHAT YOU MISSED'

On 4 May 2023, with five matches to go until the end of the season, by drawing against Udinese, Napoli, now uncatchable at the top of Serie A, won their third league title, the Scudetto, crowning an incredible campaign marked by graceful play and a kind of joy that seemed to have taken hold of players and the fans alike. The victory came after a thirty-three-year wait, and it belonged to the whole city and to all Neapolitans – even to those who had passed away and couldn't witness it as well as to those who hadn't yet been born at the time of the previous championship wins in 1987 and 1990. For that younger generation, those victories had been handed down like family lore, popular legend. It was thanks to a handful of exceptional players that the Scudetto made its way back to Naples: the Nigerian striker Osimhen, the Georgian forward Kvaratskhelia – two superstars who captivated everyone – along with the likes of the captain Di Lorenzo, the Korean defender Kim and midfielders Anguissa, Lobotka and Zieliński. The city went mad with anticipation, colouring itself blue from January, February, scorning superstition; such was the team's dominance in the league that there really was nothing to be superstitious about. Walking through the city's streets in the months leading up to the end of the season was like being part of some ongoing celebration, a continuous collective ritual in which people from all over the world took part, coming to the city to enjoy some of those moments. Because in Naples, when there's a celebration, it's bigger than anywhere else – and football is more than a religion: Maradona is God; the players are his saints. (GM)

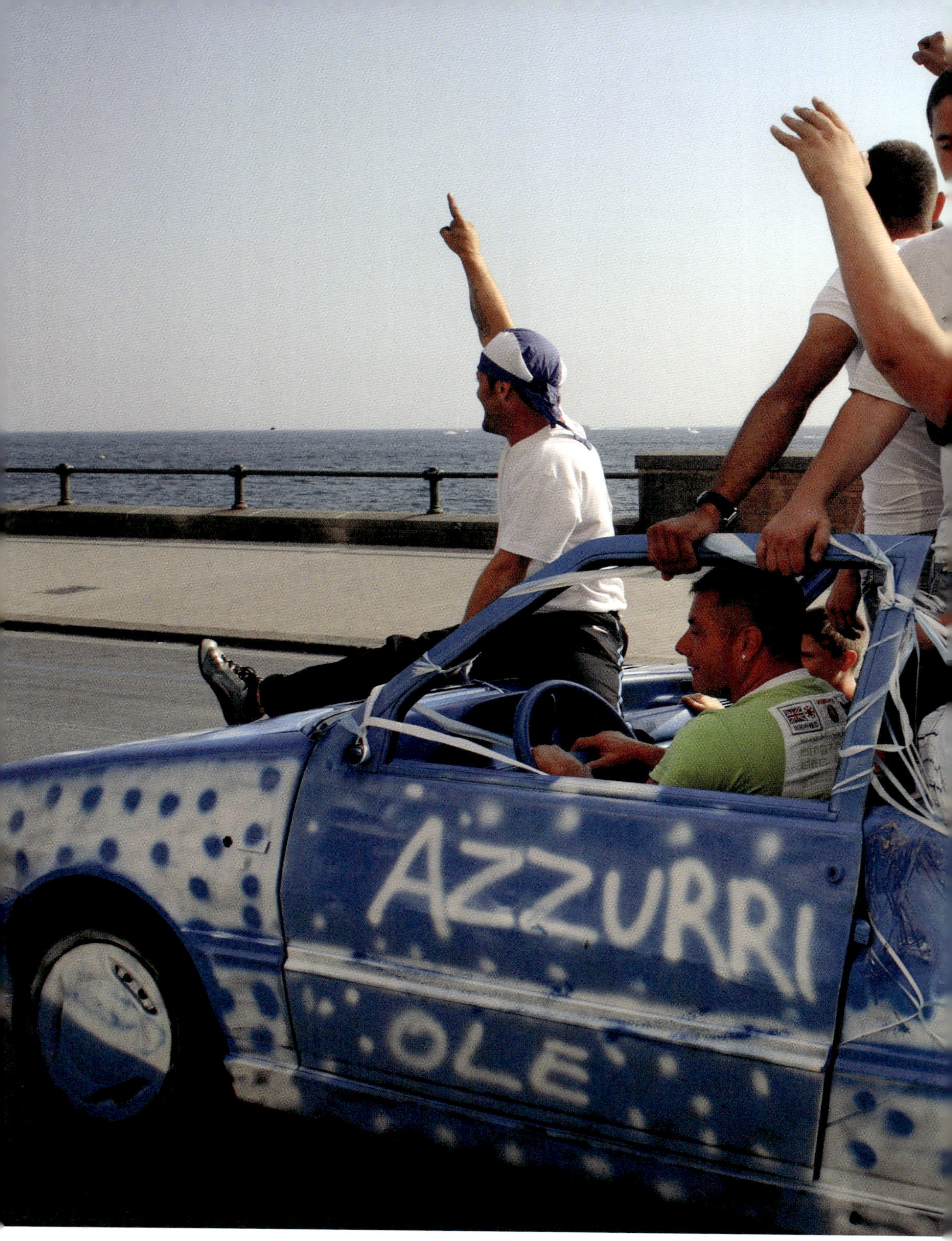
AZZURRI
OLE

Blue Voices

heads of Gioventù Azzurra, worked as a valet there. 'After a few meetings the idea of forming a single group began to emerge.' Vittorio seems emotional as he recalls this.

What's interesting is that it was in no way a given that groups of fans from areas of the city that were so close and yet so different would unite under the same banner. I again think of the bonds that form through football, which is something that I feel has been lost. Vittorio proudly claims he chose the group's name. 'Once the decision was made we had to come up with a name. A banner appeared briefly in the seventies that read "Blue Lions", but it vanished, and no one knew why. I proposed that name, and it was approved with a majority vote. That was in late 1982.' At this point in the story he is visibly moved, because those years and those steps awaken in him happy memories of a shared joy, and memory fades when you think of those who are no longer around. We are so overcome with melancholy that we have no choice but to go for a coffee – and maybe a warm *sfogliatella* pastry, too.

Ultimately, supporting Napoli means many things. It's a question of nuances and friendships as well as deep divisions. But perhaps it is a feeling of nostalgia that predominates. Every Napoli fan I know mourns a team from the past. Some miss the Sarri era, others think of Benítez and there are many who like the toughness that Mazzarri's

Pages 178–9: Napoli fans celebrating across the city.
Above: In the courtyard of an apartment building in Scampia, a child wearing a Maradona shirt and holding a ball looks for companions to have a kickabout.

> 'The name Stadio Diego Armando Maradona is perfect for it. It's as if the stadium had long worn it and was only waiting for official approval.'

squad showed. You can go back even earlier, to the times of Vinício, and I'm sure that if I look hard enough I will find at least one person who remembers with greater fondness a year spent in Serie B than the year of the first championship win, and his or her reasons would be perfectly understandable. I ask Vittorio why as fans we always miss the past, and he answers seriously, 'The future is hard work. Maybe thinking about it ages us.'

In Fuorigrotta we take a quick turn around the stadium. The last time I saw a match here it was still called the San Paolo. Like everyone else I experience a kind of flashback as I walk, engulfed in a single blue cloud, seeing hundreds of people move by me approaching the entrances. I see my Sunday-afternoon friends, the ones with whom I grew up, with whom I shared the passion of this support and spent days commenting on a goal and long nights imagining the future. The name Stadio Diego Armando Maradona is perfect for it. It's as if the stadium had long worn it and was only waiting for official approval. Before coming here I had stopped at Bagnoli to say hi to another friend who is a Napoli fan, Marilisa. I always liked her attitude to football. She's never too soft on the team, and she keeps her emotions in check. She's a critical spirit. And little does it matter that her controversial outlook isn't always driven by reason. She notices things that others, blinded by a goal, don't see. Some of the housing where she lives was built for workers at the former Ilva steelworks.

It's a territory in perpetual conflict, caught between events that were foisted upon the people and things that were promised but never materialised, proclaimed in the name of a better tomorrow that never came. When I hear the words 'rust' and 'sand', I think of Bagnoli. Marilisa tells me that during the minute's silence for Maradona everyone in the neighbourhood, no exceptions, stepped out of their houses to applaud. We were locked down, and she was struck by the fact that until Diego's death no one had left their homes to join a protest, a flashmob or anything else. When I close my eyes I see Via Cavalleggeri d'Aosta and people opening their windows, their doors, walking down the stairs and applauding, some of them crying. I continue on my walk around the stadium, past the VIP entrance, and I remember the (few) matches I watched from this section. I stop for a while at the point that Curva B starts and then at Curva A. I have an equal number of memories of afternoons spent in each section. When I come upon the Nisida Stand I spot someone within. I imagine it's a stadium employee, but then I look more closely, and I think it's Flora. I tell myself it can't be. I decide to leave, but something holds me back. The person turns around, and, sure enough, it is Flora. She smiles at me and says, 'Oh, it's you. Don't worry. We'll win this Saturday.' I close my eyes to grasp the sentence more fully, to concentrate on this figure. When I open them again all I see is a fading shadow.

Blue Voices

The Centro Direzionale

ESTER VIOLA
Translated by Alan Thawley

A void, surrounded by glass. The business district of Naples. Traffic-free, white and imbued with a contrived orderliness of piazzas and buildings that are too new and too phony. A part of the city with no friends, not even the Rione Luzzatti, the neighbourhood right next door made famous by *My Brilliant Friend*.

If there is one place in Naples that there really is no point in discussing, a place ignored by most people – especially Neapolitans – then this is it, the Centro Direzionale. Located behind the railway station close to Poggioreale prison. You get there on the Circumvesuviana, the train that never comes. Once every forty-five minutes on a good day. You could grow old waiting for that train. There are no timetables, no estimated times of arrival. As a lawyer (which I am), if you have a hearing and fail to arrive at the station an hour early, you'd be putting your case in jeopardy.

The Centro Direzionale was supposed to the be the Gulf of Naples' answer to the City of London, its administrative nerve centre. We were meant to imagine – as its architect Kenzo Tange had himself imagined – forty thousand orderly people arriving each morning to populate the city's economic hub. This was the Centro Direzionale, or the abstract idea of it formed in the mind of a Japanese architect. And abstract it remained.

A few decades later the Centro Direzionale is a deathly, defunct district. Whatever your reason to venture into these parts, you come with one thing in mind, and that is to get away as quickly as you can. To Neapolitans it simply does not exist.

It is the ultimate metaphor for Naples and the most interesting, because the hopes of a modern vision of Naples were invested in it. Not to tear it apart but to build, and build up to the sky. Like New York. If you're driving into Naples and look towards the city, it is the first thing you see – like the skyscrapers of Manhattan the first time you land at JFK and take a taxi downtown – except that here it's worse than you expect. Amid the tumbledown roofs and the most ramshackle neighbourhoods – *scarrupizzi* in Neapolitan – you wonder what it's doing there, that modern, symmetrical thing with all that glass.

Unfortunately this great metaphor remains unused, because the Centro Direzionale is not a place for writers. You cannot just observe and hope to understand. Attempting an empirical explanation of the Centro Direzionale would mean years of visits, years of despising the place.

It is the district for lawyers, for prisoners' relatives, for people down on their luck. If you have to go and queue for the social security service, for the telecoms regulator, at the regional offices, this is where you'll find yourself, in the white hell.

They called the different sections of the Centro Direzionale *isole*, islands, so it sounds like a game of battleships – *isola* A5, *isola* E7, *isola* F2 – perhaps because it's a bit like being at sea. There aren't even any signs, so you're bound to get lost. You walk around with the feeling that you're getting nowhere and always take a wrong turn. In summer the intense Neapolitan sunshine reflects off the white stone, and you wander about like a blind person, lost.

Is there anything they didn't get wrong when they built the Centro Direzionale?

The absurdity reaches new heights at the courthouse, that most noble of institutions, which occupies three blocks of glass and metal. Hundreds of rooms stacked vertically, immense columns of mirrors, the court of Naples is one of the busiest in Italy and at the mercy of its lifts. As well as queuing for the metal detectors, for identity checks, for hearings, for the chanceries and for your turn in front of the judge, you have to queue to enter a lift and – at every stop on the way up – your stomach feels like you're taking off in an aircraft. The court is divided into towers: A, B and C. The offices are shared out between them, so where you go depends on what you need to do. So keen are you to leave that you take the emergency stairs to get back down, because the overcrowded lifts have a tendency to get stuck and anyway before a certain time of day they only go up and not down. From a distance you can see hundreds of people scurrying up and down the wobbly external staircases with their old iron latticework. Like ants on a skyscraper. But given that we're people who sleep under a volcano, what else would you expect? Who knows, maybe the Japanese foresaw this.

The Dark Side of Neapolitan Cuisine

CRISTIANO DE MAJO
Translated by Alan Thawley

Pizza and mozzarella, of course, as well as *pastiera*, *sfogliatella* – two sweet treats made with ricotta – plus *babà*, the Neapolitan take on rum baba. Neapolitan cuisine as we know it in the rest of Italy (and around the world) is made up of five or six classics that are adored and much imitated – and, in fact, adored and imitated more and more frequently. In Milan in the past few years, Neapolitan pizzerias (*actually* Neapolitan) have been opening at the same rate as Chinese GDP growth during the golden years. On social media we discovered that the Covid lockdown even inspired people up north in Rovigo to make *pastiera*. And with mozzarella, no question, we're all experts: for starters, buffalo mozzarella doesn't come from Naples but from the provinces of Caserta (Aversa) or Salerno (Battipaglia), and even pizza with buffalo mozzarella is halfway to heresy, although one that gets a free pass nowadays. Truly Neapolitan dairy products are made within the province of Naples, around Agerola: *fiordilatte* (cow's milk mozzarella) and *provola*. These are cheeses that can't be imitated, and when they're 'exported' they just don't taste the same. What the Neapolitans do keep secret, however, are the numerous dishes, mainly but not exclusively street food, that have remained unknown 'abroad'. The reasons for their lack of wider recognition are not always clear, the most understandable being their strangeness to outsiders, a heaviness that means they don't travel well and the fact that they can be difficult to prepare. There certainly is a sunny, fresh side to Neapolitan cuisine, with its vegetables and seafood, but there is also a dark side, which derives from a lethal combination of the city's historic poverty and a legacy of gargantuan appetites linked to its royal past.

With *la genovese* (despite the name it's from Naples) we are already well on the way, because of all the 'strange' dishes it is perhaps the one that has started to gain the most traction outside of Neapolitan households. It is a first course, traditionally prepared at home on Sundays, made by the lengthy browning of the meat in a *soffritto* that includes insane amounts of onion. The result is a sort of sauceless ragout, dense and deep brown, that is served with pasta (preferably ziti). The actual Neapolitan *ragù* – which is more delicious and, strangely, less well-known than its 'Bolognese' cousin – is made by cooking various types and cuts of meat in a tomato sauce. It has to simmer in the sauce over an extremely low heat (Neapolitans have a special verb for this, *pippiare*) for many, many hours – a minimum of six, say the purists; the longer you cook it, the more character it will have – until it takes on a very dark (I said it would be dark) red colour. Now we are moving towards the darker side, but we are still within the realms of familiarity, and we could venture down some decidedly less well-explored paths. For instance the traditional *minestra maritata* made for Easter and Christmas, an extremely laborious broth made with many types of vegetables and cuts of meat. Or the glorious tradition of the *'o pere e 'o muss* (trotter and snout) carts that sell boiled offal (in dialect *zentraglie*, from the French *les entrailles*) dressed with oil, salt and lemon. They offer all kinds of cuts and types in addition to pig's trotters and calf's muzzle, from cow's udder to the characteristic 'book' tripe (*centopelle*), which is one of the calf's four stomachs. Offal also makes an appearance in another gastronomically extreme Neapolitan dish, *zuppa forte*, but this, along with *capitone* and *taralli*, deserves a more detailed treatment.

NOT SUITABLE FOR VEGETARIANS

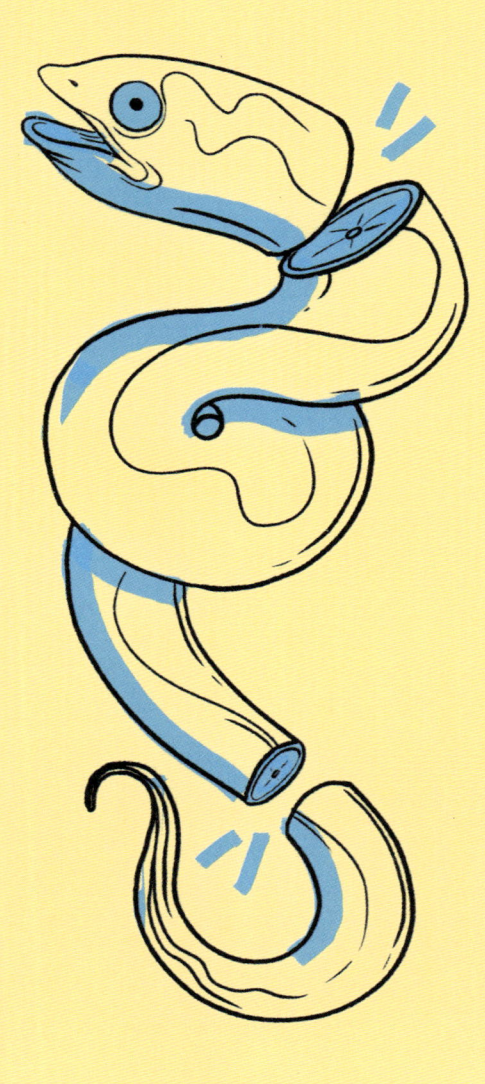

'O capitone

Looking at the tanks of desperately writhing eels outside the fishmonger's, you could imagine the beginnings of entire family legends, which, like any family story worth its salt, begin (or end) at Christmas. The Neapolitan tradition of eating eel at Christmas is something that goes beyond taste and feeds into the need to hand down customs – but it also owes a lot to superstition. Eating *capitone* – which refers to the female of the species despite being a masculine noun (whereas the male of the species, *anguilla*, is actually feminine, in a very contemporary gender twist) – wards off bad luck. The ritual, which probably has something to do with an eel's resemblance to the Serpent, symbol of evil, remains predominantly male-led. I have never seen any of the women in my family show appreciation for the dish. In fact, until my grandad died, the rule every Christmas was to ask whether we ought to make it or not – 'But do we have to have *capitone* again this year?' – but they would always be persuaded. 'Dad wants us to.' And the ritual begins long before you get to the table, with the merciless slaughter of the animal, chosen by the buyer on the day before Christmas Eve, with often tragicomic results (the eel launching itself out of the tank and ending up on the road, perhaps between the wheels of the cars stuck in traffic). Once recaptured by the fishmonger it ends up cut into pieces, with the individual sections still twitching even after having been carved up, and then put in a plastic bag. It is cooked for dinner on Christmas Eve, most often fried but sometimes also stewed. Either way, it's delicious.

Zuppa forte

While genuine *sanguinaccio*, the creamy chocolate preparation made with pig's blood for Carnival and now banned for health-and-safety reasons, must take first place among the Neapolitan foods to approach with courage, in second, just ahead of *'o pere e 'o muss*, we might put *zuppa forte* (literally 'strong soup'), which is also more simply known as *soffritto*. The dish is no longer made at home – well, one or two people probably do still make it – but is generally bought ready-made from the butcher. If you visit a butcher's shop almost anywhere in the city you will see little aluminium trays filled with a thick sauce with little bits of dark meat peeping out. On first glance you might think 'meatballs'. But no. This is pig's liver, spleen, heart, lungs and windpipe, cooked with tomato and tons of chilli pepper. All very strong flavours. Once brought home from the butchers it needs to be diluted and is then often eaten on bread or *freselle* (a sort of crispbread), but when accompanied by vermicelli it is to die for.

Taralli 'nzogna e pepe

You might be familiar with the ring-shaped biscuits known as *taralli*. Nothing particularly special about a *tarallo*, you might say. True, but you could also say that there are *taralli* and then there are *taralli*. The Neapolitan *tarallo* is nothing short of a meal unto itself, to be consumed only under certain circumstances and at a certain temperature. But first we need to talk about chalets. If you're not Neapolitan, you won't know what these are – rather, you'll know the more usual meaning of the word, a house in the mountains, but not the meaning in Naples, where the term refers, rather absurdly, to kiosks – more specifically, the kiosks along the seafront between Mergellina and the Lungomare Caracciolo. What do you do at said kiosks? You can have drinks, ice creams etc. by the sea. But, above all, they sell *taralli*, *taralli caldi* to be precise, served hot to accompany a beer. The most famous chalet is at the Diaz roundabout and is called Nas' 'e can (Dog's Nose). Neapolitan *taralli* are called *'nzogna e pepe* because they are made with *sugna* (lard) and a hefty dose of pepper. The other ingredient is whole almonds. They are eaten hot because by reheating them you reactivate the animal fat they contain and the biscuit becomes crunchy and crumbly like when they're freshly baked. Neapolitan *taralli* have a long history, possibly dating back to the 18th century, and they were developed to make use of the *sfriddo*, leftover bread dough. According to legend, *taralli* were originally dipped in the sea.

The Dark Side of Neapolitan Cuisine

The Playlist

FRANCESCO ABAZIA
Translated by Alan Thawley

You can listen to this playlist at:
open.spotify.com/user/iperborea

For almost twenty years the news that the Neapolitan dialect is going to be recognised as an official language, possibly even added to the UNESCO World Heritage list, has periodically popped up in the media and on social networks. Neither of these two things are true. If anything, the Neapolitan language, or dialect, is being added to the list of vulnerable languages, meaning that it is at risk of extinction. The persistence with which the news keeps circulating, however, testifies not only to a certain – inherent – vanity among Neapolitans in general but also to the level of importance that the Neapolitan language has assumed in arts and culture throughout Italy. Think about music: for many, many years Neapolitan music was simply what foreigners regarded as Italian music, and the development in the way it has described the city over the years has reflected the different periods that the city has been through, both historical and cultural. The use of a certain type of everyday speech, vulgar in the purest sense of the term, which becomes almost onomatopoeic, as in the 'Secondo coro delle lavandaie' from Roberto De Simone's opera *La gatta Cenerentola* or Tullio De Piscopo's 'Stop bajon', gave way to the refined *neomelodica* style of Franco Ricciardi or Maria Nazionale, who revisited the theatrical tradition of the *sceneggiata napoletana*. All through the use of a language that has never stood still but has constantly evolved right up to the modern reworkings to be found in the music of Liberato or in Neapolitan rap. A language – sorry, dialect – that is always the same and yet profoundly different depending on who is using it.

1
Roberto De Simone
Secondo coro delle lavandaie
1976

2
Tullio De Piscopo
Stop bajon
1983

3
Antonio Sorrentino
Luna lù
1983 / 2020

4
Nino D'Angelo
Senza giacca e cravatta
1999

5
Maria Nazionale
Ragione e sentimento
1997

6
Franco Ricciardi
Ed ora piove
2001

7
Clementino
L'età ré tass
2006

8
Co'Sang
Nun me parla 'e strada
2009

9
Anthony
E chiammalo
2010

10
Nu Genea
Je vulesse
2018

11
Geolier, Nicola Siciliano
P Secondigliano
2018

12
Liberato
Je te voglio bene assaje
2019

The Playlist

Digging Deeper

FICTION

Maurizio de Giovanni (tr. Antony Shugaar)
The Bastards of Pizzofalcone
Europa Editions, 2017

Erri De Luca (tr. Jill Foulston)
The Day Before Happiness
Penguin Modern Classics, 2006

Diego De Silva (tr. Antony Shugaar)
My Mother-in-Law Drinks
Europa Editions, 2014

Jennifer Egan
A Visit from the Goon Squad
Knopf, 2010

Elena Ferrante (tr. Ann Goldstein)
Neapolitan Novels Series
Europa Editions, 2016

Andrej Longo (tr. Howard Curtis)
Ten
Harvill Secker, 2013

Valeria Parrella (tr. Antony Shugaar)
For Grace Received
Europa Editions, 2009

Nicola Pugliese (tr. Shaun Whiteside)
Malacqua: Four Days of Rain in the City of Naples, Waiting for the Occurrence of an Extraordinary Event
And Other Stories, 2017

Roberto Saviano (tr. Antony Shugaar)
Piranhas
Picador, 2018

Paolo Sorrentino (tr. Howard Curtis)
Everybody's Right
Harvill Secker, 2012

Domenico Starnone (tr. Oonagh Stransky)
The House on Via Gemito
Europa Editions, 2023

NON-FICTION

Marius Kociejowski
The Serpent Coiled in Naples
Armchair Traveller, 2022

Jordan Lancaster
In the Shadow of Vesuvius: A Cultural History of Naples
Tauris Parke, 2019

Norman Lewis
Naples '44: A World War II Diary of Occupied Italy (USA) / *Naples '44: An Intelligence Officer in the Italian Labyrinth* (UK)
Da Capo, 2005 (USA) / Eland, 2002 (UK)

Local Architecture Network (eds Benoit Jallon, Umberto Napolitano)
Naples Super Modern
Park Books, 2021

Anna Maria Ortese (trs Ann Goldstein, Jenny McPhee)
Neapolitan Chronicles
New Vessel Press, 2018

Jason Pine
The Art of Making Do in Naples
University of Minnesota Press, 2012

Tullio Pironti (tr. John Domini)
Books and Rough Business
Red Hen Press, 2009

Peter Robb
Street Fight in Naples: A City's Unseen History
Bloomsbury, 2011

Roberto Saviano (tr. Virginia Jewiss)
Gomorrah: A Personal Journey into the Violent International Empire of Naples' Organized Crime System (USA) / *Gomorrah: Italy's Other Mafia* (UK)
Picador, 2017 (USA) / Picador Classic, 2019 (UK)

Desmond Seward
Naples: A Traveller's Reader
Robinson, 2018

FILM/TV

Saverio Costanzo
My Brilliant Friend
2018–

Matteo Garrone
Gomorrah (film)
2008

Claudio Giovannesi
Piranhas
2019

Ferzan Özpetek
Naples in Veils
2017

Francesco Rosi
Hands Over the City
1963

Roberto Saviano
Gomorrah (TV series)
2014–21

Paolo Sorrentino
The Hand of God
2021

John Turturro
Passione
2010

Graphic design and art direction: Tomo Tomo and Pietro Buffa

Photography: Mario Spada
Photographic content curated by Prospekt Photographers
Illustrations: Vincenzo Del Vecchio
Infographics and cartography: Pietro Buffa
Pasquale typeface: Gianluca Ciancaglini and Alessandro Latela

Managing editor (English-language edition): Simon Smith
Editorial consultant *The Passenger: Naples*: Cristiano de Majo

Thanks to: Eleonora Di Blasio, Chiara Di Mauro, Domenico Esposito, Agostino Ferrente, Anna Magnago Lampugnani, Christian Raimo, Cristina Ricotti, Viola Sarnelli, Mattia Tarantino

The opinions expressed in this publication are those of the authors and do not purport to reflect the views and opinions of the publishers. All content not specifically credited was written by The Passenger.

http://europaeditions.com/thepassenger
http://europaeditions.co.uk/thepassenger
#ThePassengerMag

The Passenger – Naples © Iperborea S.r.l., Milan, and Europa Editions, 2024

Translators: Claudio Cambon ('A View of the City Through Its Newspapers', 'Blue Voices'), Eleanor Chapman ('Minor Saints', 'Going to Naples'), Ned Darlington ('Republican Kings', 'Naples, the Sacred Ground', 'Napolisphere'), Jamie Richards ('Napuletana'), Will Schutt ('Cages of Metal and Cages of Paper'), Alan Thawley ('The Neapolitan Janus', '*Nero a metà*', 'The Centro Direzionale', 'The Dark Side of Neapolitan Cuisine', 'The Playlist', all *Passenger* texts)

Translations © Iperborea S.r.l., Milan, and Europa Editions, 2024

ISBN 9781787705319

All Rights Reserved. No part of this publication may be reproduced, stored in a retrieval system or transmitted in any form or by any means without the written permission of the publishers and copyright owners.

The moral rights of the authors and other copyright-holders are hereby asserted in accordance with the Copyright Designs and Patents Act 1988.

Printed on Munken Pure thanks to the support of Arctic Paper

Printed by ELCOGRAF S.p.A., Verona, Italy

Republican Kings
© Paolo Macry, 2018.
Extracted and adapted from *Napoli. Nostalgia di domani*, published in 2018 by il Mulino.

Minor Saints
© Alessandra Coppola, 2021

The Neapolitan Janus
© Lorenzo Colantoni, 2021

Going to Naples
The Dark Side of Neapolitan Cuisine
© Cristiano de Majo, 2021

Nero a metà
The Playlist
© Francesco Abazia, 2021

Napuletana
© Cristina Portolano, 2021

Naples, the Sacred Ground
© Carmen Barbieri, 2021

Cages of Metal and Cages of Paper
© Piero Sorrentino, 2021

Napolisphere
© Peppe Fiore, 2021

A View of the City Through Its Newspapers
© Raffaella R. Ferré, 2021

Blue Voices
© Gianni Montieri, 2021

The Centro Direzionale
© Ester Viola, 2021